Elizabeth Teissier is half-French and half-Swiss. She gained a Masters degree at the Sorbonne, became a French teacher, then a model at Chanel, an international cover girl and an actress.

She became interested in astrology in 1969 and in 1975 hosted the first daily European astrology television programme.

# YOUR STARS TO 2001

**Elizabeth Teissier**
translated by Bill Garnett

SPHERE BOOKS LIMITED

I hold my tongue about astrologers whose science, so useful to mankind, vindicates itself in the light of experience.

Saint Jerome

A SPHERE BOOK

First published in Great Britain by Sphere Books Ltd 1991

Typeset by Leaper & Gard Ltd, Bristol

Printed and bound in Great Britain by
BPCC Hazell Books
Aylesbury, Bucks, England
Member of BPCC Ltd.

ISBN 0 7474 0808 0

Sphere Books Ltd
A Division of
Macdonald & Co (Publishers) Ltd
Orbit House
1 New Fetter Lane
London EC4A 1AR
A member of Maxwell Macmillan Pergamon Publishing Corporation

# *Contents*

| | |
|---|---|
| Introduction | vi |
| 1991 | 1 |
| 1992 | 25 |
| 1993 | 51 |
| 1994 | 77 |
| 1995 | 103 |
| 1996 | 133 |
| 1997 | 165 |
| 1998 | 189 |
| 1999 | 217 |
| 2000 | 247 |
| A Glance at Your Next Five Years | 271 |
| How the Signs Divide into Decans | 276 |

# *Introduction*

## *The Prospects for Our World*

Paul Valéry, one of the most clear-sighted of Scorpios, once said, 'Our diverse civilisations today know they are destined to die.' His words were prophetic.

Our world is breaking up; our ethical and aesthetic values progressively degenerating, increasingly sinking into a tangle of contradictions, a world of confusion where absurdity reigns.

For, astonishing as our scientific and technical knowledge may be, it has not made mankind either happier or better. As Rabelais said, 'Unscrupulous science is the ruin of the soul', and this gulf between intellect and soul, between what Pascal called 'the order of mind and the order of love', is progressively deepening, till our scale of values turns upside-down and self-centredness, materialistic cynicism and indifference come to pass for a respectable creed. In short, the world seems to have lost its points of reference. Above all, it has lost Faith and Love.

But why? The theory of *planetary cycles* provides an explanation. For they are responsible for civilisations' great changes. And crises of world consciousness do not occur at random. There is a direction to the course of history, though not the one normally attributed to it. Rather than political, it is cosmic, and geared to universal order and planetary rhythms.

The most important changes in civilisation occur in tandem with a cycle which represents the lowest common multiple of forty-five astronomical cycles – every 496 years – or approximately five centuries. (This represents the length of two cycles of Pluto – which each take 248 years – or a fraction more than three cycles of Neptune – which each take 165 years.)

The sixth century BC, for example, saw the birth of great men such as Lao Tzu, Confucius, Pythagoras and the Buddha, who were to leave their mark on the world for more than 2500 years.

In the next cosmic cycle came Christ.

At the end of the fifth and beginning of the sixth century AD, five centuries later, there was the fall of the Roman Empire and the great barbarian invasions, followed at the end of the tenth century by that of the Vikings in England. This period also witnessed the advent of the Capetians in France, whose reign would last for 800 years.

At the end of the fifteenth century we have major geographical and technological discoveries, as well as the birth of such reformers as Luther, Zwingli, Calvin and Ignatius Loyola, founder of the Jesuits. (Interestingly, printing, which was invented in Europe during this period, had previously been invented in China at the end of the tenth century – exactly one cycle earlier than in the West!)

Coming to the twentieth century, we find that since 1980 – and especially since 1988 – we have once again entered a pivotal period of major celestial conjunctions: a turning-point … This will result in great changes for mankind.

There are many possible scenarios. One is the extinction of our species: either brought about by man himself through his own hellish/sublime inventions and exploitations, like nuclear power; or through a virus such as AIDS; or even through the pollution of our habitat, the planet Earth, to the point where it becomes uninhabitable.

Equally, the opposite may occur: inspired by a salutary attack of conscience, man may save himself and his world, make great discoveries – on a planetary scale – that even spread out to the cosmos as he colonises the solar system…

Whatever happens – and anything can – a determinant factor will be our own awareness; our sensitivity to urgency; our response to the influences which shape our lives – our collective karma. For though the stars signpost coming change, even indicate *when* it will occur, the *how* it will come about largely depends on our own wisdom. Or our folly.

According to astrological tradition since the time of Ptolemy, the course of existence is largely determined by whether planetary cycles are evolving (in the ascendant) or devolving. In the ascendant – which is a positive phase – the planets are spread open in their cycles in a kind of conjunction. In the devolving phase they retract and the climate of events which began with the first conjunction deteriorates. So what we have is a universal ebb and flow, a sort of cosmic breathing: inhaling and exhaling, action and reaction.

Currently, the majority of planetary cycles are devolving and will only become ascendant again in 1993 or in 1997, which could see the dawn of a new Golden Age.

A less positive vision is provided by the Hindu 'Vishnu Purana', which places us in an Age of Iron: a disastrous period of progressive global degeneration that culminates with the end of the world in 1999, though the tradition of Zohar gives the more comforting date of 2239. And the great astrologer and visionary Nostradamus forecast world's end for 3397. So we should have a little breathing space!

Returning to planetary cycles, there are four major conjunctions on the horizon between 1990 and 1997, and a fifth in the year 2000. Beginning in 1980, these have already given rise to a number of disasters, both natural and otherwise, whose frequency seems to be increasing: the eruption of El Chihón, the breakdown of the ozone layer, remarkable climatic changes, the war between Iran and Iraq, the rise of Islamic fundamentalism...

When quick planets align with slow the result is what we call planetary accumulation. And the more planetary accumulation there is in a century, the more that century tends to be disturbed. Thus the twentieth century saw planetary accumulation in Taurus in 1941, well into the Second World War; next in Aquarius in 1962, which is when astrologist and seer Jane Dixon places the birth of the anti-Christ; again in December 1989, which proved particularly significant for Eastern Europe. And finally, with seven planets in Sagittarius, there will be a short-lived planetary accumulation in November 1995. Among other spectacular developments, it could well mark our total and definitive victory over AIDS.

1993 will see the most notable astrological occurrence of the decade in the conjunction between Uranus and Neptune: a cycle that only happens roughly every 173 years. In approximately 18 degrees of Capricorn, the effect of this conjunction will be felt from as early as 1997 right through to 1991. And it will change the spirit of our times. (Just as it did when it last occurred in 1820 and the world saw the birth of the industrial era and a sea-change in the entire social, political and economic fabric of society.) January, August and October of 1993 will mark its most intense times, and the first two months indicate periods which risk being particularly turbulent for the world, while the last period will be more harmonious and constructive. Perhaps a new model of society will already be on the launching pad. In essence: the new age checks in in 1991 and settles down in 1993.

So the new form of society we are in the process of building will be born in 1993. (When astrology may once more achieve the recognition it deserves as a science.) The dawn of this new cycle promises to be decisive for our western society, with the probable advent of a new humanism in the likeness of the Age of Aquarius. It is even possible we may have a planetary council of the wise, uniting people from all corners of the world according to their worthiness and knowledge – without political, racial or professional distinction – who would have as their goal to find answers to the major problems of our changing world through worldwide, supranational laws, with particular regard to the problems of pollution, nuclear energy, famine and AIDS – all the planetary scourges which make a mockery of national frontiers. Perhaps this is the price we must pay for our planet to survive and flourish...

But it all depends on us. On how we play the cards the heavens deal us.

## *Your Personal Prospects*

In view of how long it takes for a slow planet to complete its cycle (varying between 12 years for Jupiter and 248 for Pluto) it's easy to see how such heavenly bodies remain for a considerable length of time in a zodiacal sign. And this explains why certain signs will find themselves, in the years to come, in a prosperous phase, while for others the same years could have every appearance of a run of bad luck. 'Life has its ups and downs', as popular wisdom has it, and 'There's always sunshine after rain'; but, in fact, it's worth emphasising that the cyclical nature of our lives' climate, of our destiny, is far from being approximate or vague. On the contrary, it answers to an entirely mathematical discipline – the astronomical discipline of the march of the planets.

With Neptune and Uranus in Capricorn, for Aries, Libra and Cancer subjects (and quite often Capricorns, depending on their natal charts) the coming years are not going to be any picnic. This is not to say that subjects of these ill-aspected signs are necessarily condemned to a sort of unavoidable netherland. That would be too simple for several reasons. Firstly, even if the overall outlook for these years is bad because of the semi-permanent presence of a number of slow planets, the more rapid planets will make a not-insignificant contribution to the cosmic context. And this will produce consequences which are more or less good, more or less questionable, according to the astral cocktail of the times.

Next, in the case of a really atrocious year, do not forget that the forecasts here are only concerned with one factor of your chart: your natal Sun, which, although essential, is far from alone in determining your horoscope. And the more you know your planetary positions (ascendant, Moon, Mercury, Mars, etc.) the more you can define your focus and make your forecast a good deal more precise.

But let's suppose that your particular chart puts you slap in the firing line, and for several years. For example, if you're mid-Aries with your ascendant in mid-Libra and your Moon and Venus there too, things will not go well and you'll need to be stout-hearted in the face of fortune. And this will prove especially true during certain phases which we will come to later on in this book. However:

1. Despite this discouraging overall picture, it would be astounding if you did not have some planetary positions in your chart which are well aspected in the years in question. And by using the cosmic energies specific to those planets, you can favour the positive outcome of these difficult phases. Specifically, the planetary energies are: endurance, patience, economy and foresight, in the case of Saturn; fluidity, open-mindedness and love of life, for Jupiter; intuition, even faith and prayer, for Neptune; and deep instinct, balanced sexuality and favourable social and professional encounters, where Pluto is concerned.

2. If at some exceptionally difficult time you have no recourse to support, no cosmic lifeline to hang on to (and that's extremely rare), remember that your innermost happiness depends in the final analysis on you alone. You must say *yes* to life: open yourself to the current of peace which is the distinctive feature of the cosmic spirit. Do so and you will find that all of a sudden even the most major problems lose their hold on you.

You see, planetary discords are there to test us. So we can assess our true worth in the face of adversity and progress in the knowledge of ourselves – which is our ultimate mission in life. For when all goes well, when we succeed, make money, enjoy the esteem of our colleagues and the love of those close to us, we have little natural tendency to question ourselves. These splendid periods, agreeable though they are, do not make us *progress*. Quite the contrary. If we're not careful, we regress, rest on our laurels, believe we've 'got it made'. And we forget the cosmic law which is as set as clockwork: the stars turn; after the ebb comes the flow; after action there is reaction.

Finally, if we wish to prepare ourselves for tomorrow without guilt or anguish, for a truly rosy future, it's today – in the here and now – that we must behave correctly. And if we only accept today what is good for ourselves and others, we won't have to fear for tomorrow. In the words of an ancient saying, 'Mankind is governed by the heavenly bodies – but the wise man directs his own star.' The moral is this: the more we stay sensible and

detached from destructive passions, the less we have to fear
from planetary discords. For they are only stressful cosmic
energy which tests our inner unity, our psychic cohesion.

All the same, if one does go through a dismal period for two
or three years one can – one must – be convinced that sunshine
follows rain, that the cosmic wheel turns inexorably. And never
let a human being, a situation or event, take your serenity from
you or deprive you of your inner peace.

The Greek law of eternal recurrence (though the same
configuration never does quite repeat itself in its entirety) is the
greatest lesson of humility and of hope that astrology teaches us.
Nothing is ever gained ... but nothing is ever lost either,
especially if we learn to use discord positively, to extract a 'plus'
of humanity, self-knowledge and spirituality from it. Forced to
see ourselves as we really are, say under the influence of Saturn
or Pluto, we question ourselves and learn to judge ourselves
objectively. We adjust our vision of the world and our actions to
a new reality. We can no longer pretend.

Another essential point is that quite frequently, in the throes
of sorrow or in some critical phase of our life, doors open for us
which otherwise might have stayed shut for ever. Spiritual or
professional revelations, even illuminations, can result directly
from a stay in hospital or the loss of a loved one. Forced by
some disaster to stop and reflect, we change objective and
orientation. We forget to pine for what might have been and
learn to live in the present; learn too that, if we must confront
the cosmic storm, it is only a matter of time before its black
clouds are swept away.

And astrology can tell us when.

# *1991*

## The course of the planets

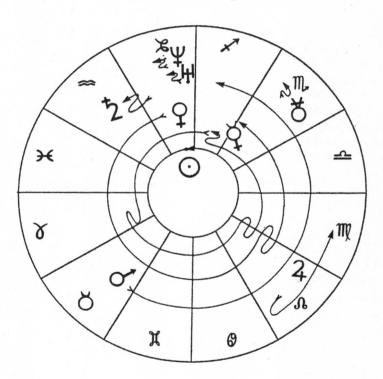

## World Events

Opening the last decade of the century and of the second millennium, 1991 falls into roughly three phases: a first term to the end of July, which will prove a lean time; a second term till the beginning of November, which will prove a neutral and calm time; and a third term to the end of the year, which will prove a good time.

Up to the end of July the civilised world will question its political structures and Europe could go through a final period of disarray (principally in March and in May) when the fall-out from different problems which appeared suddenly in July 1990 will make itself felt.

From the end of July, we will enter the second phase which will prove relatively neutral and calm, without any major planetary aspects.

Then in November a good trine will occur between Jupiter and Uranus, symbolising human solidarity and economic reform. Men of goodwill will be active and effective in the world, galvanised by a generous universal ideal.

In France, May seems to bring a godsend for the state as it profits from a litigious situation or tightened links with the European concept. May will also appear extremely profitable to West Germany in terms of trade and agriculture. On the other hand, in July France could experience a problem linked to teaching (though in November, France's best month, all will be set to rights).

Curiously, to the point where Helmut Kohl will have ridden out the cosmic storm of 1989–90, November will be extremely positive for his prestige.

Owing to a transit of Uranus, the planet of unforeseen upheavals, I can foresee great changes in the destiny and evolution of Great Britain. These changes will peak in the autumn though people may not be aware of it at the time. The autumn (October) will also see a turning-point in the history of Canada, with the possible separation of Quebec.

In general, November will be excellent throughout the world and will probably bring an important medical discovery (to do with AIDS?). There will be all sorts of manifestations of human solidarity. Electronics also should get going again after a probable crisis in 1990.

## *Your Personal Forecast*

*Note*: Where appropriate, to give more precise forecasts, we have divided each zodiacal sign into its three constituent *decans* (which are astrological periods of 10 degrees). To find out which is your decan turn to page 276.

### *Aries (21 March to 20 April)*

Whichever one of the three decans you are, Aries my friend, things have not been particularly festive for you for some time now. If you're *first decan*, you had a wounding encounter with Uranus and Jupiter in 1990 (especially till May). But now you will gather the fruits Jupiter promised you last year (between August and October): you will experience a flawless and vital optimism, your financial situation will improve, and your cup will be filled with heaven-sent opportunities! This will apply until mid-June with some particularly strong and promising moments in February and March when nothing will be impossible for you, and with luck on your side you can overcome all obstacles. In mid-January, the end of February, the end of April and mid-June, love will smile on you. And Jupiter won't be your only ally this year. Between February and December Saturn will help consolidate your position and stabilise your gains, and be especially favourable at the end of the year when your Christmas present could very well be a long-awaited, probably work-orientated, reward.

*If you were born around 29 March*: important changes which

have been germinating since last year will come to fruition in September.

If you're *second decan*, owing to Saturnian and Neptunian discords you found yourself in a tight corner last year. Now Uranus has taken Saturn's place in this contrary partnership, which means that changes in your life will be a good deal more unforeseen and abrupt. Discouraging periods of fatigue or perplexing questions will alternate with periods of over-excitement, hypertension and stress which – if not mastered – could lead to all sorts of incidents or even accidents. Be careful, therefore, especially round the end of April/beginning of May, but also at the end of June, the beginning of July and the end of September when you will be all the more vulnerable because you'll be feeling so highly strung.

As far as your heart is concerned, don't let yourself be led astray by mirages and don't believe that everyone around you has your frank and direct nature, or you could find yourself deceived and disappointed. Remember that you can't blame others for your own mistakes and lack of objectivity.

On the health side, as a discordant Neptune is quite debilitating, check yourself out to cover any possible deficiencies. It's worth knowing that your biochemical salt, in homeopathy, is potassium phosphate and that you have a particular need for manganese-cobalt.

If you're *third decan*, the year opens up relatively quietly, except if you're born after the 14th. In this case, until 10 February, you'll be subject to Saturn's influence which will tire and depress you or check your progress. But this transit will be rapid and short lived.

Between the end of July and the end of September will be a lucky period for you, both in business and in matters of the heart. And August will be a dream of a month! In love, you'll be especially ardent in September and until the middle of October, though this month will be pretty explosive on the professional level, or generally in everyday life. So cultivate flexibility, diplomacy and serenity. Otherwise, watch out for arguments and break-ups which this aggressive phase could bring on, as well as greater risks on the road.

In matters of health, it is worth paying particular attention to clean living and hygiene, to avoid the risk of renal complaints and the headaches which all self-respecting Aries subjects are particularly exposed to.

### Taurus (20 April to 21 May)

Only those *born before 12 May* are outstandingly featured this year. Other Taureans have a quiet year ahead and one of transition (apart from any counter-indications which may be found in their personal charts). There is one exception: from the start of the year till the beginning of February will prove an extremely gratifying period for those *born near the end of this Sign*. They will harvest the fruits of seeds they have sown in the past, and be rewarded.

*April Taureans*: if you've been offhand, had too much confidence in yourself and others or spent extravagantly, you can expect to pay for your mistakes during the first six months of this year. Legal disputes could be a consequence, or simply lean financial times.

*May Taureans* will experience this aspect more briefly between June and September and it will prove less malign for them. And if you're *born before 5 May,* Jupiter looks promising for you: between September and the end of the year it heralds all sorts of material and financial changes for the better, and additional vital optimism (above all in December). On the emotional level, mid-October should prove fulfilling.

Neptune and Uranus will prove powerful friends for May Taureans (*born before the 7th*) who will have every chance of evolving in a new, elevated and very enriching spiritual or intellectual dimension. They will get to know unknown realms which will fascinate them – a foreign language, a new discipline, a culture, a country – and their circle of relationships will grow considerably. Some of them will even be drawn towards mysticism, meditation or other spiritual practices, from which they will draw great benefit. Others will meet kindred spirits at the beginning of April, in May, or the end of October. Your most uplifting times will be at the beginning of January, in March, May, the beginning of July and in September. And if you're *born between the 6th and the 12th,* there's the possibility of total change in your vision of the world and your material situation too: a great turnaround is on the horizon, which should prove positive if you know how to 'let go', make concessions, be open and receptive to your destiny (particularly in February, the end of June, the beginning of August, the end of October and in November). Take particular care then of your throat, your reproductive system and your heart, and remember that in homeopathy your biochemical salt is sulphate of soda and that your sign has an affinity to the trace elements zinc and copper.

Good luck!

## Gemini (21 May to 21 June)

If you are a *May Gemini* you enjoyed Jupiter's protection last year between August and December, and it will return, greatly increased in its effects, during the first half of this year. (Those born in this period are far and away the year's winners!) Good news then, and even better: from February onwards Saturn will assist Jupiter to consolidate your gains and stabilise you a bit, which is no bad thing as you Geminis quite easily get a case of the fidgets! This planet, master of experience and time (which the Greeks knew as *Kronos*) will lend a serious durable quality to all you undertake till the end of the year (and particularly in February, the end of March, the end of May, in June, the beginning of July and the end of September): an extraordinarily constructive twelve months, then. And, especially if you were *born before 28 May,* it will be a dream of a year, when life brings you opportunities on a plate, which it's up to you to make the best use of.

As for *other Geminis,* thanks to Jupiter, their lucky period will be from mid-May to the end of September, though this will be less effective for them in concrete terms than for their fellow Geminis, as its passage will be too rapid and fleeting. Rather like them sometimes! Nonetheless, if they know how to seize their chances when they come – and Geminis do know as they're adaptable and opportunistic – they'll derive the maximum benefit from them. A perfect time this, for example, to ask your boss for a rise or make important administrative approaches; the opportune moment, too, to make financial investments ... or get married.

On the love front, sunny periods for all Geminis will be January, the end of February to mid-March, the middle of April to the middle of May (when you'll be irresistible – and it's a dream of a lifetime to honeymoon or propose), in June to the beginning of July, from the end of August to the beginning of October and in November to the beginning of January. All told, this is a year when love, leisure, friendship and art should all feature prominently.

Watch out you don't become offhand or careless – you'll really regret it! – between September and the end of the year, especially if you're *born before the 8th*. Otherwise, 1992 could bring depleted finances, legal disputes or tax problems. November and December this year will be particularly 'anarchic' so save your time and energy: organise yourself for the better and don't give way under stress. Above all, you should practise calming deep breathing – do yoga, for instance – it's the best antidote for your mercurial nervousness! Another period when things will go too quickly, or not sufficiently your way (which will irritate you intensely) is between mid-July and the end of August. Get a grip on your nerves then, or you may bring on accidents, arguments or other unpleasantness through pure haste.

On the health side, keep a check on your constitution and don't neglect your trace elements: manganese-copper and potassium chloride.

### Cancer (21 June to 22 July)

Until September, a trine of Pluto will positively influence *July Cancerians* and especially those *born between the 10th and 15th*, while the opposition of Uranus and Neptune will especially concern Cancerians *born in the first eight days of July*. And from the start of the year until mid-February those *born after the 16th* will suffer the depressing or frustrating opposition of Saturn, though this transit will quickly pass ...

From September and until the end of the year *first decans* should 'have a ball' as they'll be accompanied by an optimistic trine of Jupiter, which will raise the morale of, and increase the opportunities to make headway for, Cancerians *born before the 7th*. If you're one of these privileged few, keep your eyes open, and the opportunities which arise in the autumn (especially October) will bear fruit for you in 1992.

If you're one of those lucky people influenced by Pluto, whom we mentioned initially, you can count on a positive transformation of your living conditions, better social integration and a surer instinct for choosing the right path, while in many cases Pluto brings a marked improvement in fortune. This climate will be particularly effective in March, the beginning of May, July and September, and should be exploited to the full, seizing opportunities in both hands, without shilly-shallying – like a crab which takes one step forward and two back!

If you're born in the *first week in July* the double discord of Uranus and Neptune risks stressing you, Cancer my friend, and throwing a certain confusion into your life. Forewarned is forearmed. Be open to change in April when Mars will also provide you with overflowing energy, which you'll need to channel and master (otherwise beware of explosive incidents in your family circle, and possible accidents on the road and elsewhere). In September get yourself organised to deal with any eventuality, first of all through mental discipline: work on the principle that everything that happens is eventually useful and favours your spiritual progress. And don't let yourself get worried or depressed by phantoms, by the unreasoning and irrational fears that Neptune (inevitably) brings. October will be the last truly challenging time, so arm yourself with patience and inner calm then and let the cosmic storm blow over. This period is also worth watching on the health side, for Neptunian discords are debilitating: look after your health and ward off any possible deficiency in your mineral salt of calcium fluoride and its trace element, silver.

Fortunately, throughout the year there will be moments when your immediate circle or a loved one will help you find the right path and transform these difficult periods into stages of inner growth and expanded consciousness. Specifically these periods are: mid-February, the beginning of April, the end of May, the end of October.

Generally speaking Cancerians will be on super form when Mars is favourable in January, April–May (careful, any excess is a fault!), and in July–August and October–November.

### Leo (22 July to 23 August)

If you're *born before 4 August*, propositions or opportunities from last year will echo through this year until June. Unfortunately, there's a risk of Saturn obstructing you and giving rise to delays or obstacles to the realisation of what Jupiter promises, unless your natal chart has a planet in the first decan of Aries, Sagittarius, Libra or Gemini to more or less neutralise Saturn's frustrating effects. These will spread out until the end of the year and mainly concern Leos *born in July*. But it's worth knowing that the negative effects of Saturn will be powerfully counterbalanced by a great increase in Martian energy, and a greater freedom of action, in February, April, September and December.

Avoid overwork and stress, which this conjuncture will push you towards, at the end of May to June and the end of October to November. Equally, there's a danger of broken limbs as the result of unfortunate falls. So watch it if you're involved in sport!

For *second decan* Leos June, July and August will be the most dramatic and unsettling months when they'll find themselves grappling with an intensely overheated atmosphere in their private and professional lives. All sorts of extremes will lie in wait for them then, and this agitated time will be accompanied by a square of Pluto which changes their lives from top to bottom. Fascinating, isn't it? It will be, provided you stay morally and physically alert and on form: look after your arteries and heart regions (at risk in your Sign along with the eyes), and stay on top of it all. This will be easiest in June. But your good periods also spread over March, April, September to early October, and December. If you were *born around the 12th* your life has outlined a right-angled turn in February, which only actually materialises in August, when everything see-saws.

As for love, friendship and the pleasant things in life, *all Leos* will be favoured at the end of February, beginning of March, the second two weeks of April, in June (but with turbulence too!), in September (for *third decans* the heart side takes off) and in November.

All told then, 1991 should prove a fascinating year for all decans, even if it's not all peace and quiet.

Good luck!

## *Virgo (23 August to 23 September)*

For *all Virgos* 1991 looks like another dreamy year: a year of consolidation, of pleasant surprises and sudden strokes of luck, of better social integration, of spectacular promotions and, for single *first decan* Virgos born around the middle of August, perhaps the year they get married! Or they could be getting engaged now and marrying next spring when a sunny Jupiter returns and beams upon them.

*Second decan* Virgos especially are the 'chosen' of the year, and will find themselves sustained by Pluto, Neptune and Uranus simultaneously. This is a very rare conjunction as Pluto only comes every forty years – to augment our vital resources, link us more directly to our subconscious and favour greater social impact – while Neptune recurs roughly every twenty-eight years – to lay open a superior spiritual, mystic or artistic dimension. And finally Uranus, with a fourteen-year cycle, is responsible for unforeseen strokes of luck, enriching encounters and changes as sudden as they're marvellous. (Uranus can sometimes also originate an interest in electronics, aeronautics ... or astrology). To sum up then, a really attractive planetary trio whose convergence only happens once in a lifetime!

For *all Virgos* the best periods of the year will be ...
professionally: January, March (provided you adapt yourself to
partners and those you deal with), April to May, July to
September (this birthday month will be fabulous if you're
*second decan* and promises a year to come that's every bit as
exciting and gratifying), October (with a number of lucky
opportunities and a terrific dynamism, especially if you're born
in August) and November (apart from some setbacks in trade).

On the emotional side the best times are: February (provided
you remain in touch with higher things), the end of March/
beginning of April, May, July to August (when *first decans* will
enjoy some exciting meetings and really shine), October and
December.

As far as personal dynamism is concerned, you'll be on
sparkling form in January, April to May, July to August and
October to November. Equally, you will be tired, overworked
or nervous – watch out for clumsiness or food-poisoning – in
February to March and in December which is generally your
least good month. In fact, at the end of the year, *second decans*
especially won't know which way to turn: they'll be submerged
in offers and adrift in misunderstandings. So Virgos' renowned
organisational faculties and methodical sense can be put to good
use then!

As in the Bible, where the last shall be first, the *last decan* is
especially favoured at the start of the year when the stars bring a
just recognition of merits (until mid-February). Moreover, these
subjects will be endowed with formidable efficiency. And
athletes, company chiefs and scientists will all have extra luck.

In essence then, this is a year which many of you will
remember as heaven sent!

## *Libra (23 September to 23 October)*

Briefly speaking, the *first decan* comes out best this year and,
thanks to Jupiter, is effectively blessed by the gods – in any
event until June. Moreover, it is sustained throughout the year

by a stabilising trine of Saturn, which will bring all sorts of long-awaited satisfactions.

The *second decan*, on the other hand, is the most deeply disturbed – by abrupt changes or unsettling fundamental challenges.

The *last decan* is relatively quiet, apart from at the beginning of the year when Saturn will temporarily test it (tiring it or suddenly overloading it with new responsibilities), and in August to September when, quite to the contrary, subjects of this decan will find themselves in great physical and moral form, uplifted by the stimulating and beneficent influence of Jupiter.

For *all Librans*, but especially those of the *first and last decans*, there will be good influences in 1991. You'll be on sparkling form and galvanised with a spirit of enterprise between the end of January and the beginning of April, from the end of May to mid-July and right through December.

September to mid-October will be mixed and repercussive for the *second decan* (which risks being careless, under stress, or endangered by medical problems or food-poisoning). On the other hand, for the *first and last decans*, this period will be hyper-enlivening, stimulate luck and increase tenacity and perseverance, which will guarantee efficiency and success. However, be wary of excessive energy or possible overwork in April to May, when Mars threatens to turn your aggressive dynamism against you.

On the heart side, your emotional ties will blossom harmoniously (especially for *first and last decans*) in January, the end of April/beginning of May, in June and in September. And in November Venus puts you in symbiosis with those close to you, and gives you irresistible allure.

Things will be less good (especially for *second decan* Librans *born in the first ten days of October*) at the end of February/beginning of March and in May, while November will only serve to focus the emotional problems which could be yours this year, if that's your Achilles' heel. It's worth stressing here, though, that planetary discords are only really formidable when we're vulnerable to them. And if a relationship is in perfect fusion and health, no discord can destroy it, however powerful passing celestial tensions may be.

On both the everyday and career levels, the year holds islands of light and success, periods when everything goes without a hitch: when, especially for *first and last decans*, Librans feel themselves carried along by events. These periods will occur in February, June, August to September (apart from *second decans*), October and November to December. During these phases not only will you get new things under way, but you'll consolidate your gains, stabilise your situation, and your worth will be recognised (especially if you're *first decan*, influenced by Saturn).

Matters will be less easy in January and in July and – for *second decans* – in April and October when, ill-aspected by Uranus and Neptune in tandem, they will find everything complicated and have spots of bad luck. So if you belong to this group, react by making yourself think positively. Tell yourself that this planetary passage must help you to grow, to change what matters in yourself and your life, even though this change may be forced upon you by circumstances. Tell yourself, as the great Stoic philosopher Epictetus did: 'Do not ask that things should come to pass as you want them, but want them in the way that they come to pass – and you will be happy.'

I wish you success in this psychic alchemy!

### Scorpio (23 October to 22 November)

Looking at the evolution of this sign over the course of the year, one can say that the *first decan* gets off a great deal less well than the other two, principally because, until June, it is going to be subjected to the adverse influence of Jupiter which it had already experienced during the second half of 1990. What's more, from February onwards Saturn will join this planetary discord, prolong it right through the year, and, to a greater or lesser degree, impede undertakings, especially for those who were *born before the 27th*. Happily, this *first decan* will get relief from these trials from mid-September on, when Jupiter turns into an ally. It's also worth noting that Jupiter's influence, which is generally highly protective of enterprises subject to it, will extend to all natives of the first half of Scorpio (*born before 8 November*).

The *second decan* is perhaps the most sustained by astral conjunction, as Neptune and Uranus are your joint allies this year, opening up new and exciting horizons. If you were *born in the first ten days of November,* you'll feel the world belongs to you: you will be simultaneously uplifted by Neptunian aspiration – moments of mystic poetical or spiritual illumination – and, protected by Uranus, you will enlarge your circle of relationships in a notable way; your intellectual consciousness, too, especially if you were *born in the first week of November.*

And that's not all. Pluto, your master, will be powerfully employed on your behalf if you were *born between 10 and 15 November.* Of course, exactly how much change it brings to your life or inner being, and how agreeable that change is, will depend on your personal chart. Its influence could, for example, signify a total professional volte-face, which for some could mean spectacular promotion and greater social integration, while for others the result could be a reversal of fortune and being put out of work. Either way, however, the influence of Pluto indicates a slow, profound change in your psyche, in your conception of life. You will emerge from this period totally changed in yourself. And, in view of the astral context already mentioned (and especially the good influence of Neptune which covers almost the same sector of the zodiac), pessimistic scenarios are a lot less probable than cheerful ones.

Turning to the *last decan* we find it (especially in January) influenced by a very positively aspected Saturn which will strengthen the situation for those *born after 16 November.* Though this Saturnian influence is quite short-lived and ceases in the first days of February, it entails consolidation of social status, greater physical resistance, a more concrete impact on the environment, people and things, as well as the realisation of a long-term undertaking or a long-awaited reward.

Less positively, natives of the *last decan* will have a brush with Jupiter in August and September, which will sow some discord into their lives, finances or love, though the effect of this will be very short-lived.

For *all Scorpios* (though of course more markedly for those already singled out) the best and the least good periods of the year will be as follows. Professionally, in everyday life and in business dealings: February, May, June and August (until about the 20th) will be the least favourable times. Those that will be beneficial and fertile are: January, March, the end of July and the end of August (particularly favourable for the *first decan*), then all September, from mid-October to mid-November and finally the end of the year. Use these periods to pursue what you've set your heart on, to undertake new projects, to invest, to discover a new language, a new country, a new discipline, a new consciousness. If you want to create and undertake things, the influence of Mars will sustain you; it will be positive in April and in the greater part of May, from mid-July to the end of August, and from mid-October to the end of November. During these periods you'll be on Olympic form, want to practise your favourite sports more than ever, and nothing and no one will interrupt your momentum. These are also times when you can function twice as fast, getting a maximum amount of work done in the minimum time.

In the fields of love, emotional ties, leisure and artistic activities, the times you'll be most creative, inspired ... or romantic (though this isn't a characteristic quality of Scorpios, who tend more to all-consuming passions) are as follows: from the beginning of January (notably for the *last decan*), from 10 May to 10 June, from the beginning of July to the end of August (especially *first decans*), from 10 October to the beginning of November, and almost all December, when your magnetism will be irresistible!

But Scorpios still unattached should beware at the year's end, when Venus accompanied by Uranus could well wound them with a spiteful – and decisive – Cupid's dart!

### Sagittarius (22 November to 22 December)

From an overall point of view, this is a golden year for Sagittarians – especially *first decans* – apart from the period from mid-September to the end of the year, which will see some disturbance in the lives of those *born before 8 December*. However, this will soon pass, and in 1992 this Jupiterian discord will have gone on its way without any long-lasting consequences. The *first decan* is in the main extraordinarily gifted, especially until June, when lucky Centaurs will savour the tasty spin-offs of ideas or propositions which will have been put to them since August of last year. If you're one of these, there will be money coming your way thanks to flourishing business, and you'll also experience a flattering recognition of your merits as Saturn teams up with Jupiter to help you.

If you were *born in November*, your good fortune won't end in June either, but will continue until December, when Saturn will bring you other rewards which have been in the pipeline since May. In fact, when Saturn and Jupiter in tandem are well placed in your natal Sun, they constitute probably one of the most certain astrological assets for lasting success and solid good luck. It's hard to imagine a more propitious configuration for long-term gratifying progress, whether it's a professional promotion or simply an overall climate of serenity, optimism and moral comfort of the type that even Sagittarians – who are gifted for life – rarely see. (The word 'jovial', by the way, comes from Jupiter, the governing planet of your Sign.)

This will be a year, then, when you'll climb the social ladder, consolidate your gains, and take on whatever's going. If you're a *December Sagittarian* the best period will be between June and the beginning of October and, more specifically, on the professional and commercial levels and also in terms of travel, in June, July and August. (Actually, discordant Mars in August could make you careless or thwart certain efforts, though it can hardly have too devastating an effect if you're lounging on a beach!)

On the emotional side, you'll be totally radiant and at ease with yourself (if you were *born in December*) during June and early July. And it's highly likely that a meeting then will have repercussions at the end of August and September which involve enthusiastic reunions.

*All the Sign* will be in Olympic form between the end of May and mid-July, in September to October and right through December, when natives of the *second decan* could go wrong through excess (too much confidence in themselves and others, too much work, too many preoccupations). Take care. *All the Sign* will be too highly strung, impatient, even clumsy between the end of January and the beginning of April (when Mars is in opposition) between mid-July and the end of August and, for *second decans* only, during December. So slow down then, and calm yourself mentally and physically, or else watch out for incidents or possible accidents during these periods and also at the beginning of March (in particular for *first decans*) and the end of July/beginning of August.

Professionally speaking, you'll have wind in your sails at the beginning of January, especially *last decans*; then (for *all the Sign*) in February, April until mid-May, July (when travel is particularly favoured – it will be lucky!), in August, the greater part of October and finally the last two months of the year.

Emotionally, you will consolidate your existing ties (particularly if you were *born in November*) and have every chance of creating something new from them – and this applies to *all the Sign* – from January to the end of February, at the beginning of March, the end of April/beginning of May, in June to early July, in September if you're *last decan*, and finally in November and the beginning of December. During these periods you'll also be in super form, both morally and physically, and your good mood will communicate itself to others and draw good luck to you like a magnet. Nonetheless, (especially if you are *first decan*), Jupiter will have you trying to do two or more things at once in October when a choice will present itself which may or may not be painful...

All told, then, everything points to a very nice year and one that in retrospect might well stand out as a landmark.

## *Capricorn (22 December to 20 January)*

As the three slow planets, Saturn, Uranus and Neptune, have been ambling through your sign for some years now, you'll be aware that you're in a front-row seat in terms of astral conjunction. And this year those *born in the first fifteen days of January* will be especially featured.

If you're a *December Capricorn* the year will be more or less neutral for you: quiet until September, when Jupiter will make an appearance and spoil you rotten until the end of the year, and also favour those *born in the first week of January* in terms of business and general good luck.

If you're *born before 6 January*, you're going to change a lot of things in your life. In fact, your existence will be turned upside-down, for many of you (particularly those *born on 1 and 2 January*) as a result of something that happened in the spring of 1990. And whatever the change – whether of home or job or partner – it will be sudden and hard to reverse.

According to your personal chart, of course, this upheaval will affect you in a more or less positive way. Many of you could meet a fellow spirit, pull off a coup, discover another country or another intellectual or philosophical universe. The influence of Neptune which will mostly affect those *born from 3 to 9 January*, will bring these subjects to a greater spiritual or mystical opening; while for others Neptune's influence will mean a deep questioning of their existence, which could prove hard or depressing. For yet others still, Neptune could bring general frailty, in particular a vulnerability to viral ailments which are difficult to diagnose, such as diseases of the blood, like pernicious anaemia. Some good advice then is to have a preventive check-up to pre-empt deficiencies and organic disorders. (Your Schussler salts, by the way, is phosphate of lime. And in terms of trace elements, homeopathy associates Capricorn with the mixture copper, gold, silver.)

As the result of the doubly impactful influence of Neptune and a sextile of Pluto, *second decan* Capricorns will feel an increased need to get to the bottom of themselves, to discover or rediscover their own truth, identity and values, for this Sign is very much a seeker after truth. And the sextile of Pluto will give them a sure instinct in this inner search while, subject to a direct transit of Neptune and Uranus, they will likewise be granted very useful vital resources.

Saturn, the last slow planet passing through the Capricorn sign, and its ruler, transits the *last decan* during January and until the beginning of February. This planetary passage – which only occurs once every twenty-nine years and which is especially essential for Capricorns – also induces the concern among them to reduce their lives to fundamentals, to eliminate dross and frivolous elements which lack authenticity. This is the moment too, when they become aware of time passing and feel the need to organise it better. This phase could in theory tally with moral isolation – even separation – and trials. But, given the astral context of the beginning of the year (with its fine trine of Mars in particular), dramatic outcomes appear unlikely.

For the *entire Sign*, the most fertile and dynamic periods are: January to the beginning of February, the end of February to the beginning of March, the end of July and all August and from mid-October to the end of November, when you'll be set fair for business and travel, your dealings will be easier and you'll be inspired in action.

On the other hand, during the following periods, you should avoid taking major risks or making radical decisions: from the end of March to the end of April, from the end of June to almost the end of July, throughout September, nearly all October, and finally November. At these times journeys could bring problems or surprises, negotiations turbulent or confused, and your image go more or less down the drain.

Emotionally, there will be something new in the air: perhaps the meeting of your lifetime if you're a Capricorn of the *first week in January*; and this meeting could well take place either in February, the end of March/beginning of April – if you were *born in December*, in July to August – or in October. Conversely, emotional dramas and scenes and 'crying and gnashing of teeth' are on the horizon at the end of February/ beginning of March and in May and November, which are times to tread softly and take care.

## *Aquarius (20 January to 19 February)*

To put it bluntly and in general, you don't have a fantastic year ahead of you here.

In fact, for the *first decan* in particular, up to June things won't be easy. Saturn will pay you an extremely rare visit (his normal frequency is around thirty years) which will challenge the fundamentals of your existence – and all the more so as Jupiter is also going to destabilise your life to a greater or lesser degree. And not until November to the end of the year will you experience the repercussions (which for some of you could be quite positive) of Saturn's transit between February and May.

There is also a strong possibility of Jupiterian fall-out from the last six months of 1990: your finances could be adversely affected, or you could experience problems to do with your superiors or the authorities, or get involved in legal disputes. Be careful, particularly before the end of March, not to do anything which could subsequently rebound against you. Jupiter, the symbol of legality, won't allow any irregularities when he's ill aspected (as is the case here).

From February onwards, you'll also be subject to the conjunction of Saturn which will pressure you to internalise, fall back on yourself, and make an objective examination of your situation. And, with Jupiter and Saturn in planetary tandem, you could well experience a degree of mental agonising and stress, which in turn could rebound on your health if you're not careful. Saturn has a reputation for weakening defences while simultaneously stimulating organic hyperactivity. So resist the possible consequences of this by taking more care to look after yourself and prevent possible circulatory problems, which are your Sign's Achilles' heel. You could be particularly physically sensitive during June and also in October, November and, for *second and last decans*, the end of June to July and in November.

The *last decan* also has a stressful period in January when those *born after the 16th* risk becoming overworked or fatigued, while the *second decan* will continue to have to confront a Plutonian discordance which may slowly but surely erode the status quo of those *born between 6 and 13 February*.

*Last decans* will be particularly sensitive to the disturbing influence of Pluto during the summer months of July and August, when you could have to face up to some difficult choices. You'll call into question the foundations of your life spontaneously, or an outside event will force you to. The issue in question could be of a professional, social or emotional nature. Some Aquarians could experience a voluntary or imposed professional redeployment, or possible redundancy. (Pluto often brings repercussions from collective events we cannot control but which affect us as individuals.) Other Aquarians will experience slow but irreversible Plutonian change in an entirely different way: perhaps through an inner transformation, a radical change in their level of consciousness, or yet again through a divorce, a change of residence or some other important upheaval. Basically, only Aquarians *born from 13 to 19 February* can expect a relatively tranquil year, and if this results in relative monotony they'll get their share of Pluto in the years to come...

Happily, there will also be better periods in the year. On the level of business and life in general, the end of March and April are positive, as is June, despite overwork induced by Mars. The end of September and a good slice of October are also well aspected, as is almost all of November and December. These are times when you'll have every opportunity to transform lead into gold or, in other words, make discords fertile. For it's only under duress that man progresses and evolves, and this dynamic year could take you a long way, if not on an exterior plane then at least in terms of personal evolution.

As far as heart, friendships and leisure are concerned significant periods will be: the end of February and the beginning of March, the end of April and beginning of May, and practically all November. Your spiritual charm will be more active than usual then, and relationships with others will be harmonious and gratifying.

Emotionally, *first decans* will have a lot going on at these times, from the consolidation of existing ties to an outstanding and exciting meeting, even if this could lead to problems with regard to your current situation.

*First and second decans* will feel less up to the mark, and ties with others will be more problematical, in January (which also applies to *last decans*), at the end of March/beginning of April, in June and September (particularly for *last decans*) and in December. Aquarians *born before 12 February* especially will be confronted by situations where they'll have to make more or less painful choices; and even their well-known Aquarian shrewdness and dexterity may prove insufficient to sort out their problem.

Happily, in February, March, September to mid-October and in December, a well-aspected Mars will fill you with an enviable energy which will help you cope. And these are times, too, when you'll be most active – and with maximum returns – and when you Aquarians who already live in the fast lane will be really motoring!

## Pisces (19 February to 21 March)

Pisces, my friend, this is a red-letter year for you!

A rare year – exceptional even – and one which could be the year of your life, particularly if you're *born between 27 February and 14 March*. In fact if you belong to this region of this zodiac you'll enjoy an exciting sextile of Uranus which will enrich your life every which way. You'll undertake new ventures, experience changes as sudden as they'll be exciting. Your horizons will widen both in terms of intellectual or geographical awareness, and so will your circle of relationships. You will make a lot of new friends, shine in society and could quite probably concoct some fascinating plans with one of your friends which (if you're *born at the end of February/beginning of March*) will be sketched out early in the year and realised from the start of September onwards. If, on the other hand, you were *born around 3 March*, these plans will just appear in April and materialise at the end of the year. Another manifestation of Uranus could translate itself into moving home or a sudden professional promotion: in brief a positive break-out from the routine.

This will be even more the case as Uranus joins a sextile of Neptune and trine of Pluto this year (which especially bears on those *born in the second decan between 3 and 7 March*). Pluto's protection extends to Pisceans *born before the 13th* as well, promising them greater social integration, an improvement in their general living conditions and a deep and profound wellbeing that will make their spirits soar. The sextile of Neptune (your personal planet), thanks to a planetary harmony that only occurs every twenty-seven years, will for its part endow you with a greater serenity and a sharpened intuition as to which direction in life to take. It will also bring you a new opening which will be very positive for your spiritual progress and lead to more elevated consciousness, and even moments of philosophical or spiritual illumination unknown until now.

In brief, you really have an extremely fertile period ahead and, if you know how to use it without going to sleep and resting on your laurels (always the danger of very good influences – one takes life as it comes), it will enrich you in a noteworthy way and, later, *will* seem to you a key period in your life and a period of growth, probably one of the most pleasant to live through.

Among the slow planets only Jupiter (between mid-September and the end of the year) will introduce a little disturbance into your life. And that's if you belong to the first half of the Sign (*born before 5 March*). Even this discord, however, won't succeed in troubling you unduly, as other slow planets harmonising with Jupiter will have the effect of making its influence positive. Except in December, that is, when Mars, Mercury and the Sun oppose you in turn. As a result, you need to gather your energy then to stay effective, for you'll have a tendency to disperse yourself and waste your efforts ... and lack your legendary capacity to adapt.

# 1992

**The course of the planets**

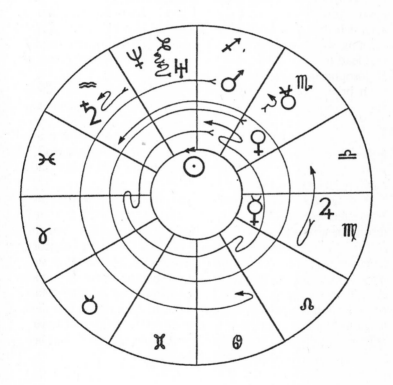

# World Events

In 1992 we should already be feeling the beginning of a new age and spirit. This will result from the important conjunction between Uranus and Neptune which is already in formation. It will give rise to an atmosphere full of hope and profound transformation, similar to that which held sway around 1821 when there was the last conjunction of the same planetary cycle. And this great cosmic encounter will put a 'certain something' in the air which will mark a new era for mankind. In 1992 itself this will only exist beneath the surface, like a watermark, as yet not precise, but will nonetheless provide an astral context and particular tone that will be superbly harmonious.

In January and August there will be numerous manifestations of interdependence and universalism, tangible proof of growing planetary consciousness (which will have been in gestation since November 1991). And the same timing holds true for all sorts of medical and technical discoveries.

In fact, 1992 should be one of the most promising, fertile years of the end of this century and one of the most constructive economically. Equilibrium and prosperity will hold sway. On a socio-political level, we'll witness the practical organisation of a number of salutary measures, especially in the field of health. The life and wellbeing of the individual will be taken more into consideration, and not only in an ideal or abstract way but through concrete implementation. Reforms will be devised and, paradoxically, the sultry month of August will be highly creative, perhaps by helping the world become aware of new social and political requirements – and then to make the appropriate decisions to meet those needs.

The conjunction of Uranus and Neptune in formation, however, will attack Germany's ascendant, possibly bringing a serious identity crisis through an atmosphere of doubt and insecurity. Perhaps the country won't yet have absorbed the problem of national brotherhood entailed by its reunification, a problem with multiple economic and social repercussions...

Queen Elizabeth II could suffer ill-health this year, which comes to a head in the autumn.

January or August could mark progress in the fight against AIDS or cancer.

It's worth noting that the big winners of this super year will be *second decan* Water Signs (Cancer, Scorpio, Pisces) and the Earth Signs (Taurus, Virgo and Capricorn).

## ☆ *Your Personal Forecast* ☆

### *Aries (21 March to 20 April)*

Years follow on ... and sometimes resemble each other. And so it will seem to you, Aries (especially *second decans*) as last year you will have already felt the ill influence of Neptune and Uranus in tandem. The focal point of this pernicious mixture has now glided on through the zodiac, and this year specifically involves Aries subjects *born between 2 and 9 April.* Unfortunately, the prospects of this influence are hardly heartening: confusion, a general atmosphere of creative fuzziness, of disturbing questions, of doubt, can all be brought on by Neptune; while Uranus adds possible dramatic turns of events which occur without warning.

In other words, Aries my friend, if you belong to this sector you'll simultaneously have to be doubly self-disciplined and methodical – to cock a snook at Neptune – and be ready to ward off the unforeseeable. So try not to provoke Fate at inopportune moments, for example, from January until mid-February, in April, in May to the beginning of June, at the beginning of July (you'll be inclined to fret at restriction and take useless risks), and from mid-September to the end of the year (with the accent on the end of October especially). These are times when events could take a completely unexpected turn which will send you off in a new direction and prevent you taking objective decisions, as a result of the confused and muddied Neptunian climate. Fortunately, throughout the year, Saturn acts as a guardian to protect your back and seal the breaches which Neptune and Uranus have caused. All the same, be wary of schemes, traps and illusions, of stabs in the back and castles in the air – they could lead you down dead-end paths and result in some rude awakenings.

Direct and straightforward Aries that you are, you probably fight much better against declared adversaries than this nebulous and irrational climate which leaves you feeling bewildered, even helpless. You who have never – or almost never – lived in a state of depression, who have difficulty doubting yourself and the world, now find yourself (and perhaps have done since last year) immersed in doubt and perplexity. So bear in mind (see the Introduction) that these cyclical trials the heavens send us are only there to make us progress spiritually and develop a more elevated state of consciousness.

Under the influence of this double discord, some Aries subjects will experience the need to turn their status quo upside down. They'll question their basic principles of existence, dream of some absolute or 'elsewhere'; or, as Baudelaire, another Aries, wrote: 'They'll dream of "diving into the unknown to find the new".' And the height of this questioning, of the quasi-metaphysical crisis which awaits you this year, will probably come at the end of the year when Jupiter in turn will contribute its share of troubles and disturbance.

Other Aries subjects, however, will experience this agitated period as the most exciting of their lives – a time of discovery and romantic passion. In fact, in December, when Venus will aid them, many still-single Aries subjects will find their soulmates. And speaking of love ... you'll bloom and, despite the astral context mentioned above, feel relatively secure, because you'll be loved and appreciated in the following propitious periods: January, the end of February/beginning of March, the end of May/beginning of June, the end of July/beginning of August, the end of October/beginning of November and also in December. April, too, deserves special mention as Venus will exert an inflammatory influence, making your charm simultaneously fiery and insolent. And this is a period when, allied to the discord of Neptune and Uranus, this planet could well produce something quite unexpected – like a break-up ... a meeting ... double involvement ... love at first sight ... it all depends on your personal chart.

Other explosive or problematic times, which will throw you into some emotional disarray, are: the end of January/beginning of February, the end of June/beginning of July, and in September, and the second part of November.

On the health side, look after yourself and be extremely restrained in your movements, your social behaviour and when driving, at the following times: the end of January/beginning of February, the second half of May, and in October. Bear in mind that, because of the concurrent discord of Mars and Uranus, there's a danger of some incident or accident – so you'll need to be doubly careful. All the same, for *the whole Sign* there are periods when you have every cosmic chance of making good the mistakes you made when led astray by Neptune; periods when it will also be possible to deal with the often untimely reactions provoked by Uranus. Thus you'll stabilise your gains and positively protect your back in February, in June, in July to August, and at the beginning of December. It's highly likely then (especially in February for *first decans* and December for *second decans*), that you'll be rewarded for your merits, perhaps by a bonus or promotion, or some distinction or other. So you see, not everything is doom and gloom in 1992 – not by a long way.

### Taurus (20 April to 21 May)

Let's start with the good news: *first decans*, who last year (particularly those born before the 27th) found themselves aggravated, delayed and obstructed by Saturn, are out of the woods. Only January and February will be mediocre months for them in that they'll still see repercussions from last year.

Saturn's 'victims' this year will be those *born before 9 May*. Thus, if you're *second decan*, you'll have to face up to delays and various obstacles thrown up by this planet which has been called 'the master of experience and time', and which presents us with the bill for our past mistakes. And if you're at the end of the second decan, *born after 6 or 7 May*, you won't get your final bill till early 1993 – for payment in full!

As you probably know, every seven years Saturn induces a phase of internalisation, of questioning our scale of values. Its influence confronts us with realities which up to this point we have neglected – and with which from here on we're obliged to come to terms. On a physical level this entails a time of maximum vulnerability, sometimes of physical exhaustion due to overwork. As a Taurean, forewarned is forearmed: you should have a good medical check-up so as to ward off eventual deficiencies, and look after your throat and vocal chords (stop smoking) as well as your reproductive system and blood circulation which is often defective in your Sign.

The most crucial times in terms of health are: almost all of February, the end of February/beginning of March (watch out for falls if you go skiing ... and elsewhere); also May, the end of June and almost all July, August and November, when the Sun teams up with Saturn to put you more at risk. These same periods could also prove to be times of trial on a professional level, where you could be susceptible to criticism from those around you at work.

If I've gone on at some length on the subject of Saturnian discordance, it's so you can enjoy the good news more! A powerful planetary trio consisting of Neptune, Uranus and Jupiter (until October) will prove strongly supportive if you belong to the *first or second decans*. In particular if you're *born before 5 May*, August will see you gather the fruits of what you sowed in the last quarter of 1991. You'll have some juicy deals, promising projects and professional success which could be as vast as it will be unexpected. The times these goodies will be most likely are: in January (for *second decan* people), March, May, July and September. The *first decan* will be especially favoured at the end of April/beginning of May and the end of June/beginning of July. Remember: Uranus and Neptune can presage a sudden, near-miraculous starring role, and their

influences serve as a powerful guard against the restriction of
Saturn.

As for the *last decan*, the periods indicated above also apply,
though less intensely. And, especially if you were *born before
15 May*, you'll suffer the opposition of Pluto this year, which
will call your status quo into question, either materially or
spiritually. Profound upheavals lie in wait for you, perhaps to
do with your spouse or partner, particularly between the end of
February and mid-March, then in May (which, depending on
your birthday configuration, could imply that these effects will
last till your next birthday) and then from mid-June to the end
of August, and finally in November, which will have repercussions in the first half of December.

So a metamorphosis awaits you, a deep, slow, irreversible
transformation of your psyche which, by the time it is done, will
have turned you into someone else. In other words, you can
expect to change your scale of values, your vision of the world;
to modify your criteria and challenge your somewhat conformist
Taurean principles. You will have every chance to make this
change positive, to see to it that it's as enriching as possible in
the following periods; mid-January, the beginning of February,
mid-March, the end of April, mid-July and September – when
Jupiter joins this cosmic concert to contribute to your inner
rebirth or material recovery.

For *all Taurus subjects* love flourishes and is gratifying (and
not only in terms of the affection of family or friends) at the
following times: from the end of January to mid-February, from
mid-March to the beginning of April, in May (do as you
please), from mid-June to mid-July; in August and, finally,
from the middle of November to the beginning of December.
These are periods which will shine like emotional beacons and
when it is highly probable that *second decans* who are still
unattached will meet their soulmates.

Some advice: if you're *last decan*, and especially if you have
Pluto in opposition this year (i.e. *born before 15 May*), it's
worth having a thorough medical check-up; for one can
establish certain correlations between Plutonian discords and
the appearance of tumours – which are most often, though not

always, benign. The planet of change, of transformation, of death and rebirth along with fundamental self-questioning, Pluto, can induce deep psychosomatic disturbance, which could well be the source of such cellular disorder.

## Gemini (21 May to 21 June)

After 1991, when the cosmic backdrop was almost entirely positive (apart from the last quarter for the first half of your Sign) this is a mixed year, two-sided like you, dear Gemini. On the one hand, Saturn continues to be on your side and brings – especially *first and second decans* – a reward for past efforts, assuring them of a generally consolidated situation and greater physical resistance; then, from October until the end of the year, Jupiter will lend a strong helping hand and favour business for the *first half of the Sign.* And yet it is precisely Jupiter that will cause problems for you if you were *born before 7 June.* In this case, you will have to suffer repercussions from late last year in terms of administrative worries, problems with authority or your seniors, and even a possible financial bloodletting!

The *last decan* will suffer few of these trials and tribulations, as Jupiter will only be very briefly – and then not seriously – hostile to it between the end of August and the beginning of October. That's the general picture. And it isn't easy to be more precise as the influences of these two planets produce contradictory effects; and while Saturn brings a perceptible consolidation of gains, Jupiter spreads disorder in your business and life, in other words destabilises your status quo, until the beginning of October.

On the positive side, you'll have unflagging energy and a galvanised spirit of enterprise – that will also galvanise those around you – between mid-February and mid-March, between mid-May and mid-June and from the end of June to mid-July. But this last period will be double-edged: you'll show unusual endurance and yet have a tendency to wasted efforts and to dissipate your energy through lack of organisation. So avoid spreading yourself too widely, which is one of your cherished faults. The other times you risk going wrong through too much stress, through hustle and bustle and lack of coherence, are in April and, if you are *at the end of the Sign*, at the beginning of January.

On the heart side, you'll want to throw propriety to the winds and do several things at a time (or at least two as you're a Gemini!) in January, the end of March/beginning of April, end of May/beginning of June (which implies that this climate could last until your next birthday, particularly if you are *first decan*), then in August especially for *second decans*, and at the beginning of September for *last decans*. Even though your sign is a past master of the art of skilfully juggling with the feelings it inspires, be careful just how far you go with your partner – or else watch out for a boomerang!

Your love life will be protected, consolidated, stabilised and restored (especially *for the first two decans*) between mid-February and mid-March, in April, from the end of May to mid-June, from mid-July to the beginning of August and in the greater part of September, from mid-October to mid-November and during almost all December – which represent the two most positive phases of 1992.

On the professional front as well, you'll gather the fruits of past efforts: in February, April, round the time of your birthday, in July (*for the first two decans*) and (*for all the Sign*) August, and finally from the end of September to the end of October. These are times when everything you undertake will have a maximum chance of enduring. In contrast, nothing will work out – briefly – in March and June (*for first decans*) and in September (*for last decans*), which are phases when everything gets complicated and you'll have a tendency to drown yourself in excess. But, as you can see, all told this is a positive year – even if in comparison to 1991 it may seem pretty insipid!

## Cancer (21 June to 22 July)

Cancer, my friend, this year's planetary backdrop will be comparable to last year's, with one difference: the planets have moved on in the zodiac and this year affect slightly different sectors.

A regenerative trine of Pluto will sustain the psyche, health and material welfare of Cancerians *born between 11 and 17 July*. It will provide them with vital reserves and act as an antidote to the double dissonance of Neptune and Uranus, whose nebulous astral climate will threaten Cancerians *born between 10 and 14 July* with unforeseen incidents and uncomfortable setbacks....

It is worth mentioning here that, while situations generated by a discordant Neptune are marked by an uncomfortable blur, an incoherent atmosphere of turmoil and doubt, Uranus acts on the contrary through sudden and unexpected upsets, break-ups, stress and possible spots of bad luck in areas that depend on your personal chart and the current planetary context. And yet ... it's often thanks to such Uranian dissonance that one has the courage to free oneself from ties which have become too tight.

Now here's the good news: what's different this year from last is a fine, clearly protective trine of Jupiter, which will bring a lucky tone to your year until the beginning of October, particularly if you were *born before 8 July* (that's to say, in the first half of the Sign). You will harvest the fruits of situations or opportunities which came about in the last quarter of last year. If you are *first decan*, the key phase of these positive repercussions will be in spring, between March and June. But watch out! Lean times will follow good if you are intemperate, especially financially, in the last quarter – which could well have ill-fated results next year. During these last three months, therefore, take care not to put yourself in an awkward position as regards the law, repayments, or the taxman, and don't take issue with your boss. You won't have the last word!

As for *second decans*, since change seems imposed by Uranus, choose the times Jupiter is supportive – with all the luck that implies – to give a new orientation to your life and improve your living conditions. The best times for this are: January, February, the end of July/beginning of August; and when rapid planets like Mercury and the Sun are favourable: between mid-February and mid-March, between the end of April and the end of May, during a good part of June, especially on your birthday (thanks to a stimulating Mars), and finally during September and November. And if you belong to the *last decan*, from the end of November to mid-December you can positively redirect the change that Pluto involves you in.

During the most disruptive periods of 1992, those which particularly for *second decan* harbour trying times and could be pretty chaotic, you must, as far as you can, refrain from making drastic decisions, for you will be totally lacking in objectivity: in January (unless you listen to those around you), in April, from mid-March to virtually the end of April, on your birthday and from the end of September to mid-October.

On the heart side, thanks to Jupiter, you will experience some ardent hours at the end of January/beginning of February, the end of March, in May, August and the beginning of October. But you'll also be perturbed and perplexed at the end of January/beginning of February (except *last decans*), in April, the end of June/beginning of July (except *first decans*), in September and the second half of November.

As far as health is concerned, a discordant Neptune can make one extremely vulnerable to viral infections. So you'll need to be far-sighted and not take pointless chances (though a sextile of Jupiter should hopefully protect the *first two decans* till August, and the *last decan* till the beginning of October, from the debilitating effects of Neptune and the risks of accident inherent in Uranian dissonance). Nevertheless, when Uranus and Mars are simultaneously discordant, one needs to be extra cautious, especially where electricity is concerned, and in handling blunt instruments or appliances. So take care in the dangerous periods of January to early February, in May and in October (especially if you're the *second decan*).

On the plus side, many Cancer subjects will meet their soulmates in 1992 – even if this could entail all sorts of complications, intrigues or mysteries – and this outstanding meeting could well be a case of love at first sight, which is most favoured in the second part of March, in May, the end of June/beginning of July, in August and in October.

And that's no bad news!

### Leo (22 July to 23 August)

For Leos the years 1991, 1992 and 1993 are all influenced by a discordant Pluto and Neptune. But whereas in 1991 and 1993 Jupiter provides a protective, expansive influence, this is cruelly lacking in 1992; though not totally as, from October onwards, the 'Great Benefactor' will light up and sustain your cosmic horizon, and this will apply till the end of the year – particularly if you belong to the *first half of the Sign and were born before 8 August*. Given this basic configuration, the rapid planets (Mercury, Venus, Mars and the Sun) will also bring their personal coloration and different tones to the cosmic picture and help trigger more or less beneficial periods.

Taken as a whole, the *first decan* gets the best of it as it's only afflicted by Saturn till February (perhaps catching the fall-out from a problem of 1991). So *July Leos* can breathe something of a sigh of relief! The more so as they will find themselves favoured from autumn on by a sextile of Jupiter which is synonymous with expansion and new opportunities. And this will apply at the end of October, in November and the beginning of December. At the beginning of the year, especially on the personal and emotional level, they will consolidate their situation, and emerge at last from the Saturnian tunnel which thoroughly tested them last year.

From February to the end of the year, the *second decan* will find itself facing the opposition of Saturn. If you belong to this sector of the zodiac, you will only completely escape this Saturnian influence in February of next year – and probably emerge enriched in experience and self-knowledge. While it's ongoing, though, this phase could be anything but rosy. As Alfred de Vigny put it: 'Man is a pupil and sorrow his teacher.' And it seems that to grow and evolve we need a certain amount of suffering, which Saturn can often supply.

So it is that this year Saturn could well bring you a problem to do with a partner or associate, confronting you with a reality which you like to ignore and whose telltale signs you might underestimate. But this influence could also manifest itself in a more precarious health (under the influence of Saturn one is liable to organic hyperactivity, functional retardation and sometimes decalcification or dental problems) or again, on a professional level, in a critical testing time in which nothing is offered or forgiven. In this Saturnian phase we are thus thrown back on our own resources and forced to discover our true identity – and thus our accounts with ourselves and with society, in all honesty.

On the heart side this process can take the form of an emotional cooling, as we become more distant and enter a period when the magic of amorous rapport seems suddenly to vanish, rubbed out by more mundane and realistic consider-ations. But then, isn't reality preferable to everything in the end? Is not truth the most desirable objective treasure? At least Saturn forces us to see things and people in their true colours – and that includes ourselves.

As for the *last decan*, especially if you were *born before 17 August*, Pluto will more or less overturn the basis of your existence this year. In fact, you are called upon to go through a total change, perhaps not only of your settled material con-ditions, but particularly of your psyche, of your world vision, which will alter entirely between now and next year. This process, of course, will take place very slowly and progressively, as Pluto is the slowest planet of our solar system and con-sequently remains for a considerable time at any particular point of the zodiac. And, in fact, only at the end of 1993 will your sector be transformed. This could very easily connect with your career, but could also influence your destiny in a general way. But whether you change your profession, your partner, your house or your country ... change there will be – for certain.

Your key periods for 1992? On the positive side, January is one of your best, as is April, most of June, October and December. So, despite the rather disturbing omens mentioned above, there are some good niches in your year. Mars, the most energising and stimulating of planets, will influence you favourably at the beginning of January (*first decans*), then in May to the beginning of June, and finally from the end of July until mid-September; it will enliven you and give you the physical and psychic strength necessary to confront possible problems.

Other people will find you likeable and you'll be warmed by affection in January, April, the end of May/beginning of June, from mid-July to August, in September and from mid-October to mid-November. Use these times to get close to others, to open a dialogue – and reduce the distance in which the opposition of Saturn isolates you. Times when your problems will appear particularly difficult to handle will be in February to March, in May, at the end of July, in October and, on the emotional side (unless you're *second decan*) in December.

Healthwise, be more careful and provident when Mars subjects you to fatigue, or makes you vulnerable to inflammation and fever, or when the influence of Saturn threatens falls or circulatory problems: as at the end of February/beginning of March and the end of June to July. These are also times of the year when you'll be more than usually lacking in flexibility and diplomacy, so cultivate these two virtues or you could easily experience a serious bust-up with friends or family. And avoid being too forceful if you can. The Leo aspiring to perfect self-mastery will take this period as a challenge to be met – and mastered.

## Virgo (23 August to 23 September)

'You can't have too much of a good thing,' the saying goes – and in your case that's right.

Virgo, my friend, 1992 will be a year and a half for you, a rare – even exceptional – year. Neptune and Uranus in Capricorn will indulge you, as will Pluto in the amicable sign of Scorpio. In fact, this trio are favouring you already and, what's more, you're lucky enough to benefit from the presence of Jupiter in your Sign as well. If it hasn't already done so, this planetary quartet can put you into orbit!

It's likely too that for the *first decan* Uranus, Neptune and Saturn have already done their work in previous years and that the result has been beneficial to you. Thanks to Jupiter, you'll still experience times of plenty, and between February and July you should be rewarded with repercussions from the previous year – such as an unexpected expansion of your business or some highly positive turn of events in your favour – all of it coming to a head in a very rewarding and flourishing period. The end of February, the beginning of March and April, May and the beginning of July will also be highly constructive in this respect, so long as you go for team-work and let yourself be advised by your partner.

The *second and early last decans* are the great winners in 1992. Neptune opens up a superior spiritual, artistic and intellectual dimension for you, gives you the aptitude to excel, be receptive to almost mystical moments of illumination and find your creativity increased tenfold. Uranus for its part will see to sudden unhoped-for luck, or sudden beneficial – almost miraculous – changes, which will come to modify the course of your existence. Promotions, rewards, providential meetings, new and exciting projects, flashes of genius – in short, in-contestable progress – are all on the cards when Uranus favours us. (Let's not forget this only happens every 14 years, while Neptune's trine only reappears about every 28!)

On top of all this, Jupiter's finishing touches will serve as a catalyst to these already fine influences. And the result of this cosmic harmony? Jupiter's contribution will only affect the *first two decans* and then only till October. But an extraordinary expansion in terms of career is in store, and perhaps marriage (for Jupiter is synonymous with official recognition). If you intend to get married, the best times to do so are late January/ early February, mid-May, the end of June and the beginning of July, which are all highly promising romantically. But even after Jupiter leaves your sector of the zodiac, Venus will favour you at the end of September/beginning of October and the end of November/beginning of December. These are times when not only are emotional matters favoured – when a love-at-first-sight meeting on a street corner could change your life – but also periods of the greatest artistic creativity, when new spiritual dimensions could open for you that you never before suspected existed.

On the business side, the best periods *for all the Sign* are: January (despite the dissonance of Mars which will make *first decans* somewhat highly-strung), then March (especially in terms of team-work or partnerships), May, July, September, October, November (with some setbacks) and the end of December. Choose these times to plan projects which you hold dear and the rest of your career could flow on from here.

As for the *last decan*, which is influenced by a sextile of Pluto (especially Virgos *born before 17 September*), the same periods indicate social success – in fact a starring role. Your potential energy will be greatly increased. And this will help you benefit to the full from this positive phase which favours the organising of your financial investments, insurance portfolios, borrowings … and the salvaging of possible loans! All told it's an invaluable period, when the context of events is almost providentially in phase with your deep aspirations. A period, then, to make progress towards what you hold dear…

All told this is a superb year – which it's up to you to get the very best from!

## Libra (23 September to 23 October)

Though the planets have of course moved since last year, they still bear on the same decans, or almost. This is to say that, broadly speaking, this year looks similar to last, with one major difference: in 1992 you'll only benefit from Jupiter's support after October. And this support will be ambiguous, as at the end of the year Jupiter will be simultaneously in opposition to Neptune and Uranus and in accordance with Saturn – which in some way may amplify already existing problems.

The *first decan* gets the best of the year: before mid-February it will reap the fruits it sowed last year in terms of a more stable situation and perhaps a long-awaited reward, professionally speaking. In private life this period could also encompass marriage, most logically at the beginning of January or end of February (though failing this, marriage is also favoured right at the end of the year) when Jupiter makes an appearance, and particularly when Venus joins it late in October.

While the *last decan* lacks either difficult or providential influences, that's not the case with the *second decan*. In fact, if you're in the middle of the Sign, Neptune immerses you in the repercussions of the nebulous climate and confused situations you've already been functioning in since last year – and perhaps even since 1990. This Neptunian discord will particularly affect you if you were *born between 8 and 13 October*, just as that of Uranus (which is currently parallel to it) will concern you personally if you were *born between 5 and 13 October*.

As you no doubt already know, Uranus in opposition can expose you to sudden upheavals, dramatic turns of events, and unexpected changes which can affect any area of your life, depending on your personal chart. It also tends to excite and fatigue the nervous system and inclines to stress, especially when Mars is involved (as it will be at the end of January, end of May and in October). So don't disregard this. And as these phases will be fraught, you must try to control yourself in order to avoid incidents and accidents – on the road and elsewhere – brought on by impulsive and clumsy behaviour; you must also be extremely careful about your diet in order to avoid a range of ailments, especially chronic ones, in connection with your liver and kidneys. Fortunately, from February until the end of the year Saturn will serve as a sort of lightning conductor for you, strengthening your physical resistance and making up for your deficiencies.

February to March and August will be the most dynamic times of your year – when, with the help of Mars and Saturn, nothing will appear impossible. Your worth will be recognised, and you could well see your merits rewarded and position consolidated in February, June, August and during the greater part of December. On the other hand (this is still if you're *second decan*), be wary of the beginning of January, of April particularly, and also the end of June and beginning of July when, as we say in France, 'You'll be cycling in sauerkraut!' You won't know which way to turn and your objectives will seem hazy and unobtainable. At times like these settle down and retire within yourself. Saturn, the planet of internalisation and authenticity, will help you find the right path.

### Scorpio (23 October to 22 November)

All in all this is a positive year for your Sign, despite the opposition of Saturn, however disturbing. The reason is that simultaneously you have Neptune, Uranus and Jupiter on your side – and this planetary trio indicates you'll overcome Saturn's hassling.

If you are *first decan*, and especially if you were *born before 28 October*, there is a possible repercussion from last year's worries. But these difficulties will vanish after February, when Saturn turns its attention on the *second decan* until the end of the year.

If you are *second decan*, your leanest and meanest times will be February, the beginning of March, and July to August. May, and your birthday month of November, are also worth special mention as you'll be subject to ambiguous and contradictory influences then: simultaneously submerged by an exhausting overload of responsibilities and work, galvanised by positive changes due to Uranus, and inspired by a fine sextile of Neptune which will help guide your footsteps.

If you're *first decan*, from February onwards your horizon will brighten remarkably, thanks to a sextile of Jupiter which enables you to profit from opportunities which arose last autumn. You will gather the fruits of these windfalls, whether socially, morally or materially – or all of them at once – between May and July, and particularly between mid-June and the end of July, which will provide a climate of growth and expansion that's highly favourable to your business and your image too.

If you're *last decan* (particularly if you were *born before 16 or 17 November*) you'll enjoy greater social integration in January, April, June to July and above all September, when

Jupiter accentuates the positive influence of Pluto. At the end of
November, too, Mars will help you take great strides in your
desired direction. Touched by Pluto, their master, Scorpios will
emerge transformed from this transit, and its effects will even
extend into 1993. A deep transformation then, particularly of
your personality and vision of the world, will take place before
and after 1992 – as you'll realise when you view your life
retrospectively.

This metamorphosis could easily take place on the emotional
level too, and, if it has to do with the choice of a new partner, is
most likely to occur at the beginning of February, beginning of
April, in mid-May, the beginning of July, end of August or end
of October. And late November is altogether a most propitious
time to meet someone.

So you can see that the year ahead looks entirely encouraging
– even exciting – despite the influence of Saturn. But because of
this you should nonetheless take certain precautions: have a
check-up to make sure you're in good health. And don't forget
your Schussler salt is calcium sulphate – which is particularly
necessary for your Sign.

Have a good year!

### Sagittarius (22 November to 22 December)

If you are *first decan* (and especially if you were *born before 20
November*) you will have already profited last year from a
stabilising sextile of Saturn which probably brought you some
reward or recognition of your merits. And if that hasn't already
happened, it will in January or the beginning of February when
Saturn returns to the same position in the zodiac. The beginning
of January in particular should be favourable for you. And as
the influence of Saturn is so positive at the time of your
birthday, the laws of astrology decree that it will continue to be
so until your next birthday, acting as a sort of lightning
conductor to channel possible negative influences. You'll need
it, too, between March and July when Jupiter, your ruler,
induces administrative harassments or financial problems (pos-

sibly resulting from the last quarter of 1991). A number of Sagittarians will also find themselves in a dilemma, either emotionally or in terms of their general activity in April and at the end of May.

Fortunately by October, when Saturn ceases to protect the *first decan*, Jupiter will have entered the cosmic dance to favour your material expansion and natural optimism, and safeguard your *joie de vivre*. This will be particularly noticeable from the end of October to mid-November and at the beginning of December. You'll undoubtedly have the opportunity then to put business matters, which have taken a turn for the worse, back on track and to straighten out shaky situations. The other good news is that the opportunities which occur in this last quarter of 1992 will have splendid repercussions on practically all the next year, if you belong to the *first half of the Sign* (that's *before 7/8 December*). So keep your eyes and ears open – and seize your opportunities in both hands!

If you belong to the *second decan* and particularly if you were born *before the 7th*, you will be subject to fall-out from Jupiter which could take the form of economic or administrative difficulties, or problems with your superiors, particularly at the beginning of the year and between July and September. In fact, August especially will find you nervous and torn by demands that are made on you from all sides, which is a good reason to be extra vigilant and not rush into decisions or actions. For many Sagittarians in the middle of the Sign, August will also be a time of emotional choice when they'll try to pursue several things at a time. Fortunately Saturn will provide a stabilising influence, which should make them less fickle...

*Second decan Sagittarians born before 10 December* will be subject to this stabilising Saturnian influence from February till the end of the year – and it will bring them all sorts of professional and personal satisfaction. Professionally, the best periods *for all the Sign* are when the Sun and Mercury or Mars are well aspected, which is at the beginning of February, the beginning of March, in April (as long as they resist irritability and temporary nervousness), then in August, October and December.

*All the Sign* will be in exemplary shape, particularly at the beginning of January (especially *second decans*), from mid-February to approximately the end of March, from the beginning of May to mid-June and – especially where the *first half of the Sign* is concerned – during the last three months of the year when Jupiter, the planet of expansion and well-being, will favour them.

All told, the year will be relatively neutral for the *last decan*, which won't be affected by deep or lasting influences, but only the rapid planets. For the *second decan* it will be mixed, apart from December (excellent for those in the middle of the sign) and May, which should prove particularly fertile. As for *first decans*, as we've said, while they will have a rewarding period at the beginning of the year and from October on, from March to July will be stressful. Still, a Sagittarian forewarned is forearmed – and I wish you a good 1992!

## Capricorn (22 December to 20 January)

As last year (especially you, *second decan*) you experienced the vagaries of Neptune and stresses of Uranus, in comparison 1992 will seem a good deal more pleasant. With Jupiter once more well aspected to your natal Sun, you'll experience a climate of moral and material expansion, new opportunities and a general improvement of your living conditions. If you're *first decan* you'll be most aware of this between March and July, when you'll reap the fruits of propositions from the end of last year. If you're *second decan* Jupiter will act as a sort of middle-man for you, a providential catalyst, to turn the influences of Uranus and Neptune to your advantage, especially in January and August. And the *last decan*, favoured by a fine sextile of Pluto, will see its subjects (especially those *born before 15 January*), firmly established in their social circle, giving them a greater professional impact – especially in September when Jupiter reinforces Pluto to provide a superbly promising time.

Favoured though it is in spring and in summer, the *first decan* (*born before 5 January*) will, from October onwards, enter a somewhat disorderly phase, which unfortunately will have repercussions in 1993. So, looking ahead, during the last three months of the year, try to avoid the mistakes you suffered from last year and be especially cautious on the administrative, fiscal and financial sides. If you take on major debts now, for example, you'll have trouble settling them later.

In sum, then, for many *first and second decans* 1992 will be a year of expansion – almost explosively so. Especially in January, at the beginning of March, in May, September and November, you'd be well advised to try everything – be as daring as you can. In April, too, Mars will galvanise you with a new strength, and throughout June, as in January, nothing will seem impossible.

Nonetheless, Mars is in direct transit in your Sign in January, so beware then of being too intransigent or inflexible, which will put the cat among the pigeons as far as others are concerned. This is equally a time on the health front when – especially if you're *second decan* – there's a danger of inflammation, viral infection, fever and migraines, if you're subject to them. This also applies to the end of May and first part of October. So take care...

The most generally difficult times will be April, from mid-June to the beginning of July, and at the beginning of October – when dealings will be difficult, confused and delayed, and you run the risk of ending up totally bewildered (especially if you're *second decan*). Whatever specific scenario your personal chart decrees, however, one thing's for sure: this year will be anything but monotonous – and it could, for many of you, prove a great time in your life.

## *Aquarius (20 January to 19 February)*

In overall terms, one could say that 1992 is going to be a better year for you than 1991 – and not as good as 1993. In other words, you're going to be a little more fortunate than last year, and a little less than next.

In fact, while Saturn continues to transit your Sign in a major thirty-year cycle – and while Pluto bears on your destiny so as to change it entirely (particularly if you were *born between 10 and 15 February*) – at least this year you won't have to count on the opposition of Jupiter, which all last year poured oil on the cosmic fire. Quite to the contrary, from October onwards Jupiter will work for you, especially if you belong to the first half of the Sign (*born before 4 February*). So if you're *first decan* (and especially *born before 27 January*) at the beginning of 1992 you'll experience the repercussions of last year's Saturnian climate. But at the end of the year a trine of Jupiter will usher in an extremely positive and expansive phase which should bring 1992 to a lovely conclusion.

The start of the year is especially significant. It could provide a magnificent affirmation of your ego, consolidate your status quo, and reward you for past efforts – if your natal Sun is harmonious. If it is dissonant, however, you'll be coming to the end of a difficult and trying time either personally, professionally or in terms of health, and this could continue until the beginning of February.

From mid-February until the end of the year, Saturn will pass into the *second decan*, bringing with it the above-mentioned trials or rewards. But in any event, whether you live this period harmoniously or in discord, whether Saturn brings you long-awaited professional ratification and the consolidation of love, or a period of isolation and reduced vitality and luck, either way this is a time to internalise, to gain by knowing yourself better, to attain inner balance and eliminate dross from your life. In other words, this is the time to take stock of your life and get down to essentials, to define your deepest aspirations and come to know your limits too, which alone will allow you to progress.

It is recognised in astrology that if one applies oneself to live through a difficult planetary influence by transforming its effects internally – by means of a sincerely increased awareness – one can algebraically reverse those effects from negative to positive. And with Saturnian influence this becomes a question of excluding superficial activity and entering into oneself so as to help the planet act in a salutary way on one's innermost being.

*Third decan Aquarians born before 15 February* will have to face up to a similar planetary climate, though in their case Pluto rather than Saturn will instigate transformation and change. So for *second and third decans* here are the most fertile and positive times of the year, when you can transform lead into gold: the beginning of January, all February until mid-March (a particularly intense period), April (especially harmonious), the end of May/beginning of June, part of October and finally December. The challenging periods will be: February to March (ambiguous), May, the end of July, August, mid-October and the beginning of November. Be tolerant and adaptable – or try to! – at the beginning of March and July, when Mars will tend to make you particularly rigid and stubborn, even tyrannical.

The affection of your family and the help of a partner will be invaluable to find solutions or make vital decisions at the beginning of January, in April, the beginning of June, in September and early November. These are also periods when you'll consolidate existing ties which will stretch into the future and bring you serenity.

The key periods in 1992, when you will have to face up to some cosmic bad weather – which could simply have to do with psychological problems – are most likely to be February to March, May, August and November. Be ready to confront them and to fit in with changes if necessary. Go all the way with your ideas and discoveries.

Good luck!

## Pisces (19 February to 21 March)

1992 will be another golden year for you, Pisces – or in any event gold-plated – as the only discord in your heavens (and that's only for the *first decan*) is the opposition of Jupiter, which will be neutralised to some degree by the astral context, and which will cease at the beginning of October anyway. In other words, once again this year you'll have the good luck to benefit from an absolutely magnificent and exceedingly rare planetary configuration, due to a concentration of planets in Capricorn and a trine of Pluto in Scorpio which extends for years. So Uranus will support you and favour the sudden, unexpected appearance of positive changes in your life; while a fine sextile of Neptune will give wings to your inspiration and intuition – to guide you surely on your path.

In this planetary context, the *second decan* won't be bothered (at the beginning of the year, or between July and September) when, in its turn, it falls subject to the dissonance of Jupiter. Quite the reverse in fact. Jupiter will act as a catalyst favouring partnerships, marriage, and all team-work. And finally, during September, when the *last decan* has Jupiter in opposition, it will be more or less neutralised by a sextile of Pluto; which means that the solution to problems will most often come through the intermediary of a friend, whose sound advice will prove invaluable.

Nonetheless, this Jupiterian opposition is a potential breeding ground for all sorts of complications and particularly financial, administrative or legal ones. It could throw up some difficult choices, especially in January and February (if you're *first decan*) and at the beginnings of June and September, in mid-August and in December. These are times when you'll have to be rock-solidly organised to get the better of a load of responsibilities and demands which will weigh you down. For you'll run the risk of dispersing yourself dangerously – especially in April and August – and of wasting your efforts, energy and time in dead-end activities.

All in all, though, with the support of Uranus, Neptune and (for the *third decan*) Pluto in conjunction, you have every chance of progressing in leaps and bounds this year, of changing everything in your life that displeases you, weighs you down or frustrates you. So *second and mid-last decan* Pisceans should take off – and leap into the unknown! For he who dares, wins. And being adventurous will be especially profitable for you at the end of February, in March, May, July, October or the beginning of November. And, if you're *last decan*, December will prove an extremely fertile and rewarding month.

If you're still unattached, Uranus will almost certainly help you meet your soulmate either at the beginning of February, end of March, May, end of June/beginning of July, beginning of October or at the end of November. These are also key periods for the *last decan* to revive a dormant romance and get back on the right track.

Good luck!

# *1993*

## The course of the planets

# World Events

The forecasts which follow are only valid in so far as the genuine birth of Europe takes place at midnight (2300 hours GMT) on 31 December 1992. For, as you know, astrology is based on precise astronomical calculations and, if its constituent elements change, so must its conclusions.

It's certainly no fluke that, remote-controlled by cosmic rhythms, we chose 1993 to found the existence of Europe: for that is when Uranus and Neptune form a planetary conjunction that only reappears every 172 years, constituting a true cycle of civilisation. And of course the effect of this most important of configurations radiates both before and beyond its precise appearances on 1 February 1993.

As you know, the period around 1821 (the date of the last similar astral conjunction) coincided with the birth of the industrial era and the beginning of socialism, but also the advent of the bourgeoisie, of capitalism and of a new European equilibrium. In essence, then, this cycle introduced a new spirit of the times – and it will again. With Uranus and Neptune in Capricorn – pre-eminently a Sign of political structures – we can expect the advent of an epoch allotted to universalised politics. We will feel the breath of a new spirit in which solidarity and humanitarianism will be at the service of society and solidly embodied in it. Or, in other words, political structures will be impregnated with this new spirit.

The twenty-first century will be spiritual, even mystical. Or it will not be. For the astrologer it is tremendously interesting to note that this most important of conjunctions is going to take shape for the first time in 172 years on 1 February 1993, and then re-form in August and in October, not to return until 2165! The first of February is one month after the birth of the new political concept – so essential for world equilibrium – of a unified Europe. And if an astrologer had been asked he would have advised October rather than the beginning of the year, as it's much more harmonious and, moreover, contains a splendid trine between Jupiter and Saturn which appears related to the European concept. As it is, the discords inherent in 1 January reflect the efforts of different countries towards general harmony and the snags and hitches which must inevitably accompany the birth of the European machine.

In a turbulent planetary context, this birth will not take place without difficulty and the delivery will be laboured. There will be an accumulation of rare celestial tension, marked especially by disturbance in Jupiter, which symbolises legality and the financial, monetary, economic or judicial character of an undertaking. Jupiter will be squared successively with the Sun, Uranus, Neptune and Mars and this indicates haphazard problems in harmonising laws or the economy, judicial confrontations, abrupt changes in legislation, a general lack of enthusiasm and scepticism, even a certain defeatism or a climate of confusion. For its part, the opposition of Neptune and Uranus to Mars points to a lack of organisation and obscure intrigues marked by diplomatic relationships lacking in frankness and undertaken in a spirit of aggressive controversy. Problems of harmonising laws and monetary questions will be the principal stumbling blocks. And the first reaction could well be disenchantment at the possibility of ever finding a solution to satisfy all member countries.

Fortunately Venus, well aspected to both Mercury and the Moon, will salvage the situation. For Venus symbolises art, culture and woman; and cultural exchanges could well be the first point on which the different countries agree. These good aspects give reason to hope that dialogue will continue, despite all obstacles, and that Europe will progress, animated by general and fundamental goodwill. Similarly, it seems that art, leisure and culture will find cohesion in its Graeco-Roman roots and Judeo-Christian ideology to embrace the fresh, all-encompassing spirit of the new age.

Last but not least, this particular Venus indicates the taking of definitive political power by women: their slow, progressive, irresistible ascension, which will be anchored in time. Saturn, in conjunction, reinforces this, and a square of Venus and Pluto indicates a far-reaching change of the role of woman in society.

Germany could have difficulty in adapting to legislative changes or the economic demands of the new Europe, which could for a time throw it into relative confusion, even a possible identity crisis! (For Uranus and Neptune in Capricorn are opposing its ascendant in Libra.) But it will still occupy a commanding position on the political landscape, as the trine Jupiter/Saturn is harmoniously placed in its ascendant – which will prove rewarding in the long term.

The same applies to France which, viewed astrologically, also seems to play an important role in the European ensemble. With Jupiter, the planet of expansion and wellbeing, in its Sun, France will probably secure the role of representative or ambassador to other world political entities. But here, too, there will be a confusing period of adaptation, with Uranus and Neptune in the mid-heavens. So, more than any other country, France will be marked by the new spirit of the times which will completely modify its internal political structures. And there's the possibility of considerable tension between conservative values and the generous surge which will eventually carry France forward ... and towards other European nations.

In May or June Prince Charles could be crowned King Charles III. It's worth noting, too, that with Venus in the Moon of Juan Carlos, the King of Spain will have an important part to play as a mediator in the European arena. And, despite all the controversy and confusion and judicial/economic complications, the conjunctions of Uranus and the Sun, and the Sun and Neptune, will preside over the birth of Europe and enlighten this ambitious political adventure.

The summer will see an irreversible change in the entity that is Canada, and if the separation of Quebec did not take place in the autumn of 1991 it will certainly happen now.

The beginning of August will prove an ideal time for political and diplomatic summits; but because of Jupiter/Uranus and Jupiter/Neptune squalls, September appears a low point with regard to harmonising European laws. And this seems to have an effect on Europe's economic situation. Ecological problems – which seem insurmountable – will arise at the end of March, perhaps in the course of an event with a European dimension. Collective consciousness will be preoccupied by the question of pollution on a planetary scale, especially in October, but a semblance of a European solution won't occur before January 1994.

By October, Europe will have attained the beginnings of a political-social balance in its new institutions and become aware of its new and original global identity. This period could mark a fresh stage in its progress, perhaps in the form of an opening to one or more new members (Austria, Sweden, Switzerland)? With the great conjunction of Uranus and Neptune in harmony with the Sun in Switzerland's constitution, this country will certainly be superbly aspected and enter a new and fertile age, perhaps for 172 years.

## *Your Personal Forecast*

### *Aries (21 March to 20 April)*

If you were *born in the first half of the Sign*, you've already made the acquaintance (sometimes painfully) of Neptune and Uranus in tandem, which since the entry of these planets into Capricorn (in 1988) has disturbed your life and shaken it to the core.

This year, this somewhat disruptive planetary team will bear on Aries subjects *born between 6 and 11 April.* You'll have to confront sometimes justified but quite often irrational turmoil due to the dissonance of Neptune, and dramatic turns of events and unforeseeable changes thanks to Uranus. Looking at the year positively, though, this could be the opportunity of a lifetime to turn over a new leaf and arm yourself in a new direction. For once the astral train is in motion there's no getting off – and however contrary or discordant planetary energy may be, you can still make use of it for the best.

If you're *second decan* you had the support of Saturn last year to give you a certain moral strength to confront these discords. And in 1993 (apart from January), Saturn will back the *last decan* right through the year. Specifically, it will help stabilise their professional situation, consolidate their gains and provide a good deal of physical resistance, which will all be extremely use to you, particularly in January, April and September, when the astral context will be difficult or stressful.

Subjects of the *second decan* will be affected by the regression of Jupiter which entered their opposite Sign of Libra last October and which will give rise to various worries or complications of a financial or administrative nature. This will apply from January to March and then again in August and September. If you're *first decan*, on the other hand, you'll have a brush with Jupiter's dissonance between April and mid-August. This is not the time (for either decan) to ask for a rise, make official approaches, or contract major debts – which you'll have trouble paying off afterwards. If you were *born between 6 and 13 April*, pay particular attention to administrative issues, as a tax audit is likely, particularly at the beginning of the year and then in September.

The most favourable periods in this turbulent period? Almost all February, June, August (with some reservations, as Mars will make you impulsive and there's a risk of making some drastic and unfortunate decisions) and finally the last part of December, which should be excellent. Mars, your ruler, will actively help you in May to June, by granting you the energy to overcome all obstacles, and in November to December as well. On the other hand, it is not recommended to make long-term decisions in January, April or July, nor in September to October, when your vision of things will be clouded and you'll lack calmness and lucidity. Physically, the double dissonance of Uranus and Mars calls for considerable prudence when driving or handling blunt instruments or domestic machinery (especially between January and April and in September). During these same periods you'll have a tendency to squander your energy, to disperse yourself in activity and lose the breathing space you need before making decisions. So take time to relax and – to be more efficient – slow down. You'll find you're a lot more effective.

Professionally, January will be relatively difficult, as will April, July and October; while on the emotional side, there's a considerable risk of putting yourself in impossible situations, either between mid-February and the beginning of June (when you'll charm all around you!), or in August, or the end of October. Many Aries subjects will want to throw propriety to the winds and set sail for new horizons. But if you're *third decan* you'll stabilise your professional gains in a noteworthy way in February, June, August or December, while your emotional life will be solid as a rock in March, July and September. So, taking everything into account, you can see this is a fascinating year – a year to tickle your sense of challenge.

Get to it!

## *Taurus (20 April to 21 May)*

While Neptune and Uranus shelter the *second decan* from cosmic storms this year (from February on), one can't say as much for the *last decan*, which will be simultaneously worried by both Pluto and Saturn.

For the *last decan* this will result in a year of confrontation with reality in an atmosphere of crisis, when you'll be obliged to make an honest assessment of your life and call your basic principles into question. This will be most apparent to you in February, May, on your birthday, in August and in November, which will be difficult phases to accept, like narrow doors of destiny that you'll need to squeeze through, to emerge enlarged and strengthened. Comfort, routine and habit-loving Taurean that you are, you'll be forced to make concessions if you want to benefit spiritually from these critical influences. For all discord has a meaning and a reason for being, even if at the time it appears arbitrary or unfair to us. And the astral context will come to your aid – especially between January and April – when Mars will give you increased dynamism, which will help you overcome all obstacles; and then in June to July, in September and at the end of December.

These same periods of time will prove fertile and promising for the *second decan* which, under the highly positive double influence of Neptune and Uranus, will in some way be guided towards a charming stranger. If you belong to this sector of the zodiac, you will have unexpected and exciting promotions, near-miraculous strokes of luck, unhoped-for professional turnarounds or long-awaited changes of residence, which comes as a sudden windfall. On the emotional level, many Taureans will find their soulmates, especially in January, June, August or October, and particularly if they're *second decan*. Finally, a warning if you belong to the *last decan*: show foresight and have a preventive medical check-up. Saturn and Pluto in conjunction can render you particularly vulnerable in terms of health.

## Gemini (21 May to 21 June)

Gemini, my friend, you have a rosy year ahead, with Jupiter and Saturn in a tandem which should prove doubly rewarding. A much better year, then, than the last, which – apart from the final quarter – had its share of harassment from Jupiter, as you'll no doubt remember, even though your sign tends to live more in the present, which has its advantages and disadvantages...

*All three decans* will have their slice of the cake in 1993, as all will be favoured at different times. The *second decan* will enjoy highly satisfying and rewarding repercussions from Jupiter at the beginning of the year until the end of March and will gather the fruits of this later, in August to September. Jupiter's horn of plenty will in all probability pour out a handsome promotion at work ... financial pluses ... unhoped-for strokes of luck ... perhaps marriage. These same advantages will fall due to the *first decan*, but in this case between April and the beginning of August, when it will gather what it sowed in October to November of last year. As for the *last decan*, Jupiter will only favour it in October, in an apparently short-lived way;

but as this sector of the zodiac will have the invaluable support of Saturn from February onwards, it won't be short changed!

More precisely, if you were *born after 6 June*, Saturn will start to stabilise your life from the beginning of the year: you will bring your plans to fruition, or your image will be enhanced; you will be appreciated at your true worth ... and property is favoured by a well-aspected Saturn. The *last decan* will enjoy these goodies between February and the end of the year. A long-term enterprise, undertaken in the spring, could be concluded in the last two months of the year to your great satisfaction, at which time you could also receive an honour or a reward (like a promotion, or examination pass) which has been gestating since the spring.

### Cancer (21 June to 22 July)

Cancer, my friend, while last year (along with the double dissonance of Neptune and Uranus which chiefly disturbed the *second decan*) you experienced a reassuring and beneficial sextile of Jupiter, this year will be quite different.

In fact, especially if you were born at the end of the *second decan between 8 and 15 July*, you will be troubled in turn by Neptune and Uranus in tandem; and Jupiter will also pose problems – particularly at the start of the year and then in September to October. These are the most difficult times of your year, in fact, when you may well ask yourself fundamental questions about the meaning of life and the value of your criteria and objectives.

*First decans*, too, will be troubled by the square of Jupiter which presents them with various problems – either financial, administrative, or to do with their superiors – between April and the beginning of August.

Thanks to Pluto, the *last decan* is the most protected – especially those subjects *born before 20 July*. This sector of the zodiac will find itself reinforced in its vital resources and encouraged and propelled towards a better integration into society, perhaps by virtue of a special, long-awaited promotion.

By the way, these positive aspects of Pluto only occur every forty years, so one rarely has a chance to profit from them more than once in a professional lifetime. And they can also transform us exclusively on the psychic plane through a better understanding and use of our potential energies.

In general, *whichever decan* you belong to, the optimum periods in 1993 are as follows: on the professional side, February to March, then May, June to July, almost all September and November – which will be particularly fertile. All the same, take care. The presence of Mars in the first four months of the year will galvanise you into action, but given the difficult planetary context, it could make this action untimely and regrettable. So think twice before you act, even in February to March, when you'll have other aces up your sleeve.

Other stressful periods occasioned by Mars will be from mid-August to the end of September and the end of December. These tricky times should be met with particular care when handling blunt instruments, or driving, as your instinct for self-preservation could well be diminished. Furthermore, when Jupiter mixes in with Mars, Uranus and Neptune, up to May you run the risk of functioning in a completely chaotic atmosphere, which robs you of objectivity and inclines you to make inopportune decisions. All the more reason to play for time, then. And be in a hurry – to wait!

On the heart side, you'll have every chance to reorientate your life when Venus is especially well aspected in January, June, at the end of September/beginning of October and in November. Choose these key periods to pursue what you most aspire to. You can count on the sympathy and support of your family and friends.

### Leo (22 July to 23 August)

In general, this year will seem a good deal more clement than last, due to a fine sextile of Jupiter which will favour you till November.

In fact, Saturn will continue to test you: confronting you with your responsibilities, and making you pay for past mistakes (especially if you were born in the first half of the Sign, *before 8 August*), while Pluto, for his part, will upset your status quo and force you to question your living conditions (especially if you were *born between 12 and 20 August*). But, nonetheless, Jupiter will sustain you with its generous and expansive energy.

For the *last decans* the dissonance of Saturn and Pluto will, in some way, make a clean sweep of the past. And, in the situations that will confront you, if you do cling onto the past, you'll only regret it. Pluto, in fact, encourages us to espouse change, however radical. And in February, May, August, October and November, you'll feel its energy strongly: which will simultaneously increase your awareness of your current situation, make you review it seriously and objectively, and counter it by orientating yourself in a new direction. These won't be easy times, but then nothing's impossible for a Leo! And the months when you'll have the most chance of positively progressing – even if at a cost – will be October and November.

The beginning of the year will be particularly favourable for the *second decan*, as it will enjoy a sextile of Jupiter with echoes from last December. Those *born during the first ten days of August* will find everything they undertake at this time has very pleasant repercussions in August to September. They'll have great plans for expansion and lucky opportunities, which will almost miraculously extricate them from problematic situations. If you're a July or beginning of August *first decan*, you will enjoy these same advantages between April and August, when Jupiter provides the opportunity for you to profit from proposals or projects which first saw the light last autumn. Nevertheless, as lean times must follow good, be particularly careful in November to December: Jupiter will be hostile then and resurrect all sorts of problems to do with regulations or the law (or simply your budget) which could well last almost all through next year. So be warned...

*Whatever decan* you are, be particularly careful what you say and do in May and June and in October, when you will be subject to the powerfully energising influence of Mars, which will tend to make you impulsive or clumsy. You should be particularly careful in sport, and also look after your heart and arteries, which are your Sign's weak points. And if you're *last decan* (which will be particularly weakened by the joint influences of Pluto and Saturn) take a long, hard look at your health to pre-empt organic deficiencies. And remember the homeopathic salt you require is magnesium phosphate.

On the heart side all goes well, and you'll be encompassed by the warm affection of your family and the friendship of others between February and the beginning of June, in July, September, the end of October and in December – which will all be propitious times for heart-to-hearts with your nearest and dearest.

In sum, then, 1993 will be largely rewarding and enriching for the *first and second decans*; while, for the *last decan*, it will prove more difficult...

Hang in there!

## Virgo (23 August to 23 September)

Another dream of a year for you! You'll be favoured by the impressive planetary trio of Pluto, Neptune and Uranus. And Jupiter as well from November on, when it enters the friendly sign of Scorpio, where it stays till the end of the year (a time when *first decans* are especially favoured and *the rest of the Sign* will simultaneously enjoy an excellent double trine of Uranus and Neptune and a rewarding sextile of Pluto).

It's worth pointing out here that this kind of planetary configuration is entirely peculiar to the end of this century. While normally the planets, more or less dispersed through the zodiac, affect all the signs cyclically, Saturn, Uranus and Neptune entered Capricorn back in 1988, and Neptune and Uranus in tandem there have favoured you ever since – especially so as they're allied to a sextile of Pluto which has been well aspected for you since 1983. Which all goes to show, Virgo my friend, just how favoured by Fate you have been for some years now.

Returning specifically to 1993, Pluto, the bringer of positive transformation and salutary evolution, will create a context of events for natives of the *third decan*, particularly those *born between 13 and 20 September*, which will be in tune with their deepest aspirations. In other words, situations will arise, socially or professionally, which will be made to measure for you. So you'll have greater impact on people and things and really progress towards your objectives. This sextile of Pluto is a rare and precious influence as it only occurs every 40 years or so. So exploit it!

If you are *second decan* – and particularly if you were *born between 8 and 14 September* – the partnership of Neptune and Uranus will reward you with benefits: you'll be showered with windfalls which will give you all the more satisfaction as they're so unexpected, even unhoped-for. You'll want to enlarge your intellectual, geographical or personal relationship horizons and – even as you do – lucky opportunities will occur which give you the chance. For example: about to move flat, you find the house of your dreams; or, caught up in a professional routine, but more or less consciously hoping to move on, your boss offers you a promotion that's as exciting as it's surprising. And many of you will all of a sudden have the opportunity to see your talents put to good use and enjoy a degree of celebrity. In brief, if you belong to this sector of the zodiac, this is truly a blessed year, particularly when Mars, the planet of action and dynamism (that of contractors and athletes, among others), serves as a catalyst for the basic influences, as it will between January and the end of April, between the end of June and mid-August, between the end of September and the beginning of November, and at the end of December. You'll feel in super form then, able to tear down mountains, and nothing will seem impossible.

What more can one say about such a superb and promising year? Everything being relative, there will be some short, less effective periods such as perhaps between February and the beginning of April – when Mercury will be in opposition to your natal Sun – or between the end of May and mid-June, or at the beginning of December, which is probably the time you'll feel least easy. But the first period mentioned (February/March) needn't even be less profitable than the rest of the year, if you know how to adapt to your partner and collaborate with, and listen to the opinions of, others.

On the whole, in this dream of a year, you'll progress with giant strides in January, May, from mid-June to the beginning of August, at the time of your birthday, in October to November and at the end of December.

And if you want to change something in your emotional life – or even if you don't – Cupid will shoot his amorous arrows at you when Venus joins the cosmic chorus (in January, June, August, from the end of September to mid-October and at the end of November). These are periods when artists, poets and musicians will be endowed with extraordinary imagination, especially if they were *born between 8 and 14 September*. And even if you're not an artist or poet, you'll be raised above yourself, as it were, and be receptive to previously unsuspected spiritual, intellectual, even mystical dimensions.

A word of advice: as we tend to be casual, even ungrateful, with regard to destiny when we're happy, remember that the stars turn, and that life will some day hand us the bill for our faults or past mistakes. As last year Saturn put you through a period of internalising, of turning into yourself, make use of this now by not resting on your laurels, or becoming too full of your own success or good fortune.

### Libra (23 September to 23 October)

Looking at your cosmic graph for 1993, Libra my friend, is enough to make one dizzy – there are so many contradictory planetary aspects! Jupiter, which the ancients called 'the Great Benefactor' and theoretically the dispenser of the most numerous benefits – either material, psychological or emotional – visits your Sign every twelve years. In theory, therefore, the year ahead should promise expansion and new opportunities. But it's not that simple. Because, particularly when it traverses the second and the last 10 degrees of the zodiac (during the first three months and August, September and October), Jupiter enters into celestial disharmony with Uranus and Neptune. So, though it will still probably provide a number of opportunities and openings in every direction, it will also inflame and widely accentuate disorder, confusion, even Neptunian anarchy, as well as provoking dramatic turns of events, abrupt changes and the impulsive behaviour which is characteristic of Uranus. The moral: during the months mentioned, be as moderate as possible – as balanced as your Sign – and especially so during the first four months of the year, then in August to September when Mars – the pre-eminently aggressive and explosively dynamic planet – adds its thunder to the cosmic concert.

In the atmosphere of confusion in which you'll find yourself, try to put the brakes on – hard – or you may find yourself carried past your desired limits into a zone you might not be able to control. Be equally self-disciplined mentally, too, so you're not taken in by hoaxers or sundry 'gurus' who'll try to take advantage of the gullibility which the dissonance of Jupiter and Neptune could induce in you. This mental confusion and stress will be particularly intense in January, April, the end of June and July, at the end of September/beginning of October, and the end of December, when Mercury and the Sun will in turn obscure your objective vision. During these periods watch out that you do nothing which could tarnish your image or harm your reputation, as the astral climate which surrounds you lacks clarity or frankness. Be especially attentive and vigilant when you negotiate, or sign a contract, for people could be tempted to mislead you: a discordant Neptune symbolises intrigues and the abuse of confidence...

But Jupiter will also be the bearer of good tidings as – and it's here that things become really complicated – it will ally itself to Saturn. Situated in Aquarius, this will protect your back and salvage things in the case of setbacks induced by Neptune or Uranus. The effects of Jupiter and Saturn together will be mainly positive in February (especially if you're *second decan*), at the end of May/beginning of June (if you're *first decan*) when Jupiter will see you gather the fruits you sowed at the end of last year, then in August (particularly if you're *second or third decan*), at the end of September/beginning of October, so long as you stay vigilant and keep a cool head, and finally at the beginning of December (for *first decans*, who will consolidate their private or professional status).

Mars will help put you in sparkling form in May and June and in November to December; but in August to September its influence will be ambiguous: you'll be in super form but, precisely because of this, run the risk of going wrong through excess and becoming rebellious. If you engage in sport, be especially sensible – or else watch out for unfortunate incidents or accidents.

Normally a wise and balanced Libran, you'll have a particular desire this year to throw caution to the winds and go for extreme solutions – especially if you were *born between 8 and 14 October* – and in essence to let yourself go in untimely impulsive acts at the start of the year and then in summer.

So be warned!

### *Scorpio (23 October to 22 November)*

Despite a square of Saturn which will impede you, if you belong to the *second half of the Sign* (born after 8 November), you have an enviable year ahead.

There's no doubt that Saturn will introduce a procession of increased responsibilities, overwork, perhaps criticism, setbacks or regrets; and no doubt at times you'll feel its heaviness or depressing effect ... but nonetheless *first and second decans*, at least, will have a very good year.

The *second decan* will only feel the effects of Saturn at the beginning of the year; and from February on, this Saturnian pressure will vanish into thin air. In contrast, from then on and right through the year (and this influence will extend even beyond the second decan to Scorpios *born before 14 November*) you'll enjoy to the full the double and beneficial influence of Neptune and Uranus, which will carry you on to unhoped-for, almost outlandish heights! You'll gain exciting new knowledge, make unexpected discoveries in every area – whether intellectual, geographical or emotional. And thanks to

Neptune you'll be exposed to artistic – even mystical – curiosities which your rational and pragmatic spirit was previously unaware of. Thus your creativity will be magnified, and you'll be suddenly interested in entirely new things (which will probably have a spiritual dimension). You'll feel the need to progress beyond mere materialism, and thrust for something else. And you'll find it in art or religion, most likely in January or June, or else in August, October or the end of November.

The *first decan* will have to wait until the final two months of the year to profit from the beneficial presence of Jupiter. But beforehand, thanks to other planets like Mars, you'll have every opportunity to progress in leaps and bounds, and be in sparkling form as you do so – as in February, for example, in July and October and at the end of December. What's more, the dynamic and stimulating influence of Mars will affect *all the Sign* between January and April; and, whatever your decan, you'll be in such superb form then that if you're involved in sport you'll break records!

*The last decan* (especially those *born between 13 and 20 November*) will be visited by Pluto (which only happens every 250 years) which, allied to a discordant Saturn, makes life anything but easy. It's worth noting that Saturn's dissonance will affect all the last decan and even extend to the *second half of the second decan* at the start of the year. As a result, they will doubtless see the conclusion of a trying process which began last spring. For some this will have been an illness, for others an emotional problem. For others still, this period will have been one of the heavy responsibilities which came to a head in overwork, even physical exhaustion. But the good news is that after February they'll be out of the Saturnian woods ... for seven years!

In February itself, the *last decan* will go through a sort of desert crossing in terms of a moral or metaphysical crisis which will call into question all the past and present. For the double dissonance of Pluto and Saturn can have a radical 'clean sweep' effect, so that one eliminates, purges, spring-cleans one's life, either voluntarily or through force of circumstance. But this very rare presence of Pluto – the planet of death and rebirth – in your natal Sun can also be put to good use to evolve and progress, even if it means turning your entire status quo upside-down.

At the beginning of February, in May, August and your birthday month you'll feel an urgent need to analyse your entire life up to now. Separations and break-ups of all kinds could ensue. But tell yourself that these upheavals, however painful, are necessary for the caterpillar to become a butterfly. There will also be times in 1993 when external circumstances will help guide you in the right direction to orientate your new life. These times will be at the beginning of January, in March, May/June and September. And if you were born astride October and November, you will go through a time of soul-searching which could culminate in a much greater determination to face the future. Your family circle, friends and much-loved ones will be in perfect accord with you in January, August, October and (more ambiguously) in November to help you with their advice and encouragement.

Especially if you're *first decan*, which Saturn and Pluto will debilitate, I recommend a thorough medical check-up so as to nip any possible problems in the bud.

### Sagittarius (22 November to 22 December)

Sagittarius, my friend, you have a superb – in fact a golden – year in prospect. *Whatever your decan*, 1993 should prove highly constructive. Jupiter will reappear in your part of the zodiac and, before September, bring the fruits of proposals, ideas or opportunities which occurred at the end of 1992 (and this is particularly so for Sagittarians *born before 8 December*). And, if you were *born between 2 and 8 December*, you can expect news, from the end of last year to the beginning of this, which will prove the source of all sorts of goodies – including hard cash! – which you will rake in next August to September.

If you're *first decan*, you will realise a project or idea which you might have perhaps abandoned, while the *last decan* will profit from the support of Jupiter, the 'Great Benefactor' of the

ancients, throughout October, when you should be on the
lookout for potential opportunities. As for *second decans*, in
January Saturn will bring a long-awaited reward which will have
matured through much of last year, particularly if you were
*born before 6 December.*

January will, in fact, be an extremely important and constructive month for the *second decan*, as it will simultaneously
unite the beneficial influences of Saturn and Jupiter. This is the
time, for example, to found a society, launch a new project or
get married, as anything undertaken in January will have every
chance of lasting and turning out well.

From February onwards, Saturn will enter the last 10 degrees
of Aquarius, where it will stay throughout 1993, apart from a
flying visit to Pisces in June, at which time it will be briefly in
opposition to very early Sagittarians, bringing complications in
everyday life and paperwork.

Throughout the year Saturn will exert a beneficial influence
on the *last decan*, favouring consolidation of gains, putting
down roots, and the bringing of all you undertake to long-
lasting fruition. This will prove especially so when Mercury,
Mars or the Sun are also clement, as they will be for *all the Sign*
at the end of January/beginning of February, in April, August
and the beginning of October, and in December. During these
times you will be particularly effective and your impact deep
and lasting. Thanks to Jupiter, good luck will assist you in a
concrete way. And when Mars joins the party – in May and
June, from mid-August to mid-September and in November to
December – nothing will hold you back in your race to success.

Emotionally, you'll feel expansive and happy to be alive –
and have every chance of meeting a kindred spirit – when
Venus joins the Saturn/Jupiter tandem, and exposes you to
Cupid's darts, which it will between the beginning of February
and the beginning of June (and how!) and in September, the
end of October/beginning of November and in December –
when you'll glitter and shine like a fistful of diamonds! In fact, if
you ever dream of getting married and founding your union on
a rock, you couldn't ask for a better configuration.

Good luck!

## *Capricorn (22 December to 20 January)*

In broad general terms 1993 can be outlined as follows: not so promising for the *first and second decans* – and very much better for the *third.*

The *first two decans*, in fact, will experience the dissonance of Jupiter, which will introduce all sorts of complications into their everyday lives and they'll also suffer considerable disturbance from Uranus and Neptune. *Third decans*, on the other hand, will benefit from a fine sextile of Pluto which will be socially or financially rewarding, and which will ensure that they profit from a co-operative climate of events that seems to favour professional progress almost miraculously.

From the start of the year until March, Jupiter will cause problems for *first and second decans*, presenting them with disturbing choices and all sorts of complications. The repercussions for the *second decan* will be felt until August/September. The *first decan* will experience these same complications between April and August (particularly April), and in June to July as well; though, fortunately, in July Mars gives subjects of this decan so much dynamism they overcome all obstacles.

The *last decan*, in contrast, is particularly advantaged, as Jupiter will only trouble it for short periods in October, when it will still be sustained by the influence of Pluto, which will last right through the year. Reversing its earlier influence, Jupiter will come to favour the *first decan* from November on and in the last two months of the year, when it will provide all sorts of new opportunities and openings, especially in the business sphere. (And there's more welcome news about that next year!)

Back with the *second decan*, it's almost certain to start the year under terrible stress, as it's simultaneously opposed by Neptune, Uranus, Jupiter and Mars! So this is in no way the opportune moment to undertake anything long-term or make drastic decisions, for you'll tend to lack objectivity and act precipitously, under the influence of brainstorms you'll come to regret. Nor is this the time to hurl yourself into legal activity, which will almost certainly end in defeat. What you must do is get yourself in hand, compose yourself and slow down until you can see things clearly. Watch out, too, for ill-considered expenditure – and this applies to both *first and second decans* – or you could wake up and find the cupboard bare.

Furthermore, if you were *born between 7 and 13 January*, you can reckon on both the excitability and dispersion of Uranus and the confusion of depression of Neptune, which will obscure your vision and tend (in April, May/June, August/September) to lead you astray and put you on the wrong track. You'll want to chuck everything overboard, change your life, throw caution to the winds, and boot out the whole load of guilt you've accumulated over the years. But, if you were *born between 11 and 13 January*, you'll be pushed to succeed, as Pluto's comforting support will be absent. And what's certain for Capricorns *born between 7 and 13 January* is that this will be a great leap into the unknown, a radical upheaval of their lives. For some time it will entail a dazzling and unexpected rise to notoriety, propelled by a providential stroke of good fortune. Others, sadly, will have reversals of fortune which could be the result of deception, breach of trust, even bankruptcy or ruin, with a possible tendency to retreat to the artificial paradise of alcohol or drugs. So caution at all times is essential – however much Uranus makes you want to rebel.

Good luck!

### Aquarius (20 January to 19 February)

Thanks to Jupiter, the *first and second decans* will have the wind in their sails this year, while in contrast the *last decan* will find itself facing a difficult astrological climate.

In fact, after an absolutely brilliant, very promising and particularly constructive January, the *second decan* continues until March to be endowed with benefits from Jupiter, which take shape mostly as proposals or opportunities which reappear from the end of last year, much to your delight! And you can expect the extremely satisfying results of this in August to September. The same applies, though with slightly altered timing, to the *first decan*, which will see a project or idea from last year re-emerge in April, and materialise more rapidly (i.e. before August).

All the same, there's a shadow over the *first decan*'s chart: from November on a previously amenable Jupiter turns its back on you; and in November and December provokes complicated situations which could well have a doubtful effect on next year. An Aquarian forewarned is forearmed! It's up to you not to incur the anger of the authorities by letting yourself get into administrative or fiscal irregularities ... nor is this the moment to begin an action at law, for the astral currents will not be with you.

While January is an absolutely excellent month for the *second decan*, after February Saturn enters the *third and last decan* and will add to the dissonance of Pluto, which has affected this sector of the zodiac since last year. This year, Pluto especially bears on the status quo of Aquarians *born between 11 and 18 February*. And from February on it enters into alliance with Saturn, which could have the effect of radically undermining the foundations of your existence at the time. You like change – and you're going to get it! You will have to face up to a reality you've tried to ignore up to now, or which you've failed to recognise. And this new reality will require adjustment or adaptation on your part. For some of you it will involve an often involuntary turnaround in your profession; for others, a radical alteration of your private life – such as divorce, separation or a health problem. On which subject, given that Saturn and Pluto relate to a lowering of organic defences and relative debilitation, you should have a thorough preventive check-up to find out and cope with any deficiencies.

Owing to the influence of Pluto you will most probably experience a transformation of personality, so that by the time this planet has moved from your natal Sun (which won't occur before 1995) you'll barely recognise yourself. You'll have changed your scale of values, your vision of the world ... have undergone a total transformation. So it's up to you to use this transit and to change positively, to progress and not regress. And this will require long, hard, level-headed introspection and self-analysis, in which you'll have to be perfectly honest with yourself – as this double dissonance could well induce a true metaphysical or existential crisis...

With regard to this, I suggest you re-read the introduction to this book in which the probable effects of planetary dissonance are discussed. For we are not powerless against these effects. And even if we cannot influence external events, we *can* modulate their influence on us and their impact on our spirits. Which is something *last decan* Aquarians should remember in the particularly delicate times which lie ahead, namely: February, May, August and October to November. On the plus side, you'll be armoured against adversity and able to weather the cosmic storms in April, the end of May/beginning of June, end of September, beginning of October and in December. These same periods will also be extremely profitable for *first and second decans* (until October) in terms of business, particularly those to do with foreign countries, publishing, advertising, journalism or politics.

Take care healthwise in May and in October and, if you're playing games, watch out for falls and fractures (particularly your ankles – which are your Achilles' heel). During these times you should also monitor your circulation, which is another weak point of yours.

On the heart side, the best times for marriage – which is particularly favoured if you're *first or second decan* – will be between February and June, in July, at the end of October, or in December if you're *last decan.* And it's worth noting that in these same phases, even the less-favoured *last decan* will have the moral support and warm affection of family, the comfort of friendship and the tenderness of a partner. During these periods it will be possible to consolidate existing ties. And where *last decans* go through a phase of interiorisation and inner retreat, they should force themselves to open a dialogue with their loved ones. It will pay dividends!

### Pisces (19 February to 21 March)

Pisces, my friend, here's another superb year in prospect!

– especially if you were born in the second half of the Sign, *after 6 March*. If you're *first decan*, you'll need to wait until the last two months of the year to benefit from a fine trine of Jupiter, the bringer of luck and expansion. And if you belong to the beginning of the *second decan* (born in the first week of March), you fall into a sort of no man's land, unaspected by slow planets, apart from briefly in June.

If you were *born in the second half of the Sign*, then, you will have every cosmic chance on your side in 1993. Thanks to Uranus, radical and positive changes lie ahead; and an intellectual and spiritual opening to an invisible dimension (to which you're already sensitised by your Sign) is quite on the cards. And if you were *born after 11 March*, Pluto promises opportunities for greater social integration, material enrichment and, above all, positive psychic transformation through a sudden awareness of your interior resources. In brief, this is a really fine year for those *born in the second half of the Sign*: you'll experience an atmosphere close to Nirvana between January and April (when you'll also be in extraordinary physical form thanks to Mars), at the beginning of May, end of June/ beginning of July, in September and November. And for *first decans* the last two weeks in December are the most positive time for the sector.

These periods are excellent for *all the Sign*, in fact, though their positive effect is especially marked on the second half of it. If you're one of these lucky Pisceans then you'll have new and original plans, and be subjected to unforeseen changes so beneficial they're almost miraculous! You can undoubtedly count on an improvement of your living conditions, and especially an extension of your field of consciousness, which will help you progress on the spiritual plane and enrich your entire life. You'll want to participate in group activity, associations, clubs, to make yourself socially useful, apt as you already are to devote yourself to others. And, as you will most of the year, you'll experience an extraordinary dynamism, first of all until April, then in October and at the end of December, when you'll spare no trouble or effort, and the outcome will equal your ambitions.

For still unattached Pisceans, Uranus (especially when allied to the beneficial influence of Venus) will let fly some of Cupid's amorous darts, probably in January, June, August and November, when there's every chance you'll meet your 'other half'. Neptune, your ruler, will carry you off on a rosy cloud then and make you even more of a mystic, dreamer and idealist than you already are!

In sum, then, a really lovely year. Without a false note – or almost.

# *1994*

## The course of the planets

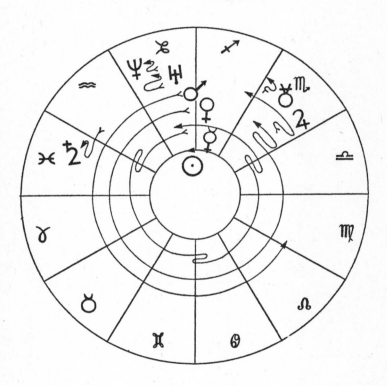

## World Events

After a rather strained start to the year as a result of the repercussions of a problem (Chinese ...? Israeli ...? to do with petrol ...?) whose roots stretch back to October, or even March of 1993, the remainder of the year unrolls in a reassuring cosmic harmony.

April and August should see the definitive consolidation of an institutionalised Europe and one that's doing admirably. Socio-political structures will be ratified in practice; and the economic, financial or legal problems which accompanied the birth of Europe will diminish and be cleared up. The general world economy is in good health.

In October, under a sextile of Jupiter and Neptune, a spirit of goodwill is prevalent, animated by ideals; and in November we will once more witness movements of solidarity, humanitarian works and perceptible economic growth. The year ends with the conjunction of Jupiter and Pluto which, if we have not already found a substitute for petrol as a source of energy, could mark an important moment in the history of oil: a rise in price ...? a politico-economic controversy ...?

Israel and China, furthermore, seem to enter a new cycle.

April will be a very promising month for France in terms of influence and economic wellbeing, and it will play an active and constructive role in the heart of Europe. At the end of the year, the French will become aware that adjustments must be made to harmonise with Europe and they will enter into an extremely positive phase of adaptation.

For Switzerland, the best period will be between August and October when it will play a starring role, perhaps on entering Europe at this time ... ? or some other exploit? October, November and December will bring its influence and economy to a peak.

In Germany, on the other hand, the end of the year will see

the conjunction of Jupiter and Pluto in Scorpio in opposition to the Sun – which could result in a problem to do with indebtedness or loans, which more or less puts a stopper on its horizons and disturbs its progress. But if Helmut Kohl is still in the political arena, 1994 will assure him a spectacular comeback.

For Britain it is a year of consolidation and expansion.

## *Your Personal Forecast*

### *Aries (21 March to 20 April)*

Taking an overview of 1994, Aries my friend, one can see a benevolent neutrality as far as the *first decan* is concerned and a sweet neutrality in the case of the *second decan* which – at last! – is liberated from the double dissonance of Neptune and Uranus, which has troubled it for years.

The *third decan*, as you'll have guessed – as a result of the logical course of the planets – will, in turn, be affected by this double dissonance for some years. Only Aries subjects *born before 17 April* will come under these influences; the rest will be 'victims' of Neptune and Uranus next year. If you belong to this sector of the zodiac, you must arm yourself with patience, calm, method and self-discipline: calm to confront the nervousness and stress inherent in Uranus (or the sometimes brutal shocks which bring on totally unforeseen change); and method and rigour to thumb your nose at Neptune, which sows trouble, confusion and bewilderment in our lives, by masking reality and making us see it as something other than it is, which in turn carries us on to mistakes and illusions and makes us prone to let ourselves be misled by others. Which is all the more reason to stay rational and as realistic as possible.

For the *last decan*, January will be one of the most agitated and confused times of the year, a period when these Aries subjects will ask themselves all kinds of questions, when everything will tend to be complicated – as on the leisure and emotional side – and there's a risk of building castles in the air. However, if you were *born after the 16th*, January is extremely rewarding, probably bringing recompense for past efforts, and the recognition of your merits.

Other critical periods of the year are: the second part of March, April, July, September and October. Uranus makes you want to rebel and to change everything in your life, while Neptune adds a low note and vague desires to this Uranian climate. Adventurous Aries that you are, you'll willingly dive headlong 'into the unknown to discover the new', as Baudelaire – himself an Aries – said. But because of the influence of Neptune you'll need to watch your step. Otherwise, watch out for rude awakenings. And during these periods you should avoid taking long-term decisions, for which you won't be sufficiently clear-sighted or objective.

In January, beware of sudden mental or emotional impulses which are very likely to result in dramas. At the end of April/ beginning of May and from mid-August to the beginning of October, Mars will also blend with the perverse influences of Neptune and Uranus to induce a simultaneously explosive and confused astral climate. Physically, these are times you should keep an eye on, periods when your chronic ailments could reappear strongly; given your nervousness and natural impulsiveness and excitability, there's a danger you may trigger regrettable incidents. The head – which is your weak point – could well be the target for these discords. So if you have a tendency to migraines, to dental or eye problems, have a preventive checkup; and cultivate caution, including on the road.

Love will be a source of tumult, complication and possible right-angled turns in January, at the end of March, the beginning of June and the end of August/beginning of September. So distrust impulsive decisions then, however you may cherish them, and also don't have too much confidence in others – there's deception in the air! And, though particularly applicable for the *last decan*, these periods we've mentioned also concern the *whole Sign*, who during these times of the year will be less steady with themselves and those around them (apart from the end of March, when the positive worth of Venus is amply manifest in increased charm and sociability). In contrast, the whole Sign will enjoy the warm attachment of their nearest and dearest and feel at ease with themselves at the end of January/beginning of February, in May and at the end of June/beginning of July, in particular.

On the professional level and in day-to-day life, you will go through positive phases of self-affirmation and have greater impact on other people and things in February to March, from mid-May to the end of June, in August and at the beginning of December. April deserves special mention as it is especially inscribed for the *first and second decans*: this birthday month, as every year, gives you more free will and puts you to the fore.

One more point: Jupiter, which is absent all year from your firmament, will make a shy, late appearance in an excellent trine in December, and then only favour the undertakings of those *born before 25 March*, for whom it will provide a most agreeable way of ending the year!

## *Taurus (20 April to 21 May)*

Following the Bible's example, where 'the last shall be the first', let's start with the *third decan*, which is the most affected by the planetary structure this year. Furthermore – and it's a great stroke of good luck – the opposition of Pluto, which affects Taureans *born after 14 May*, is going to be accompanied by the extremely efficacious double support of Neptune and Uranus, instead of being negatively reinforced by some other dissonance, as was the case last year. In other words, after a false alarm and a difficult January, when – especially if you were *born after 17 May* – you feel you are in an unendingly depressed and problematical phase, the horizon clears.

Right through the year you're going to be raised above yourself, in an elated frame of mind that's entirely new, and a lot less pragmatic and prosaic than that which characterised you up to now. You'll be bombarded with happenings, discoveries, new relationships, swept away in a whirlwind of circumstances which will favour windfalls and a widening of your mind that you've never known before. You can count on an extension of your field of consciousness, a new creativity, enlarged horizons, a feeling that the universe is vaster, more ample and rich than you ever supposed. This phenomenon will correspond with a profound change in your scale of values and criteria. A fascinating year then, especially in January, between March and May, and in July and September – which, furthermore, are all beneficial periods that promise progress for the *entire Sign*.

As far as the *first and second decans* are concerned these periods are entirely rewarding, though these subjects will also suffer the opposition of Jupiter, which is synonymous with financial or administrative worries and complications in general. But precisely during these periods (except May) their immediate circle or the circumstances of their environment will favour the appearance of a solution to their problems. In particular this year up to November, good luck might well come from either an emotional or professional partner. So it will profit you to take others' advice and guidance. Specifically, if the *second decan* has a brush with red tape or authority in general, if it has to face up to a difficult choice, there's every chance this will happen in the first four months of the year – with an effect on September and October.

The *first decan*, on the other hand, will experience the same kind of troubles and complications between May and the beginning of September. The *first two decans* will have to come to terms with negative Jupiterian influences, particularly between the end of January and the end of February, then in April/May, June (when they'll find themselves under stress and pulled in opposing directions), then in August, and finally in October and November. These are also times they should keep an eye on their health (particularly in terms of what they eat) for they'll tend to burn the candle at both ends. This appetite – almost greed – for life will be particularly keen in February, at the end of June and between September and the beginning of December, when you could equally well find yourself confronted with a difficult choice in love. Most of the time, even though you may be a faithful Taurus, you'll tend to chase after several people at a time, through fear of having to choose. And should some of you sometimes have the impression you're living through disturbing or painful times, you might like to know that 1995 is going to be a dream of a year!

## Gemini (21 May to 21 June)

While last year was particularly mild, thanks to the joint and supportive effects of Saturn and Jupiter, 1994 will, in general, appear more difficult, particularly if you were *born before 5 June*. Saturn will frustrate your plans to a greater or lesser degree, slow down the rhythm of your life, and oblige you to question yourself a little more often as a result.

Geminis *born after 5 June* are hardly affected by the procession of slow planets which form the astrological back-drop. In any case, if you're *third decan* (especially born after the 17th) January will bring a consolidation of your position, a perhaps long-awaited reward, which could very easily occur at the end of the month or beginning of February. On the other hand, if you are *at the very beginning of the Sign*, in February you'll probably experience the resurgence of a problem from last June, which could entail a separation or break-up that has been gestating since then.

Subjects of this *first part of the Sign* will feel blocked, slowed down and disturbed by the dissonance of Saturn which only occurs every seven years and often seems heavy and restrictive for a frisky Gemini. For austere Saturn, the master of experience and time, is fundamentally a stranger to you: you like to live in the present, free from all burdens, all responsibility, without ties and without looking back. Saturn, on the contrary, through events you cannot control, often plunges you back into a past which you have liked to forget and obliterate.

If you don't want to suffer too much from this Saturnian phase which starts in June (when the planet begins to regress, to hand you the bill for your past mistakes at the start of 1995), follow my advice; don't attempt to carry on regardless of Saturn, don't try to cheat, but live through this time of trial or self-analysis precisely by greater interiorisation, and turn your back on diversions or the superficial. In other words, avoid going into a daze where you're submerged in your possible distress, remorse or regrets, and don't simply stifle or put off till tomorrow the questions which come from your innermost being. On the contrary, in the silence of your heart try to find an answer. For you can live through all the dissonant phases of the

planets positively, so long as you harmonise with the fundamental characteristic of the planet in question, which will
neutralise or exorcise its negative effect.

Periods when you must turn your back on the outside world
and be increasingly attentive to your innermost being are:
March, May, the end of August/beginning of September, and
December. Don't ask too much of your nervous system, a
particularly vulnerable area of yours, in March, July to August,
and December; at these times you'll be unapproachable and run
the risk of making unfortunate and dangerous moves, either
while driving or elsewhere. Don't expose yourself to cold at the
risk of bringing on neuritis, especially in the shoulders and arms
where you are most sensitive. And if, like Atlas, you're weighed
down with heavy responsibilities which seem unbearable,
lighten your load by deep breathing. I don't mean metaphorically. For proper breathing is an essential function which you
often neglect – and it will be the best therapy for you.

For *all Gemini* Mars will put you in sparkling form in
February, May, July to August, and between October and mid-
December. During these periods nothing will seem impossible
to you and you'll eliminate whatever work is pending with
formidable efficiency. All the Sign will also profit from the good
influences of Mercury and the Sun to make desired progress at
the end of January/beginning of February, then in April, May/
June (except those *born before 5 June*, August, September with
mixed results), and in October. And if you feel less on form
emotionally (which chiefly applies to the *first part of the Sign*),
particularly at the end of February/beginning of March and in
May and July, this is because Venus will ignore you. Equally it
will favour friendly, amorous and emotional relationships in:
February, May, the end of June/beginning of July, and the end
of August/beginning of September, when your spiritual charm
will be utterly irresistible!

## Cancer (21 June to 22 July)

Cancer, my friend, I've almost nothing but good news for you
this year! If you're *second decan* you can celebrate, for at last
the tandem of Neptune and Uranus leaves you and moves into

the *third decan*. After several years of disarray and doubt, after deception, intrigues, depression, abrupt and difficult changes, after this long, disturbed and disturbing period, you are going to be liberated! Liberated and favoured too, as Jupiter and Saturn will be there to guide you, bring you new opportunities on a plate and, above all, restore your confidence in yourself and in life.

Unfortunately, this double influence only applies to the first half of the Sign (those *born before 7/8 July*), as Jupiter will only favour the end of the Sign very briefly in October and November. But all the same, for this important sector of the zodiac, the year till October promises to be extraordinarily positive and constructive. You'll consolidate what you have gained and, between February and June, see the resurgence of plans or ideas for development which you may have given up on. They will bear fruit precisely between July and October. And it's worth knowing if you belong to the *second half of the Sign*, that everything you undertake this year – especially before July – will prove extremely beneficial for you right into next year. You will be rewarded for past efforts, and perhaps receive an interesting promotion or distinction at the beginning of 1995 ... but everything in its place!

The *last decan*, for its part, will have to confront Uranus and Neptune in tandem, which may make it feel unprovided for, disconcerted and discouraged. In January, June/July, April to May and August to September you'll have the impression you're 'cycling in sauerkraut' (i.e. getting nowhere fast!) and are doomed to all sorts of dramas without any say in the matter. But, in general, Pluto will be there to sustain you: it will grant you a sure instinct of what path to follow and also give rise to events which will favour your progress. In other words, if you have a problem, you'll also be lucky enough to have its solution. In all probability Pluto's trine will also provide a positive change in your personality which will only be complete next year – that's if you were *born at the end of the Sign*. This evolution of your personality will go hand in hand with a deep enrichment, perhaps brought on by just those problems and fundamental questions you are obliged to ask yourself.

You'll have the wind in your sails and people and things will be in tune with your aspirations in February, March, May (ambiguously also in June/July), the end of August/beginning of September, and finally in November. Profit from these periods to make vital decisions, to see far and wide, to dare ...

As for love ... it will be set fair for *all the Sign* at the end of February/beginning of March, in April, at the beginning of June, in July, and from September to December – a long period in which your charm will make itself felt and you'll win widespread approval. If you're *last decan* you'll change many things as well, but this will probably result in a great feeling of wellbeing and – thanks to Pluto – have a happy outcome. While for the *first two decans* these will be blooming times, when you feel intensely happy to be alive.

## Leo (22 July to 23 August)

Leo, my friend, *whatever decan* you are, I'm afraid that 1994 is not going to be a very amusing year. Unless, that is, you were born at the very beginning of the Sign (*before 28 July*). In which case – and only at the end of the year – you will enjoy a flourishing trine of Jupiter (and we'll tell you the exciting news about it next year).

Whereas in 1993, particularly if you belonged to the *first two decans*, you experienced a phase of expansion and *joie de vivre* thanks to Jupiter, in 1994 you'll experience this planet's dark side. After times of plenty, lean times come. So watch out during the first six months of the year that you don't take on too much or get into debt. You'll have a hard time paying it off, which unfortunately could be the case between July and September.

While the *first two decans* will be troubled by Jupiter throughout 1994, the *last decan* will only be briefly bothered in November. Nevertheless, it must be all the more distrustful of the end of the year, as it will have not only Jupiter in opposition – throwing confusion and disorder into all its dealings – but also Pluto. This planet will bear on Leos *born after 16 August*, totally destabilising their status quo. It's highly likely that their problems will be of a group nature, that they'll have to take the consequences of a negative environment and so, for example, could suffer redundancy. But in general for *last decan* Leos this destabilising has to do with home life or family, which will be disturbed in a latent manner right through the year; and particularly in January, at the end of February, the end of June and in November to December, which could make life extremely difficult.

And in fact through all of February, June and from the beginning of October to mid-December, a dissonant Mars will also contribute to make you nervous, careless or stressed. You'll be quite unapproachable then, and your nervousness or lack of tact risks prejudicing the quality of your family relationships.

Some advice for the *first two decans* which are ill aspected by Jupiter almost all year long: firstly, don't break any rules or the law, and don't instigate legal proceedings – especially between mid-January and the end of February, or in May or June – as you won't have the last word. And nor are these exactly ideal times to make approaches to officials or ask your boss for a rise!

If you're *last decan* and have any choice in the matter, don't be stubbornly opposed to change, as all too often circumstances outside one's control, or fateful coincidences, play an important role in Plutonian dissonance. So embrace change and adapt to it, even if it seems you are leaping into the void. If nothing else, it could evoke a salutary awakening of your consciousness.

You will feel the worst of Pluto's influence, experience its difficulties and discomforts most keenly in February, mid-May, June and November. And, if whatever change is involved concerns your emotional life, there's a strong chance that February, April, the beginning of July, mid-October or the end of December will prove sensitive periods of the year for you.

On the other hand, you'll have everything going for you emotionally in March, May and August. And the affection, tenderness and good advice of those around you will help you face up to adversity and find a sensible solution to your problems. On the work or career side and in everyday terms, the best times of the year are April, June, October and December, when the Sun, your ruler, is favourable and supportive.

You'll be in sparkling physical form and full of a spirit of enterprise from mid-April to the end of May, in July to the beginning of August and during the last three months of the year, when you could nonetheless go wrong through excessive energy, and by trying to steamroller your family, which could set off a regrettable boomerang reaction...

As we've said, this is not going to be the greatest year of your life, but let's hope what we've mentioned here will help you deal with it.

## Virgo (23 August to 23 September)

This Sign's and 1994's winners are without doubt the *last decan.* In fact, three out of the five slow planets are 'going' for it – for you – this year (which you'll find especially filled to the brim with luck in November, when Jupiter comes on the scene). It's hard to imagine more effective or promising planetary support: at one and the same time this quartet of planets symbolises strengthened psychic resources (Pluto) ... magnified intuition and serenity (Neptune) ... an opening to unforeseen and spectacular progress (Uranus) ... and the whole lot sprinkled with the zest of Jupiter's pure good luck!

For *first and second decans* 1994 is more mixed. At the start of the year subjects of the *second decan* will be favoured by a sextile of Jupiter which will bring them all sorts of new opportunities on a plate – which could pay off in a solid and spectacular way. The *first decan* will be a candidate for maximum luck between May and the beginning of September, as the result of positive repercussions from plans or propositions made in the last two months of 1993. Yet, while in summer (June to July) the *first decan* will be in an extremely fertile and promising phase, the *second decan* (especially Virgos of the first week of September) will find itself opposed by Saturn, which will have affected the *first decan* during the first four months of the year.

Virgos *born before 2 September,* in fact, will experience the tension of a periodic Saturn (which occurs about every seven years) and will suffer its relatively difficult or problematic influence from early September to the end of the year. This Saturnian phase could well be a time of trial, a test of your worth; it's a moment for interiorisation, self-criticism and drawing up an objective balance sheet. In fact, this is a period in one's life when one can no longer pretend, when one has to confront and deal with reality. And as this opposition of Saturn can be accompanied by additional unwanted responsibilities, which often lead to overwork, it follows that you need to keep an eye on your health.

For many Virgos of the *first and beginning of the second decans* (particularly those *born before 5 September*) there will be a problem whose outcome won't be apparent till the end of the year, or even the beginning of 1995. But fortunately (even if its timing doesn't always synchronise), you'll have the support of Jupiter, 'the Great Benefactor', right through the year. It will help give you the vitality and optimism necessary to sort out your problems, often thanks to someone in your immediate circle who will provide excellent advice. This planet will also ensure you some pleasant and useful meetings, negotiations, dealings or advantageous contracts.

The *last decan* will have the wind in its sails and really shoot ahead. And if you belong to this sector of the zodiac, 1994 could well be the year of your life. You can count on this blessed period to lay out your pieces on the chessboard of life exactly the way you want to. This is the time to stake all! Dare, plan, change the things that annoy you ... you're well protected. For many of you, this period will see a professional turnaround or spectacular promotion, sometimes linked to sudden notoriety. For others this is the year they make their fortune, or definitely get their place in the sun ... and what a place!

The most promising and fertile periods for all the Sign are: firstly January, which is absolutely superb, without a cloud on the horizon (even for the *first decan*, which Saturn hasn't yet started to bother), then the beginning of May, which is excellent in every way, then July, the end of August, all September and October to November. And for the *first decan*, the end of December seems to provide a solution to the problem of Saturn.

In general, you'll be in sparkling form in January, June, from mid-August to the beginning of October and at the end of December. Your spirit of enterprise will be massively increased then and you'll have a wealth of energy which will help you resolve all your problems – if you have any! Nevertheless, watch out in July and at the beginning of August, when you'll tend to be careless and impulsive; and, especially if your birthday falls between the end of August and the beginning of September, watch out for unfortunate falls or injuries if you play contact sport. If you were *born before 5 September*, you'll be particularly aware of the checks, hang-ups or difficulties caused by Saturn: between February and the beginning of April; then between mid-May and mid-June; at the time of your birthday, and at the beginning of December. These are also the least lucky phases for the *other decans* (though they'll only be dimly aware of it, given their extremely positive astral context).

On the emotional plane there's a risk of considerable tension at the end of February, if you're *first decan*, as well as at the end of April/beginning of May and in mid-June. Try not to feel discouraged or morally isolated, which will be 'Saturn's fault'! And don't let its austere influence prevent you from becoming aware of a fundamental problem in your relationship, which will reveal its Achilles' heel – the worm in the fruit, as it were. Depending on how solid you are as a couple you'll emerge – one way or another – from this crisis at the end of this year or beginning of the next.

If you're *second or third decan* and still unattached, thanks to Jupiter and Uranus you'll have a great chance of meeting the love of your life. Either in January, the end of February/ beginning of March, in April, the beginning of June, July to early August, or in October (for the *second decan*), when a meeting could result in unexpected and very interesting developments in December, which should provide a lovely end to an overall fascinating year!

## *Libra (23 September to 23 October)*

Taking a broad view of the cosmos in 1994, we see that the *first two decans* are unaffected by the slow planets which form the year's planetary backdrop; which, in essence, simply means that those who belong to this sector of the zodiac won't experience a particularly pivotal or decisive year.

Thanks to a well-aspected Mars, *all the Sign* will be more dynamic and effective than usual between the end of January and the beginning of March, in July to early August, and between the beginning of October and mid-December. During these periods you'll be unbeatable, especially at games, and so full of go and galvanised with energy you'll be impossible to keep up with! But this energy will tend to excess and to make you careless or clumsy in January, from mid-April to mid-May, and from mid-August to the beginning of October. During these Martian, or hyper-Martian, phases, be more restrained in your movements; and live with an eye on your health (like drinking more water to cleanse your kidneys, for instance) so as to pre-empt any chronic ailments.

You'll enjoy the warmth and affection of those close to you (which you need very much more than usual) from the end of January to mid-February, from the end of April to the end of May, from mid-June to the beginning of July and in August to the beginning of September, as Venus will accentuate your appeal and refined Libran charm. Make the most of these times to get close to your loved one; organise intimate meetings or evenings with your friends. You'll shine socially and be thoroughly charming.

In your profession or career, and also in your daily life, you'll have a carefree and frequently satisfying time from the end of January to mid-February, in May and the beginning of June, in August and October and in early December. During these phases with the Sun and Mercury on your side, people and things seem to work towards your happiness. So learn how to use those periods to make progress towards your objectives.

The *last decan* will be the focus of the rather disturbing planetary duo of Neptune and Uranus this year. And – apart from January, when Saturn brings a consolidation of your situation or some reward you've been expecting since last year – this year's auspices are not very good. Owing to Neptune, you can expect a period of hesitation and confusion, perhaps distress mixed with doubt, the sort of year in which one asks oneself a host of questions in a hazy and uncertain climate, in which objective reasoning seems difficult, if not impossible.

Watch out, as Neptune is also the planet of waking dreams and a tendency to depression, and refrain from taking excessive medication or drugs, which are nothing more than a flight from reality. Try instead to neutralise the phantoms of doubt and distress by realistically analysing your problems, such as they are, in your heart and in the company of someone close to you.

Just as Neptune is the bringer of a largely chaotic climate, a dissonant Uranus is synonymous with abrupt change, rupture, nervous excitability and an irrepressible need for freedom. Under Uranian dissonance the nervous system has too many demands made upon it and enters a semi-permanent state of stress, which it's up to us to remedy. Avoid clumsiness and impulsiveness in January, in April to May and in August to September, when Mars will greatly magnify these disruptive energies. These are also times when you are more exposed to viral contagion, so take care.

If you were *born around 12 October* a problem from the start of the year will have repercussions in September to October, when in all probability it will be up to you to solve it. This could be a radical turning-point in your life which you'll have trouble deciding about, objectivity being difficult as a result of Neptunian dissonance. So make especially good use of the positive periods mentioned earlier. And, sustained by the positive influence of the Sun and Mercury, your morale will be better and your reasoning more lucid when it comes to making the decisions you have to take.

If you were *born between 15 and 19 October*, your 'low' period will occur in April to May, with the bill for this falling due at the end of the year, when you'll have to take whatever decisions are called for. It's also highly likely that events you cannot control will turn your destiny in another direction. For many of you *last decans* the problem Neptune and Uranus in tandèm bring has to do with home and the family. This area could well give you trouble: especially at the beginning of January, in March, June and the end of August – all times which focus on emotional problems. Here, too, you should take advantage of the positive phases of Venus, when the affection and support of those close to you is assured. Put to good use, calmly and objectively, they could help you sort out – or at the very least bring to light – your problems.

### Scorpio (23 October to 22 November)

It's extremely pleasant for an astrologer to be able to announce such a superb year!

Admittedly, the Saturnian dissonance, which some of you (especially the *second half of the Sign*) had to undergo last year will still have an influence in January 1994. And this could even involve a break-up or separation at the end of January/beginning of February. But this apart, the entire year for *all the Sign* promises to be cloudless. And that's a really rare occurrence! – one you must get the very best from, using your heaven-sent opportunities to the full.

*First, second and third decans* (for different reasons and owing to different influences) all end up with a dream of a year. The *first decan* benefits from the rather rare (every twelve years) presence of Jupiter in its natal Sun, where it will stay until next September. It is highly likely that propositions or plans from the end of 1993 will 'give birth', have fertile and very significant offspring. And on both the material and moral plane, the direct transit of Jupiter, 'the Great Benefactor', can't be surpassed in terms of benefits, astrologically speaking, especially when it accompanies a stabilising and consolidating trine of Saturn, as is the case for you this year.

In fact, this last influence concerns all Scorpios *born before the 4th*. So this sector of the zodiac will receive a double astral input that's super-constructive and extremely positive; while Scorpios *born after 4 November* will be favoured by Jupiter from September till the beginning of December. As this transit is relatively more rapid, it will also probably be less forceful and promising. All the same, you should feel its highly beneficial effects during these three autumn months especially, for you'll also have a well-aspected Sun, Mercury and Venus then, which will simultaneously favour business, health, optimism and love.

The *last decan* will be sustained all round this year by Neptune and Uranus in tandem, which will serve as a positive

catalyst to the influence of Pluto and render it totally constructive and fruitful. These excellent influences will be at their very
best in November when Jupiter joins this already existing planetary trio. So this is the time your opportunities progress – in
fact, all your opportunities will be at their peak. And, according
to astrological theory, because these superb influences preside
over your birthday, they'll affect all the following year ... till
your next birthday, which is good news – especially for Scorpios
of the *last and first decans.*

Given Jupiter's influence through your year, one can safely
deduce that a good many Scorpios will want to get married in
1994, for Jupiter is the planet of legitimation, which for other
Scorpios could also mean they'll have children.

Professionally, even the craziest new plans will be protected
and audacity will pay off as never before. What's more, if you
were born in the sector governed by Saturn (*before 4
November*), all that you undertake this year will be short lived.
It's worth noting that your period of greatest good fortune will
be between May and September; while if you're *second decan*
this period divides into two phases: the first four months of the
year, and September to October, which will also see the positive
repercussions of the earlier phase.

If you're *last decan* swept along by the superb conjunction of
a brilliantly aspected Neptune, Uranus and Pluto, it's highly
probable that, in retrospect, you'll consider 1994 as the year of
your life, or at least a key period in your existence, a sort of
launching pad. For this planetary trio simultaneously promises
positive and unforeseen changes, spectacular promotions,
admirable success, even notoriety and celebrity for some; while
Pluto in particular brings you the need to reshape your life, to
change in depth. And given this year's astral context, that can
only work in your favour.

The times which in various ways catalyse these excellent
influences correspond to the passage of the rapid planets which
sustain such a hyper-positive planetary background; they
are: the first half of January, March, the end of April/beginning
of May (so long as you work as a team and take account of your
partner), June to July, the end of August, from September till

the end of November, and the end of December (particularly for the *first half of the Sign*). These are lucky, effective times, in which the *last decan* will hold every trump card to enable it to change things just as it wants to and in which the *first and second decans* will have the chance to construct something durable and solid, thanks to Saturn. And over all of which Jupiter will sprinkle his zest of pure luck!

Under such aspects it's difficult to imagine any major health problems, so you should be in excellent physical shape all year long, particularly because Jupiter optimises wellbeing and grants you an extraordinary vital radiance and great self-confidence. Not only that, but the good influence of Mars will make you even more enterprising and dynamic – if such a thing is possible! – in January, March, from the end of August to the beginning of October, and at the end of December … when you'll be positively invincible, supported and galvanised as you are by this powerful combination of planets.

Emotionally, your plans have every chance of success in January, the end of February/beginning of March, the beginning of June, end of July/beginning of August, and from September to the end of the year, which will prove decisive for many of you. In a long transit through your Sign then, Venus will lead to fascinating and exciting meetings, passionate reunions, even the birth of a rare and precious relationship – one that will last.

## Sagittarius (22 November to 22 December)

Sagittarius, my friend, unless you were *born before 5 December*, this is hardly going to be the year of your lifetime! For, with the exception of Saturn, no slow planet will affect your sector for the zodiac in 1994. And, again, I've no very good news for *first decan* Sagittarians.

In fact, if you were *born before 5 December*, you'll have to deal with a square of Saturn which appears roughly every seven years and, in general, is not very heartening. The harbinger of internalisation and withdrawal of settling accounts with oneself and others, Saturn instigates introversion, which is in total contradiction with your more extrovert, open nature. This period could well be a time of trial for you, a test for your true worth, in which you have to take stock and adjust yourself to reality, even if up to now you would have liked to ignore it. A time, then, to pay the bills for past mistakes, to look back and remember. In sum, a time that can bring on an unfocussed sense of guilt, and a lowness of spirit that's hard to control.

During this period, not surprisingly, your physical resistance could well be below par. You'll be more vulnerable than usual to your chronic ills. So monitor the state of your liver, which is your organic Achilles' heel. Equally, when Mars joins Saturn, you'll be exposed to the likelihood of accidents and falls; so watch out for your thighs and hips, which will be most at risk. The periods to take special care are: March to the beginning of April (watch out if you go skiing!), then in July to August (watch out if you're windsurfing!), and at the end of December.

More generally, if you belong to the *first half of the Sign*, in March, June, September and December your natural optimism will be battered and you may well feel abandoned by what the Arabs call *baraqa* – the divine favour which gives us luck (and in which you believe so much). In compensation, though, you will have more impact on people and things and a more progressive orientation in February, April, August and October.

Your emotional ties, relationships with those close to you, friendship and leisure activities will all be particularly protected at the end of January/beginning of February, in March, May, the end of June/beginning of July, and in August. An emotional problem could arise at the end of February, end of April to May, or in July. Turn away from yourself and towards others; be tolerant and generous, as you well know how to be – though it is not always easy when one's not at ease with oneself – and you'll find you can get the better of Saturn.

### Capricorn (22 December to 20 January)

Taking a panoramic look at your Sign, Capricorn my friend, you could say it's almost indecent! For you've got a dream of a year ahead – a year with no disturbance – a year, in fact, that is absolutely *unique*. And you who generally know how to use what life brings you to the full (perhaps because you often have trouble getting it), will be offered luck heaped high on a silver plate. You just have to help yourself! So long, that is, as you take your chances by the scruff of the neck – and dare.

Opportunities and luck will rain on your daily life; there will be proof aplenty that your family appreciates your worth; and you'll be granted the esteem you've earned in the recent past. This is due to a sextile of Saturn, the planet of experience and time, which will particularly favour Capricorns *born before 3 January*. It's highly likely that these subjects will be approached in the first half of 1994 regarding an award or distinction which they'll get at the end of the year ... or perhaps at the beginning of 1995.

Running parallel to the consolidating and stabilising influence of Saturn, you'll also have the exciting influence of Jupiter at your disposal: and it will strongly favour those Capricorns *born before 6 January*, bringing them propositions or spectacular opportunities before the end of June, which will bear fruit lavishly before the beginning of November.

During November, the *last decan*, for its part, will be relatively briefly supported by Jupiter, 'the Great Benefactor', whose isolated effect might have been negligible were it not for the double transit of Neptune and Uranus which intervenes at the same time and serves to release, almost detonate, this Jupiterian influence. In other words, if you are last decan, November could bring some extraordinary unhoped-for luck, which could really put you in orbit. Thanks to Jupiter, you'll have the opportunity then to realise your latent desire for change, to alter your life totally – and in a radical, positive way.

An awareness of another dimension, thanks to Neptune ... an irrepressible need to change your life, due to Uranus ... a propensity to modify the way you look at yourself and the world, caused by Pluto ... all this suddenly crystallises at the end of the year around Jupiter, which will provide practical conditions that favour this major revolution in your life. Psychologically speaking, you've probably never been so inspired, so sure of being on the right path, so full of faith and hope in yourself and in life, and with good reason!

So there's something this year for everyone, for all tastes, and all Capricorns will get their slice of the cake. The best times? Certainly January, March, May, September, November and the end of December. Emotionally, you will have every chance of satisfying your deepest aspirations; if you're single you could find the perfect partner in the meeting of a lifetime – and make a clean sweep of the past; or if you are already one of a pair, you could consolidate your relationship admirably, even marry under the best auspices in January, the end of February, April, July or in the last three months of the year.

I've no need to wish *you* luck in 1994!

### Aquarius (20 January to 19 February)

Generally speaking, Aquarius my friend, I'm afraid that, *whatever your decan*, 1994 is not going to be an exactly festive year.

For the majority of you, in fact, it will be a year of dispersal, of complications or difficult choices, of feeling you're being pulled in different directions. When Mars becomes involved, you won't know which way to turn and will have the impression the whole world has a down on you, particularly the law and everything that represents authority. So, if you belong to the *first half of the Sign, born before 5 February*, be extremely prudent. Particularly at the end of June, make sure you don't make a legal *faux pas* or get bogged down in an administrative deadlock, for in everything to do with red tape there's a risk of serious trouble between July and December. For instance, if you were engaged in legal proceedings (either at the end of last year or the first six months of this), you will suffer the repercussions – which are likely to be unpleasant – before the end of 1994.

Given that Jupiter (which is involved here) has an affinity to money, you should refrain from indulging in ill-considered expenses during the first phase of this planetary dissonance: you'll run the risk of seriously straining your budget, and afterwards having to scrape the bottom of the barrel to make ends meet! In February, June and between October and mid-December, you'll feel this Jupiterian disorder and agitation keenly and it could lead to stress and dissipation. So, during these phases, keep your eye on your goals and try to take things less personally and be more objective in your reactions, for you'll be in a frame of mind where the least remark will seem like a personal attack. Though nervous, as an Aquarian, you have a strong tendency to wisdom, serenity, even the 'angelic', so call on these virtues to face up to the turbulence of the planets!

For many of you, this disorder and unstable climate could relate to your career, which suddenly wavers in its direction. And during this time of confusion there's a risk you'll no longer know what you want, or what to aim at. A disturbing dilemma could result, which will be particularly the case for the *last decan* in January and in November – the worst months of 1994 for these subjects. If you're in this sector – and especially if you were *born around 17 February* – there's a danger you could find yourself in an identity crisis, a state of affairs which leads you to question the very basis of your existence; and to give much deeper consideration to your essential and deepest needs. Thus for those at the end of the Sign, January could be tough to get through, unless you grapple with 'the enemy' and in some way come to terms with it. So don't attempt to escape; and avoid the 'diversion' of getting yourself so feverishly agitated you don't face up to the real issues. Sit yourself down alone and make a note of what it is you actually need. Remember who you were at the dawn of your life, when you first became aware of your personality, of your goals, and try to connect with this person across the years. Especially when it harmonises with a transit of Saturn, the dissonance of Pluto often imposes this sort of self-confrontation on us, and though seldom comfortable it's often fertile.

In fact, *last decans* will be influenced by the dissonance of Pluto all year long, especially if you were *born after 14 February*. It is highly probable that you will go through a process of profound metamorphosis, or irreversible change. It's possible, too, that this change could be brought about by events beyond your control, such as an involuntary about-turn in your profession, illness, or something radical which intervenes in your life. As an Aquarian you love change, so don't thrust aside this chance to shed your skin, as it were, and be reborn. On the contrary, embrace the changes which come to you. You'll emerge enriched and ready to pick up a new life. Don't be too forceful, though, in February, June and between October and December, when you'll tend to be dogmatic and tyrannical, and quite unlike your true self. And if, emotionally, your ship turns turtle, or threatens to, this will most probably happen at the end of January/beginning of February, in April, the end of June/beginning of July, or between September and December. Forewarned is forearmed, and you'd better work out just how far you can go, given the atmosphere of instability which surrounds you.

Happily, there will of course be clear patches and brighter periods for all of you in 1994, and these will be in April, the end of May/beginning of June (but beware of aggression), in September to October and in December.

Hang on in there!

## Pisces (19 February to 21 March)

Pisces, my friend, you're in luck. For though you'll experience a direct transit of Saturn this year (which in itself is generally not very good news, as it often brings litigation), you'll have the good fortune to be under a protective trine of Jupiter at the same time. And, as if by magic, this will transform Saturn's lead into gold. In all probability, Jupiter will thus make Saturn's influence conducive to stabilising and consolidating gains, and building on firm foundations. This double aspect of Saturn and Jupiter chiefly concern Pisceans of the *first half of the Sign*.

The other sector the stars focus on this year is the *last decan*, and if you belong to this, you have a dream of a year ahead. You'll be holding every trump card if you plan on changing your life, especially if you were *born before 18 March*. If you're at the beginning of the decan (*before the 13th*) you'll pave the way at the start of the year for a change which will only come about at the end. On the other hand, if you were *born between the 12th and the 18th*, you'll sow your crop in April to May and harvest it at the end of the year, if not in 1995.

Whatever your present position – be it humble or mighty –

you'll recall later on that 1994 was a key year, a providential time in your life. You'll change gear, climb the social ladder, increase your spiritual possessions or your aptitude for happiness. Hitherto ignored or neglected realms (which may well concern the invisible, occult or mystical) will be open to you. For example, this is an excellent configuration for getting on in the world of the arts, or becoming a politician (or an astrologer, as Uranus is the planet alloted to astrology), while Pluto's trine assures you of material growth, expansion and a better integration in society.

Protected by Jupiter, 'the Great Benefactor', the *first and second decans* won't stand still, either. And if you belong to either of these sectors you can expect lucky and unhoped-for opportunities. For the *second decan* they'll in all probability appear before April and be realised in September to October; while for the *first decan* they'll occur between May and the beginning of July, and be fulfilled before mid-September.

When Mars is well aspected (in January, March to April, June and from mid-August to mid-October) you'll greatly increase your potential and efficiency at work; while athletes will have the best possible chance of beating their opponents, as they'll be galvanised with Martian energy. There are two periods, on the other hand, when Mars cautions prudence: July to early August and the end of December, when Mars in opposition to your natal Sun will encourage impetuosity, clumsiness or arrogance.

For *all the Sign*, you'll have a wind in your sails that will sweep you on to success at the following times: January, March, May, June and November. Love will smile on you; the affection of your family sustain you; and a lot of people will fall victim to your increased charm (perhaps for life!) in January, the end of February/beginning of March, in April, June and the last four months of the year, when a trine of Venus makes you appropriately irresistible. Whether thanks to Jupiter – which will make you radiate a contagious optimism and favour outstanding meetings – or to Uranus, the bringer of unhoped-for surprises, it's a safe bet that many of you still unattached may well find the love of your life!

# 1995

## The course of the planets

# World Events

In March, and then in August, an extremely positive astral climate comes in, stemming from a very important cycle of Uranus and Pluto, whose last conjunction dates back to 1966.

This first evolving sextile – which will engender lively and constructive forces – will be extremely important for the generation born around 1965–7. This was remarkable for its reforming, revolutionary, extremist, even fanatical spirit which, at the end of the 1980s, as a result of disappointed realism, sometimes thought it right to throw itself into drugs or delinquency. But now, at last, this generation is going to feel at ease with itself and stable, having perhaps (since 1993) found a cause which satisfies its aspirations.

As this cycle also seems to preside over the evolution of Japan, this country could very well achieve true economic world leadership, while in Great Britain 1995 will prove a year of flowering prosperity and positive innovation.

Some drastic reforms will be put in hand, and finally implemented in March 1996. They will be mostly inspired by idealistic Aquarians and Sagittarians on one side, and combative and tenacious Scorpios and Capricorns on the other. Enhanced by the sextile of Pluto and Uranus, the concrete and salutary effects of the new spirit that has been in the air since 1992–3 will make themselves felt.

With the entry of Jupiter and Pluto into Sagittarius, the hermetic Sign of healing, it's highly possible that this year will see the discovery of a definitive and radical cure for AIDS.

Uranus symbolises the peak of technology and space research and Pluto symbolises power, so this sextile could well accompany a much greater conquest of space and, from 1995 on, we may well see the beginning of its colonisation by mankind.

The only black mark on the great planetary aspect of this

year is a latent tension tied to Europe at the start of the year becomes more definite in November and, specifically, seems to concern Germany and Switzerland, which are perhaps having some difficulty in adapting to new political realities.

## *Your Personal Forecast*

### *Aries (21 March to 20 April)*

To come right out with it, Aries my friend, if you're *last decan* (especially if you were *born after 12 April*) you're not going to find yourself exactly spoiled in 1995. Metaphorically speaking, there are banana skins on your path just waiting for you to slip on, and abrupt and untimely changes lie in store which will not be to your taste. Unfortunately, you'll often feel as if you're tilting at windmills and don't really know who your enemy is – which isn't easy for an Aries all set to confront his or her adversary...

But perhaps this will be because your 'enemy' will often be yourself: your own confusion, your feeling of 'what's the point?', your sudden doubts and uncertainties and queries as to which path to follow. You'll find yourself suddenly asking new and strange questions, and re-evaluating the principles which have guided you up to now. In short, a pretty chaotic, wavering, even helpless period lies ahead, and you must react by cultivating a positive outlook and a great deal of pragmatism. In other words, avoid illusions, chimera, castles in the air ... and also those reactions to escape, inherent in Neptune, which are allied to drugs or medication. For you'll be particularly vulnerable to all drugs during this Neptunian dissonance, especially when Mars adds his own discordant influence between the end of July and beginning of September, and during December.

If you belong to the last sector of this Sign, take care as well that you're not too credulous or passively negligent (which is hardly your nature in any case), or you could be the victim of intrigue, breaches of trust and deceit, either in your professional or emotional life. Professionally, be particularly on guard in January, April, July and October, which for *all the Sign* are months when you make the least impact on people and things. On the emotional side, be wary of being misled – either by yourself or others – in February, the beginning of May, July, the end of September/beginning of October and early December.

If you have moments of helplessness or depression, remind yourself that planetary discord is sent by destiny with the sole purpose of making us become more mature and aware, which in the end is always profitable. And even if the events the planets induce are often difficult or uncomfortable to live through, they'll prove spiritually productive in that they'll lead to a more elevated level of consciousness. As the famous Aries, Alfred de Vigny put it: 'Man is a pupil and sorrow his teacher.' And though this maxim may not be pleasant, it's nonetheless true: human beings only learn when they're pushed by destiny.

You'll have every chance of mastering this upheaval and confusion when the astral context is favourable, as it will be for *all the Sign* in February, June, August and December. Use these periods to take your bearings, particularly at the end of November to December, which will be especially propitious as a trine of Jupiter will give rise to lucky opportunities, put you in spectacular shape and help you redress the balance. At the end of November particularly, you'll have the simultaneous support of Jupiter and Mars (your ruler) to overcome your problems and worries.

The *first and second decans* will be gifted by Jupiter. Particularly if you were *born before 6 April*, you can expect additional material or moral wellbeing – or both – an appreciable plus in every area of your life. You'll be buoyed up by a much-increased vital optimism. And, as you know, opportunity is party to our psychic disposition, our spiritual state, and when these are positive they can to some extent 'summon' happy events. *First decan Aries* will summon them – and they'll come to you – especially in January, and again in June and September, when the year's early promises will be realised.

Special mention should be made of *very early Aries subjects* (*born around 21 March*): Pluto will be propitious to them firstly between January and April, and then at the end of the year, handing them spectacular progress on a plate! Some will find themselves almost miraculously promoted to an unhoped-for position which is favoured by a positive social or professional environment. Others, very probably in March or at the end of April, will have the meeting of a lifetime, which in November or the end of December will come to fruition in a long-lasting relationship.

For *second decan Aries* your luckiest times from every point of view will be between February and the beginning of June, when you'll plant seeds that will bear fruit in October to November. It's highly probable, for example, that extremely attractive proposals put to you in the spring will be realised at the end of the year, much to your delight. Equally, if you intend to undertake a long-term project, take this timing into account. It will prove extremely propitious. Finally, an excellent trine of Mars will energise you between February and May, when you'll enjoy one of the most expeditious and effective periods of the year.

### Taurus (20 April to 21 May)

Let's start with the good news: the *first two decans* will be relieved to hear they'll no longer have to face the opposition of Jupiter which could well have made life difficult. On the contrary, they'll be happy, anchor themselves in their gains, consolidate and savour their situation. Taurus subjects *born between 26 April and 15 May* will be subject to an excellent Saturn. As this sector largely includes the *last decan*, this too will be favoured by extremely constructive influences between May and the beginning of October, and will see its hopes and aspirations realised at the start of next year. This is the time, then, to undertake long-term enterprises that will give every satisfaction in 1996. By the way, if you were *born before 26 April*, this year's conjunctions do not affect you, either for good or evil.

On the other hand, if you're *last decan*, this will prove an important year. Those born in the last half of the Sign (*after 16 May*) will have to confront Plutonian metamorphosis. And this confrontation for many of them will be like a sort of delivery or childbirth, which could be largely painless nonetheless, as they'll have the support of Uranus and Neptune to help them mentally overcome their difficulties and come to terms with the deep disruption which Pluto implies.

If you were born in the *last sector of your Sign*, in January and between April and July you'll feel a deep need for something or somewhere else ... but be patient! There will be concrete results between August and the beginning of November. And the way you look at life will be turned, provided you learn to make concessions: let yourself be dispossessed to some extent, the better to win thereafter. In all probability, this profound change will be brought about by an event to do with a partner or associate; and your emotional life could be less than sweet in March, June, August and late October to early November.

Otherwise, if you were born in the *first half of the last decan*, you can expect a fabulous, dreamlike, expansive year! You'll be swept towards your objectives and attain another dimension, either professionally, socially or intellectually. The trine of Uranus which will affect you has the peculiar quality of simultaneously galvanising the will and endowing us with keen discernment. And willpower and good judgement are perhaps the two prerequisites for success, especially when you add the sprinkling of luck that Neptune (which will also be present in your heavens this year) can offer you.

*Almost all the last decan* will be simultaneously affected by the intersecting influences of Neptune and Uranus. As a result your creativity will be greatly increased, your consciousness enlarged either intellectually, spiritually or mystically, and your level of awareness will evolve in a spectacular way. Without any doubt your personal compass will be set towards what's 'positive'.

All this will be particularly the case between May and October, when Saturn will add its austere but constructive and beneficial influence to those of Neptune and Uranus. You'll be keen to give concrete form to your new aspirations then, rather than simply stay in the realm of the vague and ideal. And as I mentioned earlier, it's highly likely that you'll reap your just rewards for this in early 1996. The end of the first decan (those *born after 26 April*) and all the *second decan* will also be protected by a positive Saturn, which will bring them the results of their efforts last year. The *beginning of the second decan* (those born at the start of May) will have no doubt initiated a project last June or July which will be realised this February. Taureans born earlier will be recompensed at the very beginning of the year.

All the *second decan* enjoys the protection of Saturn – which acts as a sort of physical, professional or emotional shield between February and April – which will pay dividends between October and January of next year. In fact 1995 will see manna from heaven for *almost all the Sign*, especially in January, when (helped by Mars) you'll be endowed with almost indomitable energy, and also in March, May, June and July, September and December.

Taureans *born around 20–21 April*, however, deserve special mention. Between the end of March and beginning of June they'll be subject to a turbulent square of Uranus. With their lives at a major turning-point, they'll feel a frantic desire to free themselves from all cumbersome ties. If you belong to this sector of the zodiac, pay attention to events which could be outlined just below the surface in April to May, whether in terms of your profession, relationship or health (which is more at risk); you'll see the hint of a change which, in fact, will only really come about next year.

For may *last decan* Taureans, love will prove the highlight of their year. There could be an exceptional meeting, an upheaval and sublime escape to an exciting affair in February, April, early June, July, September or mid-December, which are all times to mark with a heart in your diary if you're still unattached. As you can see, an enticing slice of life lies ahead which will be anything but monotonous!

## *Gemini (21 May to 21 June)*

This is a year, dear Gemini, which will put your adaptability to the test. While last year Saturn only really bothered or inhibited the *first decan*, this year it will have a negative influence on *almost all the Sign*, apart from very early or very late Geminis. More precisely, if you were *born between 28 May and 17 June* it is getting ready to make you morally uncomfortable. And while the *first decan* will be over its bad times by the end of January, the *second decan* will see trouble dawn between February and April, which will include obstructions and setbacks whose unenviable effects and repercussions will mature in the last three months of the year.

In other words, a problem in your professional or private life will be outlined at the beginning of the year and take concrete shape in the last months of 1995. In view of Saturn's restrictive effect, this problem could take the form of a separation, or trial of some other kind ... perhaps an illness. As a Gemini, forewarned is forearmed: have a medical check-up to assess the state of your health and physical resistance, and ward off any possible deficiencies.

Jupiter, for its part, will plant disorder and complications in your life if you were *born after 24 May*. If your birthday falls *around the 24th or 25th*, watch out for legal or financial troubles which could come at the start of the year; and as they could have unexpected repercussions you may have to suffer during the summer as a result. So don't put yourself in situations which could go from bad to worse. The same applies to the *second decan*, though in a slightly different time frame: watch out for possible hang-ups or rows with your family or superiors, which could occur between February and May; and don't initiate any legal action if you can help it, or the result will be bad news in October to November. In fact, only the *last decan* will effectively be spared by Jupiter, whose dissonance only touches it – and then briefly – in December.

Some advice for *all Geminis*: look after your nervous system and don't expose yourself to incidents or accidents through clumsiness or haste, particularly in January, June and

November, when Mars will make you nervous and impulsive. At these times you'll find yourself in an abnormal state of stress, you won't know what to do with yourself, and your tendency to self-dispersal and thoughtlessness will be greater than ever. To counter this, learn to be calm, to concentrate and breathe deeply, which is especially important for you. In fact, meditation, yoga and relaxation are just the 'medication' you need.

It's possible, too, that for many Geminis an emotional issue, in terms of a painful choice, will come to the fore in 1995. This choice could be particularly prickly in January, April, June, September and November. On the other hand, *all Geminis* will have their good times emotionally too. Venus will accentuate your mercurial charm in March, May, June (though that won't suppress other problems), then in August, the end of September/beginning of October and the end of December. During these phases of the year you'll gain the attention and affection of others; so re-establish the dialogue which Saturn may have blocked.

Professionally, your best periods are in January to February, April, August, (September being ambiguous) and October, while your birthday month will spotlight the problems which concern you, especially if you're *first or last decan*. But then, being aware of a problem means you're halfway to solving it.

Good luck!

## Cancer (21 June to 22 July)

This year, Cancer my friend, you'll benefit once again – and more than ever – from the support of Saturn which shields you and brings you security, stability and the reward for past efforts (particularly if you were *born after 26 June and before 18 July*). And though (unlike last year) you'll no longer profit from a trine of Jupiter, the bringer of expansion and pure luck, you still have an excellent and constructive year on the horizon...

If you were *born at the beginning of the third decan*, which is threatened by the double position of Neptune and Uranus – a planetary obstacle you got to know last year – Saturn will now come to your aid as a sort of protective screen against the possible upheavals brought on by Uranus, and depression aroused by Neptune; for Uranus and Neptune in tandem will menace almost all the *last decan*, only sparing Cancerians of the 13–14 July. If you belong to this sector of the Sign then, you can expect a certain amount of destabilisation and a climate of general confusion in your life: at times you won't know which way to turn and will feel you are 'cycling in sauerkraut'. You'll be particularly conscious of this stressful and debilitating atmosphere in January, April, July, October and December, which are the least promising periods for the *entire Sign* as well. The same confusion, the same uncertainty, the same climate of deceit or possible illusion could also have an effect upon your love life – which could entail dramatic turns of events and sudden bust-ups – in February, at the beginning of May, in July, at the beginning of October and in mid-December.

Happily, your Sign will enjoy a massively increased dynamism and admirable vitality due to a well-aspected Mars in January, June and September to October, which are times when you'll effectively take the bull by the horns. Especially if you're *last decan*, June and October will be periods when nothing will seem impossible or unobtainable; you'll have a fantastic spirit of enterprise then and an unequalled tenacity. This same climate will affect the *first decan* in January. Other Cancerians will consolidate their ties in a reassuring way in January, April, May to June, July, the end of August/beginning of September and in October, which will bring them the emotional security they are so much in need of. These are also periods to make the most of, if you have a plan to do with property.

For those *born at the end of the Sign (after 19 July)*, a trine of Pluto will project them beyond themselves as well as fitting them even better into their social circle, where they'll noticeably go up a notch. If you belong to this sector, it's highly probable that a deep and positive change in your situation is proposed in January; you'll have echoes of this proposal between April and August and it will be realised between August and November. In any case, even if Pluto's trine is not accompanied by a radical change of events, it brings us greater inner strength and increased psychic resources: a sort of regeneration of the spirit which helps put us on the right path and guides us in the choice of our objectives. This means that, if you were *born at the end of the Sign,* you'll have a surer instinct with which to direct your life in future. For many of you this time – which one only sees once every 80 years! – will bring wealth, fame or major professional promotion. And the most positive times of your year are: March, May, July, September and November.

Make sure you get the very best out of them!

### *Leo (22 July to 23 August)*

Congratulations, Leo my friend! Unless you're at the very end of your Sign (*born after 19 August*) your horizon for 1995 is a cloudless blue. You'll have nothing more to do with last year's Jupiterian turbulence, nor the Plutonian disturbance that was mixed up with it. And with the positive spirit which characterises you, I've no doubt you'll profit from the good omens of this new year.

Leos at the *end of the Sign* will be somewhat tested however. In January and then between April and July, they'll experience repercussions of last year's Plutonian dissonance which will encourage them to change the course of their lives. Between August and the beginning of November 1995 they will complete this change and you can bet that at the end of the year they will be installed in a new personality and consequently in a new life. This process won't necessarily be very easy or comfortable. For some it will involve a change in their emotional relationships, a sort of amorous about-turn, which could happen from January on (or in March or yet again in May to June) to reach its conclusion in October. And even if this doesn't entail separation, these will be moments of crisis insofar as personal relationships are concerned; while for others there will be a total change of status quo, of home or family context.

Pluto will be beneficial to Leos *born around 23 July* (and particularly between February and April, then between November and the end of the year). A Plutonian trine will bring these Leos an increase of psychic resources, an indestructible strength, and the assurance they're definitely on the right path – which assurance will be engendered by possible social progress or a promotion. Under a harmonious Pluto, in fact, you feel in phase with your environment, carried along by events and supported by them, and as if by chance you find yourself precisely where you are needed. You are the man – or woman – of the moment.

Very early Leos aren't the only lucky ones either, as Jupiter will favour the whole of the *first two decans* in just as spectacular a way. If you're *first decan*, between June and the beginning of July you'll see the repercussions of proposals from the end of last year, or beginning of this one, take shape. Pay particular attention to them, for the opportunities concealed by these suggestions are very promising and their perspectives vaster than you could believe. Moreover you won't have to wait long to see their results. They'll fall due to you before the beginning of October.

For subjects of the *second decan*, opportunities will arise between the beginning of February and the beginning of April (particularly if you were *born before 8 or 9 August*) and without doubt you will enjoy their benefit after October.

As for the *last decan*, given that Jupiter does not retrogress in this sector, its passage will be more rapid and therefore have less effect. However, it will take place between November and December when you must prick up your ears and seize your chances in both hands (particularly in December in business and November on the heart side).

The best times of the year for *all the Sign* will be as follows: the planet Mars, which influences our physical form, will be clement between the end of January and the end of May (especially if you were *born before 8 August*), when your immediate circle will find your positiveness leonine! Martian energy will also fill you between the end of July and the beginning of September, and from the end of October to the end of November. You'll feel particularly fit at these times as Mars (the planet of muscular strength among other things) invites you to participate in sport and use your surplus energy in a positive, organically stimulating way. You'll be the driving force of your group and doubly effective. And given the existence of a positive tandem of Jupiter and Mars in these periods one can deduce that you will profit from extraordinary strokes of luck – when everything will simultaneously go both quickly and well – and enjoy the best of all worlds.

Due warning, however: at the beginning of September and the end of October, Mars will make you more nervous than usual, which could incline you to false moves or resort to a force in your relationships. So be tactful and diplomatic, which are not always leonine virtues! And when someone cuts in front of you on the road, don't turn a hair. Simply smile in a superior way and you'll have perhaps avoided an accident.

Your free will is going to be diminished in the period January to February, when I suggest you listen more to other people, (especially if you were *born at the end of the Sign*, in which case you could have to confront a fundamental problem to do with a partnership of your family). At the end of April, in May and in November, the Sun and Mercury will toss out a problem which you will surely pick up; these are your less good periods, especially in the case of Leos *born from 18 August on*.

As for the good times ... the heavens favour *all the Sign* from the end of March to the end of April (particularly the *second decan* on account of protective influences of Jupiter and Mars); then in June (especially the *first decan* this time); in August which will be extraordinarily dynamising and positive; October (*second decan*); and in December, which is most propitious for the *last decan*. During these periods, Leo my friend, you will be particularly radiant and on form both mentally and physically. Your good humour will be infectious, your luck as well. You'll enjoy much better relationships with your family and those dear to you and many Leos still single will find their *alter ego*, and this exceptional meeting could well take place at the end of January, in March, at the beginning of May or end of June, in August – the month when you'll really shine – or yet again at the end of September/beginning of October, or in November. And if you're single, it's worth knowing that Jupiter, the planet of legitimation, may well invite you to a wedding – your own!

## Virgo (23 August to 23 September)

The years succeed each other and are rarely alike. Sometimes one regrets this, sometimes one's glad...

Frankly, Virgo my friend, this year will be somewhat less good than last, especially if you belong to either of the *first two decans*. In which case, there's a strong chance that the double dissonance of Saturn and Jupiter (particularly if you were *born between 25 August and 17 September*) will play some rotten tricks on you: you will feel yourself pulled hither and thither, simultaneously slowed down, depressed and obstructed by Saturn, which will strew your path with obstacles; and also disturbed by Jupiterian imponderables, which for many of you will take on a legal shape, but for many more will present themselves as financial problems.

There will be a possible stream of these major inconveniences. So when the influence of these two planets comes into play – which it will before March – avoid false moves which could create all sorts of complications; be extremely prudent in choosing what business you undertake; and cultivate your natural virtues of clear-sightedness, organisation and self-discipline. You will thus escape the regrettable repercussions of these planetary influences which in the case of Jupiter will occur from April on (and affect first the *second decan*, then the *first*), and which in Saturn's case will start at the beginning of July (especially for the *last decan*) and end in November, after having disturbed the *second decan* a good deal as well. Now, while the shambolic effects of Jupiter may occur in the last three months of 1995, the doubtful effects of Saturn (especially for the *last decan*) will only fall due at the beginning of 1996, which is a good reason to stay in a state of expectancy; avoid taking on too great responsibilities at the start of the year, and don't commit yourself through thoughtless promises which in due time you'll find you can't keep. Be careful, too, to keep your administrative paperwork in the strictest order for, as far as the authorities are concerned, no slip-up of yours will be pardoned.

You most risk getting fined, penalised or hit with back taxes between the beginning of March and mid-April, between the beginning of May and mid-June, during your birthday month (especially if you are *first decan*) and in December (particularly if you are *last decan*). Forewarned is forearmed, so don't go through any amber traffic lights and don't rile the constabulary!

If you're *second decan*, many of you will experience this period as one of emotional crisis, a test of amorous ties. Or you might, as a result of Jupiterian tension, find this a time of difficult, even painful, choice. Paradoxically, in fact, you'll at times simultaneously feel cut off from others and uninvolved – yet also appealed to and pulled in all sorts of directions. The key periods emotionally will be at the end of January, in April, at the end of June, midway between August and September, and in November. In these phases which could well be delicate or trying, remember that planetary tension is only sent to us to arouse in us a better understanding of ourselves and the world, and to help us evolve towards greater perfection. For its part, Saturn often obliges us to examine our past: it plunges us in a climate of nostalgia, even regrets or remorse. So, sort out these confused or morose emotions and above all try – through sincere and objective self-criticism – to find your inner reality and that of your relationships to others which, thanks to Saturn, you will then see in its true colours.

The *last decan*, on the other hand, enjoys some excellent influences thanks to a tandem of Neptune and Uranus which seems to give it wings. Neptune, in fact, opens a hitherto unknown spiritual or intellectual dimension: art, poetry, religion or humanism beckon with open arms and an invitation to excel; while Uranus helps this decan to widen its circle of relationships and acquaintances. You'll find new hobbies, make intellectual discoveries – a brilliant invention isn't out of the question under such an influence! You'll have the wildest, most original plans and pioneer innovations which will open up a whole new path. A well-aspected Uranus is excellent for inventors, engineers, technicians, computer scientists, film makers, people in the media, movements which show solidarity ... and astrologers! If you belong to the *last decan* you can expect changes as positive as they're unforeseen, which will suddenly reveal the world to you from a different and more elevated point of view.

If you were born at the end of the Sign (*after 18 September*) you'll enjoy a fine sextile of Pluto, which occurs roughly every 40 years and which will install you comfortably in your social circle, where you may go up a notch. And that's not all. It will also give you an inner psychic strength which can help you overcome all obstacles, if there are any. You can expect to change or expand your vision of the world in 1995, to open yourself to new and enriching philosophical attitudes.

The most splendid periods of the year for one and all (and of course especially the *last decan* which is so favoured by this planetary backdrop) are the beginning of January, from the end of April to the end of May, your birthday period (but only the *last decan*) and November. Use these times to the full to make headway, solve possible problems and progress towards your objectives.

One warning: in January, June to July and in November, be extra prudent all round, for you'll be more vulnerable than usual; more vulnerable to falls, fractures (especially arms, shoulders, feet and thighs) and also to inflammation or digestive ailments, which is a weak area of yours.

Have a good year!


## Libra (23 September to 23 October)

On a global scale, 1995 is a year of transition between periods of great conjunctions, which from 1997 onwards will extend to the end of the twentieth century. And as far as Librans are concerned, this will give them little cause for complaint.

The most fortunate Librans are probably those at the *very beginning of the Sign, born around 23–24 September,* who will find themselves almost miraculously in phase with events: they'll seem projected above or beyond themselves, placed on a launching pad that's unique in their existence. Furthermore, apart from the *last decan* (which is still ill-aspected by Neptune and Uranus in tandem) *all the Sign* will find itself protected and lucky. And even the *last decan* can take heart as the heavens will bring it a very positive year's end: after November its horizon will clear considerably; and it will profit from providential meetings and good advice from the family, which will help it out of difficulties. The *rest of the Sign* will benefit from a fine sextile of Jupiter which will last right through the year. And this excellent protective influence (which, according to astrological tradition, is the most desirable of all) will inject its quota of pure luck into their lives.

If you're *first decan*, stay extremely alert for opportunities, business matters and propositions which could appear before the beginning of February; you'll have news about them after June; and from August on things will take a turn for the better which will be extremely satisfying.

The same scenario applies to the *second decan*, but with different timing: interesting business opportunities occur in February and until the beginning of April (particularly if you were *born before 10 October*), to give concrete results in October to November. (The *last decan*, meanwhile, will only get Jupiter's protection at the end of the year.) These are ideal times to put new ideas in place, to launch oneself on an adventure, to plan a marriage or business association ... and why not even a year off travelling around the world? (Jupiter symbolises travel, especially when located in its own Sign of Sagittarius.)

In any event, *whatever your decan*, you'll be caught up by the need to move, the desire to communicate, to break loose from all restraint, and the planetary context will help you.

Mars will appear in the heavens to add its dynamic and stimulating influence between January and May, between the end of July and beginning of September, and from mid-October to the end of November. During these periods you'll be on sparkling physical form and, if you play games, will be definitely unbeatable. These are also times of the best possible luck: when things will go both so swiftly and well it's almost as if they're telepathically guided by your wishes.

However, if you're *last decan*, you should mark the period from the end of July to the beginning of September in red in your diary, as you'll be in a phase of turmoil which could be prejudicial: allied to the dissonance of Neptune and Uranus,

Mars will simultaneously render you more vulnerable to contagious and viral illness and expose you to confused situations, which are difficult to untangle, and where deceit could intervene. For its part, Uranus could serve as a sort of detonator in a family bust-up or possible mechanical accident, so have your car serviced and take particular care when handling blunt instruments or anything electrical. This also applies to December, when Mars becomes dissonant again. During these explosive periods, stay tolerant and relaxed in your dealings with others – as you, more than anyone, know how to.

Returning to those fortunate few at the *very beginning of the Sign*: simultaneously favoured by Pluto and Uranus, they'll enjoy an astral climate favourable to their aspirations from the end of January till April; but there's no doubt that it's the much stronger and more meticulous influence of Uranus, present from the beginning of April till June, which will serve as a catalyst for their ambitions. You'll need to wait till the end of the year (November) for the results of these good influences which could well extend into next year too, which is good news. You'll certainly have climbed the social ladder by then, or increased your personal development. Professionally and in everyday terms, you'll have optimum luck in February, June, August and December (and that even applies to the less favoured *last decan*).

In contrast, the most difficult times for the *entire Sign* – and particularly the *last decan* – will be the beginning of January, July and the end of December; while for the *last decan* we must add April and October. You will be less at ease with yourself in February, the end of April/beginning of May, July and the beginning of September. And if you had an emotional problem during the year, the beginning of October could really inflame it.

Venus, however, will bring comfort and put you right with yourself and others in January, March, June, August, September to October (except the *last decan*) when you'll really shine, and finally in November and at the end of December. If you want to organise some festivity, choose one of these times:

your circle of friends will especially appreciate you, and your Libran charm will be at its height!

All told then, Libra my friend, apart from the *last decan*, which unfortunately will find its light somewhat under a bushel, you've a really fine-looking year in prospect, a lot more pleasant than the last – and one you must try to get the very best from!

### Scorpio (23 October to 22 November)

Scorpio, my friend, you must be in league with the heavens to enjoy such superb influences! There's not a cloud on your horizon in 1995, any more than there was last year – and as for next year ... but I'm jumping the gun.

In fact, Saturn consolidates your gains, gives you physical resistance and encourages long-term enterprises, especially if you were *born between 28 October and 18 November*. It stabilises your situation by helping you gather the fruits of past efforts. It rewards you and sees that your merits are recognised. Neptune and Uranus, for their part, take charge of your fortunes – and how effectively! – if you're *last decan*, by giving rise to events which are tailor-made for you and by placing you in a starring role in the year's conjunction, which will help you attain your objectives. And you'll attain them all the better as these two planets (accompanied, what's more, by Pluto, your ruler) will open you to superior realities and make you receptive to an unsuspected world or worlds. You'll find fascinating hobbies, intellectual or spiritual discoveries, which will change your life. Many people under the good aspects of Neptune become poets or mystics ... or (especially under the influence of Pluto and Neptune in tandem) successful businessmen or politicians of some standing. Just precisely how this influence will become manifest, of course, depends on your natal chart, which reflects the tendencies of your innermost being.

Scorpios at the very beginning of the Sign, *born around 23–24 October*, merit special mention. From very early April till June, Uranus opposes their natal Sun, implying the beginning of a radical change in their lives. It's possible that this change is not finalised till 1996. But in any event, it's a safe bet that if you belong to this sector of your Sign, radical upheaval will be gestating in the spring of 1995, in particular on the career or business levels, from mid-April to the end of May; or emotionally in mid-May. According to your personal chart and the general stability of your situation, one or other area will be about to be turned upside-down. Remember, this Uranian dissonance has a 21-year cycle, and try to recall what particular change struck your life around 1974 ...

Mars will galvanise *all Scorpios* in January, and from the end of May to the end of July; it will make you unbeatable in September to October and in December, which are all periods when your vitality will be at its peak. Take advantage of these phases to speed up your activity, deal with all current business and, if you're keen on sport, benefit from your extra pace. You'll have a rare efficiency and perseverance, a capacity to work that will be invincible, especially for *first decans* in January, and for the *last decan* in June and September to October. The *second decan* will only experience this frenzy of efficiency in December.

For *last decans*, these are also times when your intuition will be particularly keen; when you'll know exactly what's good for you, thanks to an almost mediumistic sense of reality. What's more, these periods, simultaneously so well aspected by both Mars and Uranus, will literally galvanise you into action; they may even make you impossible to live with in the eyes of your family, as your self-assurance will know no bounds. So try to be just a little subdued, to stay in tune with humble mortals!

For *all the Sign* the rosy periods of 1995 are: the beginning of January, March, July, September, November and December. These are the times which (according to the specific influences which apply to your decan, as already described), will be the most busy and promising. Particularly if you belong to the *second or last decan*, initiate a project between March and June, and you'll see results before November; while the final realisation of the enterprise will most likely occur in 1996.

Emotionally, you'll be particularly in sync with others and yourself in January, February, April, July, September, October and the beginning of December; thanks to Saturn, you'll consolidate exciting ties but, if you're *last decan*, you're also quite liable to create something new and impromptu from them!

## Sagittarius (22 November to 22 December)

A superficial analysis might lead an astrologer to say that, given the presence in your zodiac of your ruler Jupiter, the planet of expansion and good luck *par excellence*, 1995 will be the year of Sagittarians. Unfortunately, however, this is not quite the case. For while Jupiter has indeed been in your Sign since 1994, a square of Saturn also affects you this year, and its dissonance will markedly spoil your Jupiterian chances. Happily, this won't apply right through the year. But during the first four months you should particularly distrust any ideas of grandeur, and watch out for false promises (those of others and those you make yourself), especially if you were *born after 8 December*. For Saturn is waiting round the bend to constrain and limit you, and at the year's end will present you with the bill for unfortunate choices.

If you belong to the *first two decans*, it's highly likely you'll feel ill at ease, pulled hither and thither by the planets, at the beginning of the year and up to August. For you will be subject to the broadening, radiant and promising influence of Jupiter, yet at the same time hampered or limited by Saturn, which will throw up an obstacle to every opportunity. It's as if the stars take back with one hand what they give with the other. Fortunately the horizon clears between the beginning of May and the end of September, especially if you were born in the *first half of the Sign* where Jupiter alone affects you, as Saturn will move on to the *last decan*. As a result, you'll breathe easier and feel mightily relieved. Consequently, I advise you to get your plans under way between May and the end of July. If you do they'll have truly positive results between the beginning of August and the beginning of October. From October on, Saturn comes rushing back to constrain you and cause problems.

To complicate the picture, between the end of January and

the end of May, you'll enjoy the support of Mars, which will inspire you with an extraordinary energy to overcome all obstacles and thumb your nose at Saturn. On the other hand, it also risks plunging you into restlessness, self-dispersion and overwork between the end of May and the end of July. It is excellently aspected once more from the end of July to the beginning of September, after which it energises *all the Sign* between the end of October and the beginning of December – but with one reservation: the second decan will feel itself literally under fire. This, in fact, is the most difficult time of the year for this decan, one in which prudence is really called for. And there's a danger of acting out of impulsiveness or over-excitability and of missing a chance in initiatives blocked by Saturn. (This could also very easily apply to your emotional life as Venus will be in evidence.)

Special mention should be made of the *very beginning of the Sign*, which Pluto will visit in a transit these subjects will not see again in their lifetimes (Pluto's revolution takes 264 years!). As a result the lives of Sagittarians *born between 22 and 25 November* will be completely altered, for Pluto symbolises metamorphosis, death and regeneration.

If you belong to this sector of the zodiac, you can expect your existence to change completely, especially your vision of the world. And your basic standards could well be strongly modified in the course of 1995, probably under the impact of events which will alter everything. It's impossible to say here (because it depends on your personal chart) what precise form this metamorphosis will take, except that it will be slow but irreversible. The process will begin between January and April, with a key phase between November and the end of the year, and this change will continue through all next year. What's certain is that, whatever appearance these influences take in your life, you must go with them: must wed yourself to change, as it will further your spiritual evolution.

For some of you this could entail a spectacular change of direction professionally; for others a change of residence, even of country; for others still, it could involve a separation or divorce. Watch out, for Pluto is allied to the appearance of tumours (though fortunately this correlation is far from being systematic) and you'd be well advised to have a complete medical check-up and know exactly where you stand in terms of health, and particularly your immune system. This is because Pluto often induces a climate of guilt, a deep identity crisis and a sort of existential anguish, from which psychosomatic problems can arise. Fortunately, however, the vital and optimistic nature of Sagittarius is a widely known and hopefully sufficient antidote.

The manifestations of a transit of Pluto are not always negative, of course. In fact, quite the contrary. They can be linked to explosive and spectacular emergence on social or material planes: in other words, a better integration into society as a result of suddenly finding oneself in harmony with one's environment, with the economic or cultural consensus of the time. A noteworthy promotion linked to an increased and powerful social impact is thus one of Pluto's manifestations and not the least. This influence typically favours the emergence of political or business factors which are unique in a lifetime and prove highly rewarding for entrepreneurs or businessmen.

February, April, the greater part of August and October are the most fertile periods for *all the Sign*; and if you were *born at the end of the Sign*, Jupiter will be propitious on your birthday (which should have an excellent effect on all the following year). These favourable periods are times when you'll take the bull by the horns and best know how to cope with difficult influences. This will also be particularly the case for *last decans* in March, June and September, and in November to December for *December Sagittarians*.

Love could well be the year's latent problem, especially in January, April, June, September and November, when you'll feel yourself torn by an extremely difficult choice. In November (especially for *second decans*) there's a danger of flying crockery! But you'll also experience this choice in a highly positive and expansive way in March, May, August and the end of September (especially *first decans*), which are phases when you'll know how to extract the very utmost (one of your talents, this) from an amorous relationship. Take care, though, for these are also times when earthly food will tempt you the most and, *gourmand* Sagittarian that you are, you risk putting on weight.

## Capricorn (22 December to 20 January)

Capricorn, my friend, after the dream of a year you had in 1994, you'll agree that it would be hard to do better. But 1995, as you'll see, is scarcely less good a vintage. In fact, only Jupiter's influence – though sizeable – is lacking from the cosmic prize list. That's to say that those finishing touches of pure luck will be somewhat lacking, except for *last decans* for whom Neptune will take Jupiter's place, but only if you have an extremely harmonious natal Sun.

On the other hand, Saturn – as it did last year – will continue to protect you; and in February bring rewards that were promised last June (if you were *born at the beginning of January*). Your ruler and the master of experience and time, Saturn, invites you to pave the way between January and the beginning of March (if you're *second decan*) for a long-term undertaking, which you'll greatly profit from in the last three months of the year. It is also highly likely that a promotion which has been in the melting pot since spring will be awarded you at the end of the year.

The *last decan* (particularly those *born before 15 January*) will be affected by the same configuration, though with a slightly different timing: things will fall into place, and your merits be recognised, in May and June; you'll have gratifying news of this in the autumn; and the effective and concrete conclusion of these promises (the presentation of a diploma, for example, or the publication of a book) will only take place next year. So it's up to you to organise your activity according to this time schedule, which should help you lay out your pieces on the chessboard of your life.

The *last decan*, protected as it is in May to June (and even July) by Saturn, will have even more support as Uranus, Neptune and even Pluto will work for its evolution and progress. It's worth noting that the planetary partnership of

Neptune and Uranus, which will still prove difficult for *last decans* in 1995, will suddenly take on an extremely positive manifestation then, with the result that potential distress or chronic instability (which are the negative form of this double influence) will alter dramatically and will be simultaneously channelled and defused by the powerful tandem of Saturn and Pluto. This will take place in spring and also between August and the end of October, which means that, for the *last decan*, this will be a much more rewarding and constructive year than last. If you belong to this sector, you'll find a remedy for a possible identity crisis in your environment and the opportunities of everyday life, thanks notably to those around you who will actively contribute to your progress.

If you're at the end of the Sign (*born after the 17th*), Pluto will endow you with a sure instinct how to direct your life (here, too, you will be aided and supported by your friends) and also act to promote long-term plans and further your deep aspirations.

All told then, this looks an especially favoured year, without a false note – or almost. Mars will add a touch of dynamising spice in January, June to July, September to October and in December, and give you the impression that for a motivated Capricorn nothing is impossible. Saturn will contribute perseverance, tenacity, the necessary physical resistance to overcome all obstacles and make your objectives easily attainable. But Mars will oppose you between the end of July and the beginning of September. This is a period when you'll be particularly nervous or scatter-brained and – especially if you're *last decan* – vulnerable to accidents or viral infections (which you should also watch out for in December).

Many single Capricorns will discover their soulmates in January (especially the *last decans*), or in February, April, October (for *January Capricorns*), and at the end of May/beginning of June, July, the end of August and December for *last decans*. During these periods you'll feel very much in harmony with your environment, in tune with those close to you; and relationships with your friends and family will flow on naturally. Thanks to Saturn, you will consolidate existing ties and ensure that they are long-lasting.

Your most effective and lucky times in 1995, phases favoured by a well-aspected Sun and Mercury, will be: January, March, the end of April to May, September, November and the end of December (especially for the *first decan*).

Good luck in your exploration of this superb year!

## *Aquarius (20 January to 19 February)*

Broadly speaking, Aquarius my friend, I reckon you'll be extremely happy to have finished with 1994, and be starting this new year full of hope. And that hope won't be misplaced, as this year looks a great deal more promising than the last.

If you were born at the very beginning of the Sign, *around 20 January*, it's worth knowing that you are entering a long-term phase, which will last until 1996, and which looks extremely positive and rewarding: a sextile of Pluto will help you put your potential energy at the service of society ... and see to it you're well repaid! In other words, you're in a phase of progress in which you'll be harmoniously integrated with your environment; and events will contribute to your positive material evolution. What's more, this sextile of Pluto will intensify your vital resources, give you a sure and certain instinct as to which initiatives to take and how to direct your life.

*Very early Aquarians* won't be the only 'chosen' ones in 1995, either. Thanks to Jupiter, which also forms a superb sextile with the entire Sign, *all Aquarians* will get a helping hand from 'the Great Benefactor'. Keep an eye open and be on the lookout for proposals made – particularly if you were *born before 6–7 February* – from the beginning of the year until the beginning of April. You'll hear news of them during the following months and concrete results will follow between August and November.

Especially in the second half of the year, then, you should be raking it in – quite often in the form of hard work – as the direct result of this fine Jupiterian influence. More specifically, it will make it possible for you to pave the way ahead professionally (for example, by instigating a plan you hold dear) in January to February, April, or May to June – so that you can reap the rewards in September to October, or in December.

Many Aquarians will decide to get married in January (if they're *first decan*), in March, the beginning of May or the end of June (if they're one of the *first two decans*) and will put their decision into practice in August or September or – better still – in November, which is a very 'amorous' month.

In this excellent overall picture there are, all the same, one or two times when you'll need to exercise caution. Mars, the planet of aggression, and sometimes accidents, will be in opposition – especially to the *first and second decans* – between mid-April and mid-May, and for *all the Sign* in September and the greater part of October. So you'll need to get a grip on your nerves then, to avoid actions which may have unfortunate consequences. And watch out for fever, burns and inflammation of any kind; you'll be the more vulnerable according to your own physical sensitivity. While if you tend to circulatory problems (which is often the case with your Sign) or genital, ocular, or neural disorders, you should especially take care.

## Pisces (19 February to 21 March)

Pisces my friend, let's hope you're charged like a battery with last year's fine influences – the better to confront those of 1995.

The *first two decans*, especially, will be given something of a rough ride by the astral conjunctions. It seems there's a curious change taking place with regard to last year, particularly if you were *born between 25 February and 3 March*. Specifically, the influence of Saturn you were under last year – and which probably manifested itself in a positive way then, owing to a well-aspected Jupiter – is going to change and turn against you. And, especially in the first two months of the year, there's a chance it could make life difficult. Fortunately, after February you'll have had the worst of it, at least as far as Saturn is concerned! But take care what you initiate in January as it could well bring a load of problems in the spring. In fact, January will also see you subject to a square of Jupiter, the sower of complications and financial or legal problems. And, if you're *first decan*, everything you undertake then will most likely have negative repercussions between June and October. My advice is: don't instigate legal proceedings in this first month of the year and don't play it out to the bitter end with fiscal or administrative authorities. You won't have the last word and could experience some cruel repercussions in the months we've mentioned.

The same warning applies to *second decan* Pisceans, but with a shift in time: be especially prudent in your decisions and actions between February and the beginning of May; or the fall-out you'll get in the last three months of the year won't be jolly.

As for the *third decan*, it will find itself, in contrast, largely protected by a splendid double sextile of Uranus and Neptune, as it has been since 1993. What's more, it is also sustained by a magnificent trine of Pluto, which one only sees once in a life-time!

This trine of Pluto only bears on those *born after 16 March*, to whom it grants fantastic new energy (which humanitarian Pisceans will very often put to the service of society). It also offers wealth or fame, a starring role and extraordinary expansion of business activities. For their part, Uranus and Neptune will jointly bring the *last decan* a psychological, intellectual or spiritual opening, which could also be artistic or mystical. You will surpass all boundaries and excel (precisely in what field depends on your natal chart). So once again this will be an extremely fertile year for you if you're *last decan*. And especially so when Saturn, in turn, adds its rays to this already promising trio between May and October. There's also a strong chance that, between May and early July, you will be given an inkling of an outstanding award, even a sort of consecration, which will fall due to you either between July and October, or later next year. So, if you belong to this section of your Sign, now's the time to undertake a long-term task, which will give you exceptional satisfaction in the periods mentioned.

You will have the wind in your sails in January, March to April (but only the *last decan*), in May, July (one of your best months), November, and at the end of December which looks particularly propitious.

On the other hand, the times you'll feel most stretched (especially the *first and second decan*) are as follows: the end of May and June, August to September, and at the beginning of December. While January, from the end of May to the end of July, and late October to the end of November deserve special mention. During these phases, you'll be given a really rough ride by the planetary influences, find yourself pulled hither and thither and not know which way to turn. So to regain your inner peace, turn in on yourself and review the problems which preoccupy you, if necessary on paper, which clarifies things. Above all, don't act impulsively, as a dissonant Mars is a poor counsellor. Don't take chances physically either, as falls and fractures are more than likely under the threefold negative influence of Saturn, Jupiter and Mars. And as the feet are a particularly vulnerable area in your Sign, take care – and watch where you put them!

# 1996

## The course of the planets

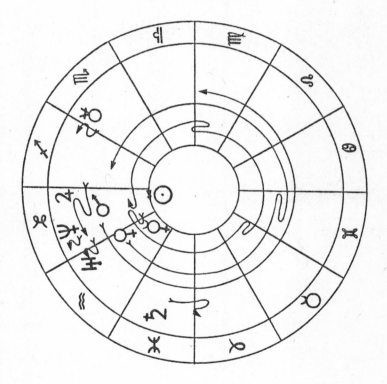

# World Events

At last – a really fine year in prospect for the world, unlike preceding, more tumultuous times...

While 1993 may have been a key year – probably the most important in this century's end – because of the conjunction of Uranus and Neptune (albeit extremely ambiguous in its manifestations), and while 1994 may have been extremely positive, 1996 is the first year of the decade to be so harmoniously aspected. And comparing this year with the last six months of 1989 (in which these forecasts were written) in particular, this can only be a strong cause for hope. For just as the end of 1989 appeared as a period of total upheaval and global soul-searching – especially in the communist bloc, which went through precisely the phase of profound mutation which I foresaw – so 1996 looks as if it ought to pass smoothly, as a sort of calm and snag-free staging post, on the way to the third millenium.

In spring, or more precisely March, a sextile of Uranus and Pluto could be particularly favourable to Japanese progress and prosperity. There will be appreciable repercussions from the preceding summer when we perhaps became aware of certain social necessities with regard to worldwide solidarity; and it's possible that salutary decisions were taken in these areas. It's a bet that, with the stars in the generous Signs of Aquarius and Sagittarius – which are inventive and open to progress – the planetary climate will be extremely fertile in social and legislative terms. It is likely, too, that the concrete results of these spring decisions will make themselves felt in September, perhaps through the application of new decrees or laws. And for once a new year may well be concordant and calm.

What's more, March 1996 ought to be particularly positive in its political climate, in its influences on worldwide society, as a fine sextile again takes shape between Saturn and Neptune. This

Saturn–Neptune cycle, as we've said before, relates to Marxism (and therefore particularly governs the destiny of the USSR). It formed a remarkable conjunction at the end of 1989 and the configuration of communism since then has changed enormously throughout the world. To what extent it will have taken on yet another guise, or have even disappeared in the form it had over most of this century, is difficult to say at the time of writing. But change is certain and whether politically, economically, or culturally, in 1996 the USSR will be in an extremely positive, constructive and evolutive phase.

In a more general way, this sextile will probably accompany a period of solid social progress. And it's likely that political structures will evolve in a favourable and generous way, which will be rewarding for the masses. In any event, the political climate in March will result from excellent decisions that were taken in June 1995.

Another configuration which will favour the application of positive reforms will be the trine between Saturn and Pluto, which will take place in April and bear fruit in October. (All decisions taken in this springtime month will be supported by the cosmic conjunction, so they're as effective as possible.) This 23-year cycle is also in phase with the destiny of the Arab world and China, and will prove excellent for them, as it will also for Germany, favouring changes in, and even the positive metamorphosis of, these countries.

Finally, a sextile of Saturn and Uranus will form in May (between the beginning of Aries and Aquarius), which will have the effect of adjusting reality to current necessities, through intelligent use of past structures. More specifically, enterprises begun in May will have concrete and excellent repercussions in November in terms of solidarity and both intellectual and technical progress, while this period should be equally favourable to everything to do with electronics.

In brief, then, a very fruitful year, particularly for the very beginning of the Fire Signs (Aries, Leo, Sagittarius), the Air Signs (Gemini, Libra and Aquarius) and the last decans of the Water and Earth Signs.

So almost everyone will have a slice of the cake.

# *Your Personal Forecast*

### *Aries (21 March to 20 April)*

Whatever happens this year, it's good to know you'll be compensated next, in the sense that 1997 will be a much better year, especially for the *first two decans.*

In fact, if you were *born around 10 April* you are still in a rut. And if you were *born before 8 April,* in the first four months of the year you'll suffer the first phase of a dissonant Jupiter, which will unleash all sorts of complications, especially financial, judicial or fiscal. You'll have repercussions from this first phase between May and December. So watch your step during the first quarter of the year: don't overestimate yourself – or other people or situations, either – or you could find yourself well and truly embarrassed by the consequences.

If you're *last decan,* you'll only be sensitive to Jupiter's disturbing climate in December, but a Neptunian coloration will mix with it, so that you'll have trouble seeing things as they really are, and you may end up duped, deceived, even robbed. So this will hardly be the time to finalise a partnership, get married, or undertake anything important to do with the future.

And that's not all. From April onwards you'll be visited by Saturn, which (as every 29 years) will be passing through your sector to bring all sorts of restrictions or limitations, though in exceptional cases, consolidation or even 'consecration'. Unfortunately, in view of the difficult Jupiterian context, this last scenario is unlikely unless your natal Sun is totally harmonious and you belong to the *very beginning of the Sign.*

If you were *born before 25–26 March,* you have a configuration at your disposal which will be a real launching pad. Your every hope could be realised, despite the spokes Jupiter puts in your wheels. You can count on the most supportive conjunctions in March, April to May, September, October and November. And you'll be particularly favoured, thanks to the concerted action of Pluto, Saturn and Uranus which will keenly negate Jupiter (and all the more so as they won't all intervene at exactly the same time). So, if you belong to this *first half of the first decan*, give free rein to your natural audacity and boldness: dare ... invent ... press forward – and nothing will prove impossible for you.

I have some good news for the *last decan*, too. The opposition of Uranus and Neptune has disturbed your equilibrium and serenity since 1994. But after a final assault in January on the *entire Sign*, Uranus will leave you in peace and pass into Aquarius. Neptune, however, will continue to send disturbance and distress your way, especially if you were *born between 13 and 18 April*, in which case try not to take too tragically – even if you do take seriously – the periods of doubt or depression which this Neptunian climate can evoke. Be careful not to build too many castles in the air and not to let yourself be taken in as a result of your trusting nature, as those around you won't always be entirely frank. The times you need to be particularly prudent and on guard are: the beginning of January, April, and the end of August/beginning of September, when Mars will make you particularly vulnerable. You'll also be liable to encounter deceit, intrigue and stumbling blocks on your path in mid-January, the beginning of April, July and October, when the Sun will be opposed to you. Look after your image then as it, too, will be vulnerable, and keep clear of criticism, scandalmongering and calumny, which Neptune can provoke.

The luckiest periods of 1996 (most particularly for those well-aspected subjects already mentioned) will be: February, the end of March, June, August – even though the dissonance of Mars makes you impulsive and likely to make telling decisions that lack organisation – and finally November and the beginning of December.

Venus will put you on good terms with yourself and others, favouring emotional harmony and increasing your charm, in January, February (even though Jupiter introduces a notion of excess here, which might be to your taste!); then from April to August, when for *all decans* Venus acts as a protective cushion against the blows of life you could suffer, especially as a result of your attachment to friends and near ones; and finally in September and December. If you're *first decan* you will have time then to meet new people, to strike up important and exciting ties which could also prove stable and long-lasting. In fact, you could find your 'other half', with whom to forget Jupiter's disturbance and mundane pestering.

### Taurus (20 April to 21 May)

Broadly speaking, dear Taurus, it's only those of you *born before 25 April* who could find themselves disturbed by an 'uneasy' square of Uranus. The remainder of the Sign will be lucky and very much protected in 1996; and all the more so as Pluto, the bringer of tension and forced change, has left your sector and no longer concerns you. Since its entry into Scorpio in November 1983, Pluto has been in opposition to your Sign – in an extremely progressive way – and during these 13 years has given rise to many changes in depth, whether tied or not to exterior events, including an upheaval of your psyche, which may have been salutary but will not have come about without pain. To sum up, then, 1996 looks very well aspected, apart from the *very beginning of the Sign.*

'The last shall be first' says the Bible, so let's consider the *last decan* first of all. In the first three months of the year, it will gather the fruits of past efforts and find itself rewarded, perhaps by some distinction or other, or for some by a veritable consecration.

If you were *born before 15 May* (especially *between the 8th and the 15th*), the concrete and rewarding effects of Saturn will be very powerful at the beginning of the year. More than ever, you'll consolidate your place in the Sun. Neptune, for its part, forms a masterly trine with your native Sun which especially affects Taureans *born between the 10th and the 17th*, as they'll profit simultaneously from the beneficial effects of Neptune and Jupiter. And in December they'll hit the jackpot! This will be the time to get your craziest-ever projects underway ... unless you wait for the conjunction of the Sun and Mercury in Capricorn, which will take place at the beginning of 1997...

Many still unattached Taureans will experience an idyllic

love, especially if they belong to the *first two decans*; and this could happen in January to February, March, August, October or December. During these periods *all the Sign* will feel in phase with those close to them, loved and appreciated by others and in perfect harmony with themselves. Thanks to the alliance of Jupiter and Venus, you'll appreciate food more than ever, which you already have a talent for. So if you tend to put on weight, watch out for Jupiterian excess!

There's no doubt that this year is highly recommended for marriage, particularly if you are *first or second decan*. And good Taurus organiser that you are, you could plan your marriage in the first four months of the year, and have it in the last four. While if you are *last decan*, the very best time to do this will be at the end of December, or January 1997.

You'll be in blazing form between mid-February and the end of March, from the beginning of May to mid-June (when nonetheless the *beginning of the Sign* should be prudent, as a square of Uranus could bring all sorts of untimely excess), in August and finally in November to December. Your vitality will be at its utmost then and nothing will stand in the way of your spirit of enterprise or enthusiasm. What's more, Mars will team up with Jupiter then, whose pure luck will be catalysed by Mars' hyper-stimulating influence: so events will go really quickly and in unexpected right directions.

*All the Sign* will, generally speaking, find itself under very beneficial influences in March, May, July, September and December, which are all periods when you'll be appreciated professionally and make progress towards your objectives. On the other hand, you will be less on form and supported by events (frankly thwarted and disturbed if you were *born before 25 April*) in February, August, and from the end of October to mid-November. But as you'll have seen, apart from these few least lucky periods, you've got a superb year ahead of you!

## Gemini (21 May to 21 June)

You'll probably be breathing a sigh of relief that last year has ended, and be looking forward hopefully to the year to come. And you'd be right most of the time. 1996 will be superb, at least for *almost all the first decan*, so especially for Geminis *born in May*. If you belong to this sector of the zodiac, you can celebrate, for the world is yours! You are especially fortunate that the opposition of Pluto – which could be a source of serious crisis – will be modelled on the hyper-positive astral context of harmonious aspects which Uranus and Saturn simultaneously form with regard to your natal Sun. This means that your friends, in particular, will play an extremely important role in your life this year, and that they will enable you to find the solution and remedy to your problems and a possible identity crisis. In other words, materially speaking, it's thanks to those near you, to your friends and family, that you will change the effects of Pluto on you – and most probably in a positive way.

Especially when Saturn mixes with a positive tandem of Pluto and Uranus, between April and the end of the year, you'll have the maximum chance of catching up on your arrears, as well as breaking new ground in your life in a spectacular way. You'll probably broaden the perspectives of your world vision and your present status quo. This extremely stimulating trine of Uranus will propel you forward in an exciting way, as its harmonious aspects (which reappear about every 40 years) usually do. And with pragmatism from Saturn, it's a safe bet you will be endowed with discernment and willpower from April on, which will also help you bring Pluto's change about positively. (While this applies to May Geminis, those *born at the beginning of June* will have to wait till 1997 to receive the doubly excellent influence of Uranus and Saturn.)

The *second decan* will be more or less neutral in terms of the influences it will receive this year, apart from the very beginning of January when it could feel somewhat hindered by the square of Saturn. The *last decan*, in contrast, will see itself hampered, hindered or inhibited in the pursuit of its objectives, though fortunately only until the beginning of April.

So all told, from April on, only the *first decan* will be affected by the backdrop of slow planets responsible for fundamental astral climates. The rest of the year will be more a period of transition, an unremarkable phase in the lives of the *last two decans*. Nevertheless, there will be highs and lows, especially physically and in terms of effectiveness, as a result of the movements of Mars. To go forward in life, take care to make decisions when you're sure you're in great form: choose January or the beginning of February, April or from mid-June to the end of July, or from mid-September to the end of October. On the other hand, be wary (especially if you're *last decan*, but also if you were born in the *very first days of the Sign*) in February to March, when Mars will be hostile to you, pushing you towards regrettable carelessness, or making you physically vulnerable to overwork or disorganisation. This will also be the case – for the *very beginning of the Sign* only – in mid-June; and for *all the Sign* in November to December, when you'll again be highly strung and therefore susceptible to blunders of greater or lesser consequence.

In contrast, life will go swimmingly in January to February (except for the *last decan*), then in April, June, August and October, when the Sun and Mercury will appear in the heavens to back you with their beneficial rays, and facilitate the course of everyday life. As for love, the presence of Venus in your Sign between the beginning of April and the beginning of August will make you more charming than ever – and it's highly likely you'll meet your soulmate at the end of April or between June and July, especially if you're *first decan*. But other periods almost as good emotionally are: the beginning of January and the end of February, the end of September and almost all November.

Good luck!

### Cancer (21 June to 22 July)

I must say, dear Cancer, that this year's configuration is hardly the most exciting ever. Apart from the *last decan*, that is, which will see itself rewarded for past efforts, perhaps by some distinction or extraordinary professional promotion, which in all likelihood will fall due in February or March.

June Cancerians, especially, will have a brush with the duo Saturn/Jupiter. And this will most probably tend to destabilise your status quo by introducing all sorts of turbulence and complications into your life. Particularly between June and November, there's a danger of financial, fiscal or judicial complications, which will result in paperwork, red tape, administrative hassles and other pleasures of a similar nature. So you'll need to be extra patient then. And it's worth knowing, in any event, that Saturn will air its grievances to you before mid-July, bring them up for consideration between July and December and make you pay for them in December and the beginning of next year. Accordingly, I advise you to be particularly careful during Saturn's first discordant passage, between April and July. And before that, during the first two months of the year when Jupiter will be in opposition, you should observe the same degree of prudence with regard to the authorities and your superiors at work. Avoid making important official approaches, which are unlikely to end in success (unless you can get one of your friends or family to act as an effective intermediary for you at the end of January).

While the Saturnian restrictions which affect Cancerians of the *first decan* follow the time-scale I've indicated, problems caused by Jupiter (excess, complications, turmoil, difficult choices) will bear on the *first decan* during the first two months of the year, and their repercussions will make themselves felt between the end of July and the end of October. As the opposition of Jupiter unfortunately favours financial problems, try to economise, or at least don't throw your money out of the window during this first part of the year. If you're *second decan* the same advice applies, but for the period from March to the end of April, which without doubt will affect the end of the year. This also means that, if you intend to take legal action during these early months, the year's end will bring you news in a similar way.

Physically, if you're *first decan*, try to avoid overwork and exhausting your strength, which for some of you could result from squandering your energy, or simply a surfeit of responsibilities which are hard to accept. You should know, too, that Saturnian dissonance – which returns roughly every seven years – is in no way generous. So you'll need to adjust yourself to a reality which you might have wanted to ignore up to now. And this could result in a disagreeable confrontation imposed by critics, obstacles, or events outside your control. The best way to counter these difficult influences in the first six months of the year will be to undertake a serious and sincere process of self-analysis, which is a good means of establishing one's true measure and adapting oneself to what's real.

For other *first decans*, a square of Saturn will correspond with stagnation or obstructions to their plans. And as this dissonance accompanies that of Jupiter, which is synonymous with excess – and which amplifies the consequences of possible events – you can bet that Saturn's discordance will be more than usually restrictive and will coincide with a period of turmoil and stress.

*Last decans*, in total contrast, can celebrate. For even if their best influences end in April, they have little to contend with right through the year other than the opposition of Neptune. (Apart from in January, when a tandem of Uranus and Neptune may disturb them.) And again this Neptunian dissonance will only affect Cancerians *born between 15 and 20 July.* For these subjects, this tension may bring a chaotic period of disarray, doubt or distress, when they'll question themselves fundamentally.

If you belong to this sector, get straight to grips with any problems rather than try and escape in some artificial paradise of drugs or alcohol, or simply a negative spirit of thinking 'what's the use'. For the best remedy is to analyse your situation objectively. Chase away the chimera of your doubts and fears and have confidence in yourself, for Neptune can take away our self-assurance. And try to think of your advantages and talents, rather than your weaknesses.

But take care, as the organism can be weakened by the opposition of Neptune, and a lowering of our defences is often associated with this planet's dissonance. So adopt a positive attitude and have a medical check-up to discover any physical deficiencies. It's worth knowing too that brass, gold and silver are particularly necessary and beneficial trace elements for you, as is calcium fluoride in terms of Schussler salts, as you will be more vulnerable than usual to contagion – especially viral – when Mars is also hostile to you (at the beginning of January, in April and in August). You'll also be more exposed than usual to deceit, intrigue, cliques, slip-ups and breaches of trust. So don't tempt Fate by taking risks during these periods.

Insofar as the influence of the rapid planets is concerned, the favourable and unfavourable periods are as follows: March and May will be coming up roses, and August will be splendid for travel; September, and from the end of October to the end of November, will also be favourable. You'll feel very much alive, despite other planetary influences, when Mars stimulates you at the end of February/beginning of March, in May, at the beginning of June and during the last two months of the year. The period from the end of July to the beginning of September is worth special mention: in direct transit in your Sign, Mars will make you particularly impulsive, sulky, crazy, sullen, aggressive ... in short, impossible! But other people could well behave in the same way towards you then; so it'll be a chicken and egg situation, where you won't know which came first. Either way, though, this is a time to go easy and take cover from the untimely vibrations in the air, which will be crackling with electricity! Fortunately, there will also be some soft and gentle periods, when those close to you will appreciate your tender, serious qualities: these will be at the end of January/beginning of February, from about the beginning of March to the beginning of April, in October and at the start of December.

Finally, if you were *born before 26 June*, try to refrain from travelling at the end of August/beginning of September, when journeys appear somewhat menacing. Otherwise ... chin up! and console yourself with the thought that, all things considered, 1997 will be a lot less complicated year.

## Leo (22 July to 23 August)

If you were *born in July*, dear Leo, you can expect the lion's share of 1996. In fact, yours is the only sector to be fundamentally influenced by the slow planets. And you're rewarded by no less than three out of five of them in our solar system, which isn't bad going! They'll work for your progress, your evolution, in a spectacular way and, in sum, will be 'going for you'.

If you were *born before 27 July*, the opposition of Uranus will have the effect of destabilising your life, and making you want to send everything packing. This isn't necessarily negative, though it often leads to disturbing consequences. In the planetary context of 1996, however, thanks to a trine of Pluto and a consolidating and stabilising trine of Saturn, there's nothing to fear. On the contrary, the changes which you'll bring about in your life, if you belong to this sector, will be coloured by the influence of Saturn and Pluto, a guarantee of stability and fine opportunities. This means that these changes were necessary and that you make them in the right way, to further your deepest aspirations. The trine of Pluto will smooth your path and at the same time favour your long-term social impact, intensify your vital resources and reinforce your psyche, while Saturn, for its part, will serve as a sort of guard-rail against shocks and spots of bad luck that Uranus can give rise to when it is ill aspected.

Nonetheless, you must watch out for sudden changes of mood, possible arrogance and lack of physical caution from January till mid-February, from May until mid-June and in the middle of September, at which time you'll be more vulnerable, and even more unpredictable, than usual. At the same time you'll also be in danger of some sort of accident, which is worth knowing, the better to avoid it. Have your car checked out, as mechanical breakdowns often occur under such astral configurations. From April on, though, Saturn will lend you a helping hand and act as a shield against the combined discordance of Mars and Uranus.

Mars will galvanise *all the Sign* in April, from the end of June to mid-July, and in September to October, filling you with a dynamism which will enable you to overcome all obstacles. From April onwards, blending with the influence of Saturn, Mars will give the *first decan* in particular the assurance that no goal is inaccessible – and endow it with physical resistance, a spirit of enterprise and indomitable willpower. These are (for *all the Sign*, but especially the *first decan*) the most effective periods and the most satisfying in terms of action. And if you're involved in sport, these are also the times when you'll be, in all probability, next to unbeatable.

The leanest propitious phases, those when you'll have to slog to get the same results, are as follows: for *all the Sign* – and particularly Leos *born before 27 July* – January to February, May, November and round their birthday in the second half of July. And it's worth a mention in passing that the opposition of Venus, which is in evidence at the time of this birthday means that – according to the laws of solar revolution – changes, visible in outline since the beginning of this year, will have repercussions on all the following year up to the next birthday.

It's possible, even probable, that love will be the focal point of your Uranian turnaround this year, and once again this will only happen if you were *born before 27 July*. The most likely months for this to occur are February, April, at the beginning of September, the end of October/beginning of November or at the end of January, which are all times that Venus will smile on you and there's a strong chance you'll meet the person of your dreams. *All Leos* will be affected by these Venusian periods, which will put them in accord with themselves, their emotional environment, their family and their friends.

And from the beginning of April till August will also be a salutary period for them, with their Sun well aspected by a fine sextile of Venus, which will cause them to radiate and beam with charm.

### Virgo (23 August to 23 September)

Virgo, my friend, rest assured – you've a great deal better year ahead than the one that has just gone by – except perhaps Virgos *born from 10th to 15th September,* who at the very beginning of the year must, in their turn, confront the opposition of Saturn. If you belong to this sector of your Sign and look into your past a little, it is quite possible that you'll realise that life and events will make you pay, at the beginning of this year, for problems that appeared last spring – problems which already had repercussions in early autumn 1995...

From the end of February, however, a trine of Neptune will enter your zodiac to neutralise the frustrating effects of a dissonant Saturn, and in March will bring *last decans* a solution, or in any case a very effective balm, for their possible wounds, perhaps simply through a widened vision of life, a new-found serenity. It's worth noting that this problem thrown up by Saturn could well have to do with a private or professional partnership. But, in any event, after the first three months of the year you'll be rid of it – and rid of the restrictive and depressing, even physically weakening, influence of Saturn as well.

For their part, Virgos at the very beginning of the Sign (*born before 26 August*), will be ill aspected by a square of Pluto. Symbol of profound change, of death and regeneration, it will oblige you to go back to the basic you; to question your scale of values; and to change the principles which rule your life. You could well find yourself the victim of events which sweep you up in their wake, such as a laying-off or redundancy, for example. Or the profound and irreversible changes summoned by Plutonian energy could be manifest in almost any other area. Depending on your personal chart, they could affect your family situation ... a partnership ... your profession. On the health side, too, Pluto can coincide with a weakening of resources, chiefly psychic, which could lead to possible psychosomatic illness. It's important, therefore, to keep yourself in good mental shape, which will help you keep things in balance. Learn to think positively!

A superb trine of Jupiter will make the task easier: mainly in January to February, and then in August to September, when you'll be animated by an increased vital strength, a fine – and contagious – optimism. At the beginning of the year this trine will give rise to all sorts of enticing opportunities – you can count on it – which you'll have news of in summer, and concrete results in the autumn. And this same influence of Jupiter will be centred on the *second decan* in March and April; and will bring these subjects attractive proposals or business opportunities on a plate, whose repercussions – often in the form of hard cash – will in all probability occur in November.

As for the *last decan*, it too will be favoured by Jupiter, though briefly, in December; though at the same time it will be subject to a trine of Neptune which will excite its luck in a spectacular way. So, if you have to organise an important project, wait till December to do it.

Virgos of the *first and second decan* will find their year stamped with the seal of luck in January, March (provided you listen to your partner, let yourself be advised by him or her and take advantage of his or her luck), then in April to May, at the end of August/beginning of September, the end of October/beginning of November, and the end of December. During these phases, you should speed things up with a view to making better progress – and you'll find luck on hand! These are times to discover the house of your dreams, to unearth the job you were made for – or the person who makes you complete. With regard to which … Venus will favour you in March, August, October and the beginning of December. Many Virgos still single may find themselves at the altar then, and are advised to choose one of these times, which are simultaneously blessed by Jupiter and Venus, to enter on this great adventure.

## Libra (23 September to 23 October)

For the *last decan*, freed from the dissonance of Uranus, the astral climate of this year is clearly better than last. But unfortunately it's not the same for the *rest of the Sign*, which is simultaneously under fire from both Jupiter and Saturn.

After being spoiled in 1995 by fine aspects of Jupiter which perhaps inclined you to rest – if not go to sleep – on your laurels, there's a potentially rude awakening in store. Especially if you're a *September Libran*; you'll be under attack from the astral conjunction. And (chiefly during the summer) you will experience cosmic disturbance in your everyday life; buffeted by events and perhaps confronted by difficult choices, you'll feel yourself slowed down, inhibited and hindered by Saturn. So you'd be well advised to be extra attentive to your decisions and actions at the start of the year; don't sign up for any long-term commitments and don't get outrageously in debt, as repayment in August to September could be awkward. And the same applies if you intend to take legal action – the result could be decidedly uncertain.

If you're a *September Libran*, a problem will arise between April and July to do with a partner or business associate; and between July and the end of November it will develop in a way that's hardly encouraging, to have repercussions at the beginning of next year. For many couples whose relationship is built on sand, this Saturnian time will bring a grave crisis, and quite possibly separation.

But here's some good news: if you were born at the *very beginning of the Sign* (*before the 27th*), Pluto will act as a powerful shield in 1996; and will have the advantage of muffling life's shocks, if only by strengthening your counter-balancing psychic resources, and making you react positively. In other words, even if at certain times of the year you may have reason to give in, you won't. Thanks to Pluto. This planet's fine sextile will help you, on the contrary, to cope with an important turning-point in your life, which in the final analysis will prove positive. Try therefore to consider your everyday problems as passing disturbances – the price you must pay for your final evolution and spiritual or intellectual progress – and keep your eye on the distant horizon.

As for the *last decan*, which for a number of years has found itself seriously disturbed by the double dissonance of Neptune and Uranus, here's some good news: from January on, Uranus will cease to be in opposition to you. And it will even positively help the *first decan*. In fact, if you were *born before 28 September*, it will favour a new blossoming and give rise to unexpected and productive opportunities, which will widen

your social, intellectual or material horizons. So this first sector
of the Sign is truly privileged by the astral conjunction of 1996.

If you're *last decan*, even if Uranus has ceased to bother you
and upset your life, Neptune will still sow trouble and confusion. This will be particularly so if you were *born between 15
and 20 October*. You could find yourself in disarray, in a state
of irrational turmoil, insecurity and uncomfortable psychological instability, in which there's a danger of not knowing
which way to turn and it's hard to hang on to principles and
values. Try not to lose faith in yourself then, or let go and think
'what's the point anyhow?' And don't be tempted to turn for
refuge to the phoney paradise of drugs.

My advice is to be absolutely strict with yourself, banish Will-
o'-the-wisps, and kick irrational fears straight out of the
window! You should also cultivate a certain wariness, to
counter a tendency to credulity which could lead you astray.
And be specially on guard in December, when Jupiter and
Neptune gang up against your objectivity and make you more
than ever susceptible to illusion and vulnerable to breach of
trust.

On the health side, take equal care to avoid contagion, to
which you'll be particularly liable at the beginning of January,
end of April and end of August. What's more, you'll be a
potential victim then for theft and deceit. So, without getting
paranoid, don't spontaneously trust anyone during these
periods. Above all, don't be discouraged. Keep in mind that,
although this is a difficult phase to live through, like all the rest
it will pass. And being obliged to confront certain, possibly
brutal, aspects of reality should help you make progress on the
journey to self-enlightenment.

In fact, many Librans of this zodiacal sector will discover that
they have been deceived, that their credulity, good faith, naivety
or simply thoughtlessness have been abused. If you are one of
these 'victims of Fate', take it out on no one but yourself, and
don't decide that all mankind is no longer worthy of confidence.
Simply note that this type of experience increases our realism –
and that's good, as lucidity and truth are worthy ultimate goals.

In general, Librans at the *very beginning of the Sign* get the best of 1996 as they're protected by the astral conjunction, while effectively *all other Librans* will find this a somewhat testing year.

On the heart side, Venus (your planet) will be favourable in January, from the beginning of April to the beginning of August, in September and at the end of December – which are times it will greatly augment your charm and appeal, while also ensuring the affection of those close to you. On the other hand, emotional problems could well come to a head with resulting confusion (for the *last decan*) and other problems (for the *first and second decans*) in February, August and November, when only *very early Librans* will be emotionally favoured.

Professionally, and in terms of the positive evolution of everyday life, February should prove propitious, along with the end of June, August and December; while the most critical phases occur in April, early June, October and at the end of December (especially for the *first decan*).

In sum, if you were born outside the small privileged niche at the *very beginning of your Sign*, as 1996 begins ... take a good deep breath. Fill yourself with positive thoughts and determination; and dive into what lies ahead, with the firm intention of transforming its lead into gold.

Good luck!

## Scorpio (23 October to 22 November)

It's unfortunately true that one gets used to the better things in life, and the recent past may have spoiled you a little. And in 1996 (apart from *very early Scorpios* who'll have to tangle with Uranus), you'll enjoy good luck again that's even more outstanding than last year's. But don't let this incline you to arrogance, for the 'astral wheel' turns...

In fact, next year will be considerably less comfortable than this one, so whatever mistakes you make in 1996 you'll have to pay dearly for in 1997. This warning is particularly applicable to Scorpios *born before 27 October* who will be subject to the dissonance of Uranus. Moreover, if one considers things on a wider philosophical level, it is a general rule of the cosmos that one makes one's 'tomorrow' along with one's 'today' in accordance with karma, or the law of equilibrium. In other words, what we do – or don't do – now will come back in the future like a boomerang.

As far as 1996 is concerned, dear Scorpio, I have only good news ... or almost. In fact till May, the first half of your Sign, Scorpios *born before 10 November*, will find themselves highly favoured, blessed with Jupiterian opportunities and the general expansion which characterises this planetary influence. If you belong to this sector, you can celebrate: everything that happens before May will, without any doubt, have fortunate repercussions on the following months and bear extremely significant fruit between September and the end of November. Open your eyes then, seize your opportunities – and you won't regret it at the end of the year.

This lucky Jupiterian influence can take various forms: for example, a child could be conceived in the first phase and born in the last, a promotion that has been in the pipeline since the spring could be realised in the autumn; or a business venture launched early in the year could come to fruition at its end.

The *last decan* will be especially favoured during the first three months of the year, in many cases as the result of something that happened last summer. A distinction, a long-awaited promotion, or the achievement of a long-term undertaking could result at the beginning of 1996. In fact the beginning and very end of the year will be most profitable for you, as at the end of the year Jupiter will team up with a very well-aspected Neptune. This planetary partnership will raise you above yourself and you'll finish the year in a near-mystical grand finale, which for some of you will be crowned with a kind of glory. There's little doubt you will experience a time of rare happiness and fulfilment. And this could be of an emotional nature, as Venus will add its gentle rays to this planetary tandem in December.

In fact, Venus will favour *all the Sign* from mid-January to mid-February; and also in August and October it will be on your side, increasing your magnetism and surrounding you with the exquisite warmth of your loved ones and those close to you. If you belong to the *first or second decan*, you should choose these periods if you want to propose or get married.

In terms of health, you'll be in sparkling form at the beginning of January, from mid-February to mid-March, from the end of July to the beginning of September, and finally during the last two months of the year, when you'll be so dynamic no one will be able to keep up with you. And you'll be lucky too!

Life will flow on smoothly and you'll have more impact on others when the Sun and Mercury enter your heavens in January, March, July, September, November and the end of December. Profit from these times by really throwing yourself into the pursuit of your objectives, as boldness is sure to pay dividends for you in 1996.

It's worth noting that these phases of the year are applicable to *all the Sign*, even early Scorpios pestered by Uranus. Though this sector will be pushed not to feel unsettled in February, April to May, at the end of July and end of October. These are without doubt key moments in the year when you'll feel seized by an entirely new and unsullied future which is radically different from your past or present. Nevertheless, in mid-January, the beginning of May and mid-September – when Mars and Uranus team up against your serenity and status quo – avoid all carelessness and untimely decisions. You should also be especially careful on the road and have your car checked out to avoid any unpleasant surprises.

*Very early Scorpios* could find that their emotional lives are subject to radical change. From time to time you'll want to free yourself from all ties, turn your back on the past and in some way or other rebel. This will be particularly so at the beginning of March, in mid-September and the end of November, which are the most emotionally explosive periods. It's quite likely that this cosmic turbulence could result in an incredible shock meeting that, like a bolt of lightning, sears your past away with it. And as you're not one to do things by halves, Scorpio, my friend, you'd better beware of those who cross your path!

## Sagittarius (22 November to 22 December)

If you're a *November Sagittarian* you can run up the flag. For it's very likely that 1996 could be the year of your lifetime. A dream of a year ... when you could realise your life's ambition. It's simply up to you.

In fact, thanks to Pluto which favours major change, to Uranus which pushes you beyond your limits and helps you surpass yourself, and finally to Saturn, which gives the clarity of judgement necessary to turn ideas into reality, you are all set for success. *Your* success. And it's highly likely that this notion of success – so dear to Sagittarians – takes on a much less materialistic meaning for many of you, one that's more refined and spiritual than you'd have believed up to now.

This will be the revolutionary and reforming work of Pluto, whose influence transfigures what it touches, so long as one is ready in a sense to die, to be born again. You may have to stay on the straight and narrow in March, possibly also between May and July, and even in September and at the end of November, when you'll feel that this influence is uncomfortable because it's so radical. But in each of these periods retain your faith and hope and be sure that, with Uranus and Saturn as allies, you have nothing to fear by diving into the unknown. This planetary duo will take you to the heights in April, and the end of July, the end of September and the end of November without fail. And from February onwards you will probably pave the way for your later evolution.

What's more, in view of the important aspects of Venus this year, it's more than likely you'll be shedding your skin, emotionally speaking, which could start in mid-January (through a meeting?), develop in mid-April (reunions?) and end in a radical change at the beginning of October (an engagement?). Of course, this could also concern Sagittarians tied to a partner by loose or fragile bonds, in which case there is the possibility of separation. It's very probable that a profound change of personality provokes a shift in their relationship which could degenerate into a yawning gulf. In any event, the period between April and August will be particularly constructive and have repercussions on the beginning of 1997, unhoped-for repercussions, as you will see.

Sagittarians *born in the first 12 days of December* won't be unduly affected by the planets in 1996. They'll live a year of transition which will be calm and tranquil, and in which they'll prepare to gather the fruits of 1997, which will provide a rare harvest.

*Last decans*, however, will have problems with Saturn, for the most part in terms of repercussions from situations which came about last year between spring and autumn. According to their age and background, the effects of Saturn will be manifest in different ways, of course, and its influence will also depend on their natal charts. For some, Saturn will affect health in terms of major fatigue that has been building up over the years. They'll feel so beaten down or depressed it'll seem like the onset of old age. But if they react with vigour, knowing that there's always sunshine after rain – as in this case – 1997 will be set fair.

For other *last decans* Saturn will bring responsibilities which are heavy and hard to bear: such as having to nurse someone old in their family, or to finish a difficult and demanding work. For others still, this will be a time of isolation, solitude, retreat and interiorisation, which is hardly compatible with the outgoing nature of their Sign. They'll feel this austere climate particularly in March, June and September, when they won't be really up to the mark. Criticism, lack of understanding, distancing from their family, a sudden cooling or hardening of relationships with others, will all lead them to reflect on themselves, which they must do in all honesty, as the search for truth is one of the attributes of Saturn's influence, and you mustn't miss this opportunity to progress.

Nonetheless, like *all the Sign* you'll be in superb form – which will help you face all your problems, whether moral, physical or material – during the first two months of the year, in April and in September to October. On the other hand, from mid-February to roughly the end of March, from mid-June to the end of July, and the last two months of the year, I caution moderation; the *last decan* in particular should be extra prudent, especially in March, when both Saturn and Mars are ill aspected. Watch out for possible liver problems then, for accidents involving your hips or thighs, for dental or skin problems and falls and fractures.

And if *all the Sign* feels it's losing momentum emotionally and in its relationships between the beginning of April and the beginning of August, it must simply grin and bear it, as Venus will have nothing to do with you throughout the spring. Which is all the more reason to take advantage of its gentle rays at the beginning of January, the end of February, in September and in November, which are veritable islands of sunshine in your year. And during these periods, if you're a *November Sagittarian*, you'll consolidate your existing ties marvellously – and ensure that they are long-lasting.

## Capricorn (22 December to 20 January)

Capricorn, my friend, the year you're starting now is exceptional, as Jupiter is back once more in your firmament.

In fact, until the end of November it will be involved with a little more than half the Sign. More specifically it will lend its magical influence to Capricorns *born before 10 January*, and only affect part of the *last decan* very rapidly – almost absent-mindedly – in December, though it will have considerably more effect when its influence mingles with that of Neptune, to literally magnify the lives of those *born around 15–16 January*.

This conjunction of Jupiter and Neptune, which will affect *last decan* Capricorns at the end of 1996, will make some of them mystics, wealthy or famous overnight; while there's a danger it will bring others deceit, deception, even ruin or bankruptcy. Paradoxically this decan opens the year with a flourish. Thanks to a fine sextile or Saturn, the first three months bring it greater organisational ability, objectivity and judgement which allow it to see clearly in all situations. And there's every chance of a well-deserved and perhaps long-awaited reward resulting from the period April to October 1995. Between January and March, therefore, you'll experience the quintessence of 1996 (if you're *last decan*). The remainder of the year, however, is extremely difficult to determine, given a direct transit of Neptune whose very ambiguous influence – harmonious or the reverse – will depend on each of your natal charts.

On the positive side, it could result in increased consciousness – whether spiritual, mystical or artistic – an extension of the imagination, a greater disposition to serenity, and a more philosophic way of looking at life; which all adds up to a sort of elevation of the spirit towards unknown realms, a phenomenal increase in intuition that touches on the psychic, and a greater disposition to altruism, even philanthropy. For others the result could be the attainment of notoriety or fame that's as sudden as it's resounding.

On the negative side, this influence could entail a host of problems: confusion, the spectres of distress and of fixed ideas that lack a rational basis; a propensity to be duped (by oneself or others), and to be robbed or entrapped. Along with this come slander, jealousy, treacherous rivalries and unexpected stumbling blocks. So distrust the month of April and from August to September, when you could be taken unaware and risk losing yourself in pipe-dreams.

*December Capricorns* should be extra prudent at the same times, but for different reasons: they're in danger of falls and fractures, especially of the knees where they are always more vulnerable than other Signs. So take care in contact sport or games where the knees are at risk (as in football, hockey or skiing). During these periods you will also be particularly intolerant and intransigent and your relationships with others could sour as a result. So dilute your intensity and you'll get a great deal more out of those around you.

Between April and the end of the year, *December Capricorns* will have business that will rebound on next year, as a result of Saturn's discordance. So, gifted with foresight as you are, it's worth knowing that in this Saturnian phase you must avoid making mistakes you'll have to pay for at the beginning of 1997.

For other *December Capricorns* Saturn's influence could take the form of sudden overwork or an increased load of responsibilities, which may well seem inconceivably heavy. In fact, when Jupiter, the planet of expansion and bringer of all sorts of benefits and openings, visits this sector during the first two months of the year, you must take care not to accept – in the euphoria of the moment – everything that's handed to you on a plate. Problems could appear on the horizon which take on a really critical dimension after mid-July. So ... between July and October you risk being seriously snowed under and regretting commitments made in the heat of the moment. In any event, whether through stress or unexpected obstacles, you will find yourself in a difficult situation then: bombarded with obligations, and forced to perform, to put up a good show – in public in some cases – while at the same time feeling tired or physically overworked, and perhaps thwarted or restricted by obstacles which you haven't foreseen. So take care! especially as for many subjects the problem could originate with your family, who oppose what's required for the accomplishment of professional tasks.

If you're *last decan*, you won't have all these problems ... at least not this year. On the contrary, your image will be enhanced and your prestige heightened between March and July, and then between October and the end of November. These will be phases when you'll put new plans into orbit: for example, complete your life as a student and enter adulthood or reach an important turning-point or phase of expansion in your adult life. If you work for someone else you could go independent, could spread your wings and launch your own business.

On the emotional level, too, this could be a time of departure, a take-off into married life with the *alter ego* you meet either in January to February; or in March, October or December. In any event, even if you haven't decided to take the plunge, these are periods when you'll find yourself marvellously at ease with yourself; when you'll radiate a contagious vital optimism; when you'll have suddenly lost all self-doubt, and your self-assurance will captivate one and all. People will see then that you have a sense of humour – which you too often hide – that you know how to charm in a subtle way, and have a clear and original outlook on the world. You'll be on a launching pad from mid-February to mid-March, in May and

November to December, your most dynamic and effective months, when everything will go a lot faster and better than you'd have thought or hoped.

But, in your euphoria, don't lose sight of your realism and natural scepticism, which are extremely good for you and probably help you avoid overvaluing things or being unduly optimistic, which could have regrettable consequences next year.

### Aquarius (20 January to 19 February)

Only Aquarians *born before 28 January* are really affected by the zodiac in 1996. The others will lead a nice calm life without great change, which, if you're not one of January's 'chosen', may be disappointing as you're all for change, almost fanatically so. But be patient! For next year will be a great deal more lively, with a lot more going on than this one...

If you were *born in January*, with the entry of Uranus into your Sign you're going to be over the moon, reaching for it – and getting it! You'll surprise yourself, not to mention those around you who will be literally staggered at the total transformation of both your personality and your life. They won't recognise you – and neither will you!

Your life will be turned around. You'll be freed from all sorts of annoying restrictions. The ideal you're pursuing will be within arm's reach, and all you'll have to do is know how to hold out your hands and grab it. And you'll know. Thanks to Saturn you'll know the right practical direction to take and Uranus will charge you with astral energy which your powers of organisation and calm lucidity will sustain. In other words, at one and the same time you'll have the willpower and discernment, self-discipline and daring to realise your wildest dreams.

If you were *born before 27 January* – and particularly *before the 25th* – April will be extremely promising, as will June to July, October and December, while January and the beginning of February deserve special mention. You could go wrong at this time through excess, as the balancing influence of Saturn only appears in April; and in January the conjunction of Mars with that of Uranus risks over-energising you and leading you to immoderate behaviour you'll regret. What's more, this Martian influence bears on *all the Sign* in January to February, from mid-May to mid-June, and from the beginning of September to the end of October. You could find yourself in a situation of conflict or family rivalry then; so be tolerant, if you want to avoid a break-up.

Physically, too, these are times of overwork and irritability, when the chronic ills you are naturally exposed to are likely to reappear; in your case the circulation in your legs and ankles could cause problems. In January, if you were *born at the beginning of the Sign*, this configuration could also threaten a broken leg – so be careful if you go skiing.

If you were *born in January*, it's quite possible you'll have an unexpected and decisive meeting in April, which you'll have news of at the beginning of July; this could be for a good reason and a relationship could ensue which, thanks to Saturn, will be solidly anchored in time. In any event, Venus will favour all Aquarians in January, at the end of February, from the beginning of April to the beginning of August – when your charm will be irresistible and you'll make a number of conquests – in November and at the end of December. During these periods you should have a beauty treatment, entertain your friends, get out and about to theatres, concerts, exhibitions ... art beckons and friendship smiles on you.

When the Sun and Mercury are well aspected – in January to February, at the beginning of April, in June, October and the beginning of December – you'll make progress towards your objectives and win the ear and attention of your friends and family. And if you're one of those Aquarians (*born after 28 January*) who are somewhat in the shade in 1996, keep your eyes on the horizon of 1997.

That's going to be your year.

## Pisces (19 February to 21 March)

It's a safe bet that, if you are *first or second decan,* last year was no picnic and you probably think this year could hardly be worse. And you'd be right! In general, 1996 is going to be very good indeed – except, that is, for those Pisces subjects *born before 25 February,* who will be unsettled by a square of Pluto.

If you were *born around the 19–20 February,* you will have already started a process of complete rebirth last year, of a change in your personality and perhaps your life. You'll feel the effect of this particularly in the summer, which could well see a total alteration of your destiny and where you are headed. Many of you will change job, house, country – everything that up to now made up your life. If you intend completely altering the standards with which you assess life, you mustn't worry if at times you barely recognise yourself. And don't bridle against destiny at the end of February, end of June, or beginning of November, when it may seem particularly hard or even cruel.

In sum, then, if you were *born at the very beginning of the Sign,* Pisces my friend, you'll be touched and disturbed by the tension of Pluto, in particular at the end of February, end of May, end of August and end of November (when the astral conjunction will give you a rough ride and you may want to give up). So try re-reading the introduction to this book and the section about how to understand planetary tension, and use it in a positive way. Besides, with a sextile of Jupiter favouring *almost all your Sign* right through the year, you should be sheltered from major bad luck or catastrophic setbacks. What's more, you'll also be the beneficiary of Uranus, which brings additional material or moral wellbeing, optimism, *joie de vivre,* good humour and self-confidence.

If you were *born before 8 March,* you'll easily accomplish all tasks as if swept on by events, and will lay foundations before May for goodies to come in November and December. For example, there could be a business proposition put to you which will only see daylight and turn a profit in November; or you could apply to sit an exam which you'll pass at the end of the year; or yet again, you could decide to get married or have a child in the first three months of the year, and see the happy outcome at year's end.

These good omens aren't confined to just the first two decans, either. The *last decan* will be favoured by a double sextile of Uranus and Neptune, as in preceding years, and until the beginning of April by the conjunction of Saturn. Which means the seed you planted last year between April and October will bear fruit at the beginning of 1996; you will be rewarded for past efforts and emerge from the long tunnel of work which seemed to shut you off from the pleasures of the world around you. You will be rewarded now – or at least by December (with February to March the best time of the entire year). And the year's end will see you buoyed up with enthusiasm, serenity; a subtle, almost mystical happiness. In fact, this will be a time of rare, almost idyllic, festivity. And if you are an artist, this phase should see your inspiration at its peak, and be a real moment of illumination.

*All the Sign* will have other positive phases in 1996, as well: January, March, May, July, September, the end of October/ beginning of November, will all be good for you professionally, and facilitate your business and day-to-day life. Emotionally, you have everything to hope for between mid-January and the beginning of February, from mid-March to the beginning of April, from the beginning of August to the beginning of September, and from the end of November to mid-December. You'll be totally in step with yourself and others then, in balance and in harmony and with no inner tension. You'll experience the joy of living and forget your troubles and natural insecurity.

So, as you can see, this will be an excellent year for most of you, and one from which you'll most probably know how to get the very best.

# 1997

## The course of the planets

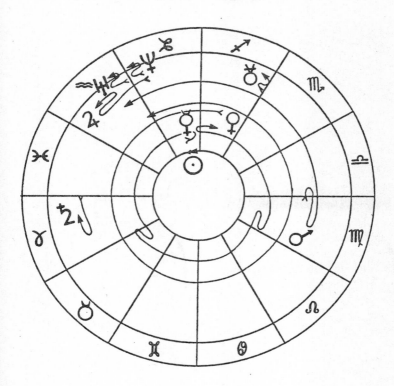

# World Events

Since the end of 1994 no major conjunction has appeared in our heavens which, globally speaking, have in general been clement. The energies of transformation which the great conjunctions of 1989 to 1994 contained should now be flowering and, thanks to Uranus and Neptune, preparing a new era, a new spirit on a planetary scale.

1997 marks the return of a major conjunction: namely Jupiter and Neptune at the end of Capricorn (in January), which will prove very important for subjects of this Sign and many others as well. The last time we witnessed this cycle was in 1984; and in France, which it symbolises, it coincided with the end of left-wing unity. From that we can deduce that this year will see important political changes in France. The bringer of a climate of expansion and liberalism, this conjunction nonetheless also seems to hinder Germany in its relationships with associated European nations, or to stir up a latent conflict involving the opposition in that country itself.

# Your Personal Forecast

## Aries (21 March to 20 April)

First of all, Aries my friend, here's some heartening news: you're clearly in the ascendant in relation to last year. In fact, taken as a whole, 1997 should be superb ... except perhaps for the end of the Sign – that's to say those subjects *born after 15 April.*

Ill-aspected since January by the dissonance of Jupiter of Neptune, these Aries subjects will find themselves in the thick of things. Everything will be complicated for them; they'll feel they're 'cycling in sauerkraut' and won't know which way to turn. So try and stay cool, if you belong to this sector. Take time to relax, go for a walk in the open air and let things settle in your mind, to work out just what's important and what isn't. Don't let yourself be engulfed by problems that are in essence one-offs and short lived. And remember that, after January, Jupiter will cease to be a problem.

Neptune will remain one, just below the surface, as it were – especially between the end of June and mid-August, then from mid-November to mid-December – when it will disturb you by perhaps making you ill at ease with yourself or by causing a sort of gulf to open between you and others. In other words, you won't have a very clear idea of where you stand and you'll have a lot of questions about yourself and the world. As a frank and straightforward Aries who hates things complicated or obscure, however, you ought not have too much difficulty neutralising the spectres which threaten to engulf you. Avoid building castles in the air and, if you can, don't let yourself be taken in by pleasant-seeming but deceitful promises. You'll be particularly vulnerable to trickery or breaches of trust, to theft or loss, in the periods mentioned above.

During these times watch how you behave, for people will not be indulgent towards you and will have a tendency to run you down behind your back. But, in consolation, you'll also have your slice of the cake next year when it will be your turn for Jupiter to favour you. And you can profit from this disturbed period by reviewing yourself, discovering why you are so dissatisfied, and energetically starting to put things right. Avoid laxity, letting go, or defeatism (which is hardly your way anyhow) in April – when you'll be particularly sensitive to this troubled and disturbing climate – and also in June and October.

If you belong to the *first two decans*, on the other hand, you can run up the flags in 1997! You'll be fortunate enough to experience the passage of Saturn (which takes place every 30 years) through your natal Sun. And this can hardly be lived negatively, as its influence will be sustained by a rewarding and exhilarating sextile of Jupiter. In other words, you've an extremely fertile, constructive and vitally important year ahead.

You'll go straight to the heart of things, instinctively eliminate the dross from your everyday life. Thanks to Jupiter, you'll spring-clean your house – metaphorically speaking – and have the change to redecorate while you're at it! In other words, you can make a brand new start if you seize your opportunities, which – alert and lively Aries that you no doubt are – I'm sure you'll do. As a result, you should have things in place before summer, which will bring the reward and recognition of your merits at the end of the year and beginning of 1998. So this is the time – if you want to – to apply for a better job or ask for a rise, which you'll hear good news about from October on.

Aries subjects *born before 27 March* deserve special mention. They are literally blessed by the gods in 1997. The year's 'chosen', they will be transported by great planetary cycles. Pluto in Sagittarius, Uranus and Jupiter in Aquarius, and Saturn in Aries ... this entire planetary concert will play in your favour and take you to the top. You'll have splendid turnarounds, spectacular developments, promotions as unexpected as they're providential: in brief, success, and all of it placed, moreover, under the long-lasting auspices of Saturn. If you belong to this sector and want to alter your life from top to bottom, don't hesitate. Do it. Whatever you undertake in 1997 is destined to end well, to succeed and advance your interests to the utmost.

For all Aries subjects the most promising periods are: between the end of January and the end of February, from mid-March to the end of April, from the end of May to the end of June, from the end of July to mid-August, and from the end of November to mid-December. So go for it!

You'll be glad you did.

### Taurus (20 April to 21 May)

Frankly speaking, Taurus my friend, 1997 won't exactly be the most tranquil or serene year of your life, unless you were born at the end of the Sign, *after 15 May*; in which case, you'll benefit from a reassuring trine of Neptune, which will broaden your horizons and distance you from the prosaic in everyday life. You will see the world from far and wide and appreciate the finer things in life – such as art, poetry, music and philosophic or religious ideas. You will raise your level of consciousness. Those subjects at the end of the Sign will effectively float on a rosy Neptunian cloud, and in January, thanks to Jupiter, will come back down to earth, to translate Neptune's beneficial influences into concrete form, and a possible resounding success. But apart from these very late Taureans, the outlook for the year isn't much to write home about.

There's instability and disorder in the air, which won't please the methodical and organised Taurus you no doubt are. All the same, you'll have to put up with it. And you can exorcise these problems by taking certain precautions: until the beginning of June – particularly if you're *first or second decan* – avoid putting yourself in risk situations with regard to the law or regulations; avoid all legal matters, incurring debts or crossing your superiors at work. Whatever happens, you'll have repercussions from this period between June and November, but you should see to it that they are as harmless as possible. It's entirely up to you.

If you're *first decan*, you'll have to face up to the simultaneous dissonance of Uranus and Jupiter together, which will bring definite change that in all probability will only be finalised next year. It's highly likely that, before summer, events will have moved in such a way that a total turnaround of your life results. Perhaps you'll find the house of your dreams and only move next year? Or perhaps you envisage a radical change in your profession, which will also only come about later?

In any event, even if you're by nature resistant to change, and a lover of permanence, stability, even routine, you'll have to adapt yourself. Try to make the best of possible bad luck by using these planetary influences to alter everything in your life you don't like. There will be times, though, when you must avoid making drastic decisions; when you won't be up to the mark, will feel yourself pulled this way and that, and won't be either objective or disciplined in your reasoning. These times will be: February, April to May, from the end of July to the beginning of August, and from the end of October to the beginning of November, while both *first and second decans* will be unapproachable and feel extremely stressed from mid-August to the end of September. Restrain your impulses at this time and control yourself, as acting out of impatience or haste could lead to accidents. Keep an eye on the state of your car as well, for mechanical foul-ups are all too likely under the dissonance of Mars and Uranus; and if there is anything electrical that may need attention in your home, you should take every necessary precaution.

For many of you an emotional choice could disturb your status quo and prove a source of torment (for though you're the faithful type there's also a dormant sensualist in you and this can sometimes put you in an invidious position). February, April, May, July and the end of September/beginning of October could well be times of emotional confusion and, for some of you influenced by the square of Uranus, periods to mark in red in your diary, when a meeting could hit you like a bolt from the blue.

Physically, you are on your best form between the beginning of March and the end of June and from mid-November to mid-December.

Take care!

### Gemini (21 May to 21 June)

You're really lucky, Gemini my friend: if you were *born before 15 June* an absolutely superb year awaits you. I'm not exaggerating. Uranus, Saturn and Jupiter together – three out of the five slow planets of our solar system – will be 'going for you', at your service and propelling you forward in 1997.

It's highly likely that last year you got some daring project under way which you expected a lot from. And you won't be disappointed. In fact, if you were *born before 26 May*, Uranus will bring concrete positive change at the beginning of the year ... or else in October. A spectacular promotion, an exciting new home, a new activity which fascinates you are just some of the possible manifestations of a well-aspected Uranus. If you were born a little *later in May*, the same windfalls are waiting, either at the end of the year or next year. In any event, things move – and move fast and well – as Jupiter and Saturn come on the scene. Jupiter gives even more expansion to business matters and brings you all sorts of enticing propositions before March; and Saturn rewards you for efforts you made during the summer of 1996.

In brief, if you are a *May Gemini*, the first three months of the year will be extremely fertile and constructive and harbour all sorts of gifts from the heavens, whose spin-offs you could harvest after October. *June subjects born before the 15th*, however, are somewhat out of sync with this celestial timing. Their good period starts in March and extends to the end of July: they'll pave the way then and lay their foundations. From October on, when Jupiter affects you again, you'll glean the fruits of enticing propositions put to you in the preceding months. And if you began a long-term undertaking between April and the beginning of August, you'll reap the benefits and prestige either at the end of this year or the beginning of next. The same applies if you've been recommended for some sort of award for past merit. What's certain is that you're in a phase where your value will be recognised, when people, things and events will seem in league with your progress and expansion. So this is a precious year that could bring you a lot.

Even the opposition of Pluto which affects Geminis *born before 28 May* (and is normally unsettling and often extremely uncomfortable) won't lessen your serenity or cramp your progress. In fact, concurrent with this cosmic tension, Uranus, Saturn and Jupiter are all well aspected, which will have the effect of turning the change Pluto enforces in a positive direction. This means that you'll know how to bend with the wind and your legendary adaptability will overcome all obstacles.

The best times for *all the Sign* – which will bring longed-for opportunities on a plate, the recognition of your talents and originality, and the consolidation of all you've built in the past – are as follows: emotionally ... February, the beginning of April, May, July, from mid-August to mid-September, and the end of December; professionally ... you'll progress with giant strides in

February, April, May to June, July to August and in September to October.

All told, then, 1997 is a remarkable year – and it's up to you to make a success of it!

## Cancer (21 June to 22 July)

In all fairness, you're not in a very promising phase of your life just now, Cancer my friend. And 1997, I'm afraid, is not going to see any massive improvement. So my advice is to keep your sights firmly fixed on the blue horizon of 1998, when you'll finally be over this tricky hurdle.

In fact, *almost all the Sign* will be in a tight corner this year: the last decan (particularly those *born before the 17th*) on account of Neptune; and the *first two decans,* thanks to an opposing square of Saturn. Only one small niche at the beginning of the last decan – those *born before 16 July* – will be spared this celestial sullenness or astral ire.

The *last decan* is most affected at the start of the year. The 'tail of the Crab', so to speak, really seems to have to confront all sorts of problems. Things become gradually more complicated, especially in your private life, with your partner, or perhaps a business associate. In brief, it's someone else who causes problems for you at the start of the year.

A very few Cancer subjects *born after 17 July* and depending on the ascendant in their natal charts could experience the reverse of this negative planetary dissonance. So, in their case, the month of January promises an unexpected windfall in terms of a partnership or possible union. And luck will come to them by way of other people.

For the majority, however, January will prove eventful in terms of all sorts of complications: you will feel submerged in a general haze which you could well do without. So be careful not to take refuge in some artificial paradise, and avoid taking drugs or too much medication which would be very ill-omened for you. The same applies at the end of July/beginning of August and at the beginning of December, when Mars will make you more vulnerable than usual to narcotics and toxic substances. Beware of food-poisoning, too. The dissonant influences of Neptune and Mars also favour aggression, theft, and abuse of trust and losing things. Forewarned is forearmed...

Cancer subjects at the *end of the Sign* affected by the dissonance of Neptune will feel especially vulnerable and exposed to the outside world, which you'll attempt to escape from to protect yourself. So some of you will retreat into sleep, others into alcohol, but this is all just totally sterile escapism. Be tough with yourself. Admitting that you don't like to confront an adversary head-on (but, like a crab, go forward sideways), you should still know that to face up to an enemy and acknowledge it is already to have half won. So avoid cradling yourself in sweet illusions or sinking into idle fancy. Face up to reality! If you don't, you'll suffer for it next year. And as knowledge is the best counter to future threats, it's worth knowing that, if you're not alert and even a little distrustful, if you let yourself nod off into nonchalance, you'll have a rude awakening.

The end of the Sign isn't alone in being threatened by this conjunction. If you belong to the *first two decans*, Saturn will put you to the test (as it does every seven years) by obliging you to turn back and confront certain realities, which you might have liked to ignore. It's highly likely that in April, June to July, October, and November to December, you'll have a crisis of awareness, a pretty brutal shock in the face of hard facts. Avoid self-indulgence, contemplating your navel or hypochondria then, which your sensitivity often inclines you to. No, people don't have a down on you. You're *not* the victim of destiny. You're simply having to face the twists and turns of fate which affect us all.

From August on, you'll be accountable for all you've done, or left undone. If you're *second decan*, you'll have to suffer for past mistakes, and continue to until next March, unless you can exorcise Saturn's influence. Of course, it's quite likely that the long phase of self-analysis and taking stock, which Saturn has forced you to go through, isn't simply the fruit of the recent past but results from what you did in former years. For this is the law of karma, of cosmic balance. We only suffer under the influence of planetary dissonance to the degree that we previously failed to respect the universal law.

On the concrete physical plane, this is a year of setbacks and limitation: you'll feel in financial difficulties, have the impression you're not progressing, or having to make infinitely more effort to get the same result. You'll be burdened with responsibilities which will be difficult to take on board and perhaps be too heavy to bear. So – especially if you were *born between 2 and 10 July* – from April to the beginning of August, try not to take on too great a burden for the future.

If you want to derive the maximum benefit from this Saturnian phase, trying though it may be, live it positively by turning in on yourself and carrying out an in-depth self-analysis (get to know yourself in your objective reality … and make whatever corrections may be needed). You should also temper your relationships with your family and friends, as you'll be more grumpy than usual and want to sulk and crawl back into your crabby shell. But that's no solution. Whereas if you open yourself to others and show tenderness and caring, you'll be rewarded a thousandfold. You'll also be helped out of the rut in which you find yourself in March, the end of April/beginning of May and the end of September/beginning of October.

Good luck – and here's to next year!

## Leo (22 July to 23 August)

What turbulence in your heavens in 1997!

But paradoxically, side by side with the turmoil and destabilisation caused by the double opposition of Jupiter and Uranus, there's an equally stabilising celestial climate emanating from Saturn. Which means … you have every chance of making a superb recovery; of accomplishing a sort of acrobatics which will enable you to change your circumstances and status quo – either emotionally or professionally – and install yourself in a new situation in a durable and comfortable way. So though this is a time of trial, it's one in which you have every opportunity. What's more, you'll only be affected by this conjunction if you were *born before 15 August.*

Two sectors of your Sign are particularly targeted.

*July Leos* will find the opposition of Uranus highly disruptive. If you were *born before the 26th,* your life will have completely changed by next October. While if you were *born at the end of July,* you'll only be permanently settled in your new life at the end of December or in 1998. But, backed by both a trine of Saturn and of Pluto, you'll have powerful protection and there's little danger of your losing balance. So the change which awaits you has every appearance of being a sweet one. Whether you change profession, partner or home, things should go as you want them to. Obviously there will be stormy periods (February, May, June to August and November) but, given the support of this planetary pair, you'll know how to cope.

*August Leos* (*born before the 15th*) will have to deal with destiny and their family circle at the times already mentioned; but sustained by Saturn – which will give them judgement and the necessary concentration and tenacity – they'll attain their goals without problems and come out on top. However, it's highly likely that Jupiter will present them with tricky choices or other administrative or legal problems in the first five months of the year.

Saturn, meanwhile, will protect the *first two decans*: the *first* will be rewarded for past efforts during the first three months of the year; while the *second decan* will see its worth and esteem recognised in true leonine measure after August, or possibly after December – when it will probably win some distinction or long hoped-for promotion – though it might have to wait till the beginning of 1998 to get it!

### *Virgo (23 August to 23 September)*

Here's a nice peaceful year in prospect. Except, that is, if you were *born in August,* in which case you'll be subject to a disruptive square of Pluto that could destabilise your status quo.

In fact, a degree of change will be forced on you by events which will upset your living conditions, and the extent of this will in some way be the product of your psyche. If you're an *August*

*Virgo*, you'll no longer be the same person by the end of the year. And if you were *born before the 26th*, Pluto paved the way for this metamorphosis last year. Summer should be particularly significant in this respect, obliging you at the end of July (emotionally) and at the end of August/beginning of September (professionally) to make drastic decisions which will affect your entire future.

Other significant aspects in 1997 affect the *end of the Sign*. If you were *born after 16 September* you can celebrate: right through the year Neptune will open you to superior realities, elevate your level of consciousness, and show you new intellectual, spiritual or artistic curiosities. You'll suddenly discover a fascinating hobby which will occupy all your spare time. And in January, when Jupiter's influence will blend with the radiance of Neptune, you could find yourself suddenly – and very much – in the limelight, with an unexpected windfall either materially or in terms of prestige.

Between March and June, when Mars transits your Sign, you'll be active in a simultaneously feverish and controlled way, hyper-efficient in fact; as you'll also be in mid-August to the end of September, and in November to December. During these phases you could be impossible to keep up with, so these are good times to involve yourself in sport and work off some of your surplus energy...

A warning, however: if you're an *August Virgo*, be careful in March and at the beginning of October, when Mars could make you particularly dogmatic, abrupt – in a word, unbearable. And under this sort of Martian influence, one can also (through brutishness or rashness), cause regrettable accidents or incidents.

So be warned!

### Libra (23 September to 23 October)

If you're a *September Libran*, you can get set for a golden year!

Expect to be literally carried away in 1997 by events which are tailor-made for you. It will almost seem as if some supernatural being waves a magic wand over the dawn of the year, to reward you with all sorts of presents and benefits. And though you'll have Saturn in opposition until the beginning of April, the setbacks or worries that could result from this will be conjured away, as it were, by Jupiter, Uranus and Pluto. So if you have a problem with your emotional or professional partner which dates back to last year, it will without doubt disappear at the beginning of 1997, thanks to the joint aid of these three powerful planetary allies. What's more, while Saturn will go on to disturb the *second decan* from April onwards and cease to concern you, Uranus and Neptune will continue 'working' for you, favouring the positive evolution, even revolution, of your life. So, if you've ever wanted to change something, the time is now or never: if you've ever been tempted to move house, start a new relationship, move abroad, found a club, play a more extensive social role ... dive in and do it! You won't regret it one bit. For the world is your oyster and vast horizons are open to you.

The *second decan* in contrast will find itself facing a period of setbacks or frustration due to Saturn, from April on – and especially after August. Fortunately, running parallel to this difficult influence, a trine of Jupiter will provide you with dynamism and vital optimism which will prove extremely useful in this case. Its influence won't only be appreciable psychologically either, but also in terms of events: providing all sorts of opportunities to extend your field of activity and launch new projects. So you needn't worry too much about this influence of Saturn (on *second decan* Librans) as you'll benefit from the almost providential support of Jupiter, though this double planetary configuration could well present some of you with a problem with your private life (which you'll be most aware of in March to April, at the beginning of July and in October) and phenomenal expansion, professionally.

*Last decan* Librans, especially those *born after the 17th*, will be influenced – particularly in January and less obviously throughout the year – by a square of Neptune. This will seem especially hard to bear in January and will give you a very gloomy vision of the year. But, don't worry, what follows won't be anything like as bad! All the same, certain periods won't be easy and will bring doubt and irrational distress, which could trip you up. But don't make anything of it; cling to your deep beliefs, to providence, to the love of others, and you'll clear this hurdle as you have so many others. If you have moments of depression, tell yourself it's Neptune's fault and it will be easier to get over them. On the physical side, avoid the misuse of any sort of drugs, to which this planet makes you more than usually susceptible. And don't expose yourself to theft or aggression at the beginning of August or beginning of December. Remember, too, that Neptune is on the point of leaving your zodiac, after which it will no longer disturb you.

### Scorpio (23 October to 22 November)

A year of respite, and perhaps your most harmonious before the year 2000.

If you were *born after 16 November*, Neptune forms a fine sextile with your natal Sun, and as a result you should profit from the beneficial consensus of this year. Especially in January, you will be plunged into the heart of current events and given an extraordinary push into the limelight. Or else, if you live more modestly, this will be a time of great serenity, of almost perfect happiness, and probably a period of much greater material and psychological wellbeing. It's possible that you will be affected by a positive event outside your own sphere from which you will draw some advantage. And then, when January is over, the fine influence of Neptune will remain right through the year, to sustain your morale, extend your intellectual or spiritual perspectives and make you thirst for something else; it will see you advance beyond everyday trivialities, thanks to art, perhaps. Your intuition will guide you more surely than ever and you may well suddenly feel the need to devote yourself to a cause, to do something for others. So it's a good year in prospect and one in which Neptune could bring some of you resounding success or even fame, and to others promises the surely greater reward of serenity.

In contrast, if you're an *October Scorpio* a square of Uranus will cause a tidal wave in your life. If you were *born at the beginning of the Sign*, you have without doubt already experienced the potential disruption of Uranus last year. And you're sure to feel its upheavals in the autumn, if you haven't already at the very beginning of 1997. If, on the other hand, you were *born at the end of October*, the beginning of this radical change in your life will appear in May and only come into operation fully in December, or even next year. For many of you, the double dissonance of Jupiter and Uranus – which will be active until mid-March and extremely destabilising – will bear on their family status quo, which will be upset from top to bottom. But it could also entail a change of residence or even country (which in itself could be accompanied by all sorts of administrative or practical complications).

Be that as it may, a square of Jupiter affects the *second decan* from March till the beginning of July. So, if you belong to this sector, keep a cool head; don't engage in ill-considered expenditure, and don't make promises you won't be able to keep. Equally, stay out of debt before June as you'll have difficult pay-days from October on.

Fortunately, Mars will give you a tremendous 'punch' between March and June and from mid-October to mid-December. It will give you almost too much energy between mid-August and the end of September, when no-one will be able to touch you with a barge-pole; your caustic irony will be limitless; and you run the risk of making enemies through gratuitous and untimely aggression. You should also be extremely careful when handling blunt instruments and watch out for burns and other injuries, as Uranian dissonance plus Martian tension is in no way a safe combination.

And if there are times you feel discouraged – which isn't very Scorpio-like – remind yourself that next year, thanks to Jupiter, will shine with a bright new light.

## *Sagittarius (22 November to 22 December)*

Sagittarius, my friend, you've thrown the dice, and come up with an unbeatable double six. And it's downright good luck which characterises 1997! And that's the case *whatever your decan* (unless you were born near the end of the Sign, after 15 December, which isn't in the picture). You have an absolutely sublime year ahead. It's a rare occurrence for such a planetary consensus to work for a Sign. So you should know that you can dare to do *anything* and follow the advice of Danton: 'Boldness, more boldness – boldness always!' – which goes with your conquering arrow. For it's certain that audacity will really pay dividends this year.

If you're a *November Sagittarian*, Pluto will turn your life around completely, overturn its foundations and impose a radical change on your psyche, if not your existence. And to make this total change positive, you have a sextile of Uranus to carry you beyond your previous limits – to project you forward, effectively putting you in orbit. You'll have new adventures, make all sorts of fascinating new discoveries. Under such an influence, why not learn a new language or visit a continent you've not been to before? Travel-loving Sagittarians won't be able to resist it. If you want to go off in search of adventure, though, do it after March. For during the first three months of the year you'll also profit from a stabilising trine of Saturn, which will help you put your new life in place. And, especially in the context of the upheaval brought about by Pluto, this extremely constructive influence should definitely not be neglected.

As if this wasn't enough, at the beginning of the year Jupiter will enter your zodiac and sprinkle all your undertakings with his heavenly manna, so as to give them a positive turn. Mars, for its part, will dynamise you in an extraordinary way in the first two months of the year to venture in every direction. In other words, nothing will stand in your way. You will be a veritable steamroller, and it's a safe bet that whoever you find yourself in competition with, you'll come out the winner. And don't think that once the first two or three months of the year are over, life will turn dull on you – far from it.

*December Sagittarians*, for their part, will have precious little cause to envy their November cousins. For they'll simultaneously be favoured by a lucky and exhilarating sextile of their planet Jupiter (which will bring them all sorts of extraordinary opportunities on a plate) and by a stabilising trine of Saturn, which will help them realise their wildest dreams. There isn't a more constructive mix in astrology than that of Jupiter and Saturn. And, between April and the end of the year, this will be at your beck and call. As a result, you can expect to feel a much greater sense of wellbeing, both psychologically and materially. You'll be in sparkling form and, thanks to Saturn, enjoy physical resistance that's up to anything. All your chronic ills will disappear as though miraculously and your *joie de vivre* will be infectious. If you've ever toyed with the idea of buying a house, this is the time to do it. You'll surely find what you're looking for before August and be installed in your new abode, either at the end of this year, or beginning of next. The same time applies to the *second decan* who find themselves rewarded for their merits and gather the fruits of past efforts: everything they sow before the summer will give unhoped-for results from October onwards.

As you can see, this is truly an exceptional year, a year which it's up to you to exploit as is right and proper. My advice is: in this dream of a time, try not to live too egotistically – which, generally speaking, is not your strong point. Think of others, of other Signs, other countries, other ethnic groups, and others worse off than yourself. Show a generous goodwill. For you know, the astral wheel turns and next year there's a danger you could come down to earth all the harder, the more you rest on your laurels egocentrically this year.

### Capricorn (22 December to 20 January)

January will be marked by the important conjunction of Jupiter and Neptune which will take place at the end of Capricorn, your Sign. And, according to how well aspected – or otherwise –

your natal Sign is, the repercussions of this conjunction on your psyche, in fact your entire life, could be radically different.

In a positive mode, it will put you spectacularly to the fore and bring many Capricorns *born after 14 January* popularity, or notoriety, and in any event appreciable success. Some will pull off a golden business deal, often of an international nature; others will play a starring role in bringing something to a successful conclusion, such as a book, film, or whatever their profession calls for.

On the other hand, in its negative mode, this conjunction indicates total chaos – depression, anaemia, even possible bankruptcy or scandal. Without wanting to play Cassandra, these things have to be said, and Capricorns appreciate the truth. And fortunately these extreme scenarios are rare, the exceptions which confirm the rule.

At the beginning of January, confusion, disorder, a tangle of legal complications and confused situations could well be the lot of Capricorns *born at the end of the Sign*. And those with an ill-aspected natal Sun will have to experience other difficulties (although they'll be less dramatic) in mid-April, July or October. Still ... at least they can console themselves that they're not the only ones in 1997 to be tested, as the periods mentioned will also be difficult for the *first and second decans*, who'll be ill favoured by Saturn, the ruler of Capricorn, and master of experience and time.

If you're *first decan*, you perhaps had a brush with a Saturnian problem last year, though only in outline, as Jupiter will have acted as a sort of guard-rail or lightning conductor for Saturn's difficult influences. At the beginning of 1997 until March, however, you'll be exposed head-on to this dissonance which, especially in January and at the beginning of February, will barely spare you. There'll be misunderstandings, setbacks, difficulties of all sorts; while your family put you to the test and won't be handing out any prizes. You'll feel awkward and hampered in your initiatives. And the wild goat in you detests that. Happily, you'll be over the worst from the end of March, which one can't say for the *second decan*, which will be given a rough ride by Saturn between April and August, a period which will have disagreeable repercussions until the end of the year. So if you belong to this sector, try not to take on too many responsibilities during this phase; by July they'll already seem almost unbearable and they'll really make life difficult and put your patience through the mill, in October and then at the end of November/beginning of December.

Some good advice: to defuse a negative Saturn and transform lead (your metal) into gold, try to live this intense period not in an extrovert, mundane or frivolous way – which is not your strong point anyway – but through interiorising and self-analysis. And as a result, you'll learn to know yourself better, to concentrate on yourself, not in sterile contemplation of your navel, but in a productive consciousness of your true reality, which in itself will exorcise the effects of Saturn. For example, you may be more than usually sensitive to passing time, to the certainty that we're mortal and our days are numbered. While this is testing enough in terms of vitality, you could also feel beaten down, both physically and mentally, by a real attack of old age. So give yourself a shake – and react. Remember that Capricorn is the Sign which improves as it gets older, like good wine, and that after you have passed through this time of trial you'll come out stronger, clearer and more lucid.

On the health side, I recommend you take what precautions you can to remedy the problems inherent in Saturn, which are: decalcification and debilitation due to lack of mineral salts; under-functioning of organs which need more stimulation; a general tiredness which could easily become more pronounced; and skin, teeth and bone problems such as rheumatism and arthritis...

And in times of melancholy, moroseness or nostalgia, bear in mind that the stars turn, and that next year a fine sextile of Jupiter will give you back your enjoyment of life.

### Aquarius (20 January to 19 February)

It's an unalloyed pleasure for an astrologer to be able to decipher auguries as exciting as yours in 1997! In fact, however you look at it, if you were *born before 13 February*, I've only good to tell you. Good news and, especially, exciting changes: unadulterated change if you were *born before 28 January*), and change in continuity, which you won't mind at all, if you're a *February Aquarian*.

In fact, if you're a *February Aquarian*, I can promise you a golden year. For Jupiter enters your Sign (which occurs every 12 years) to reward you with all sorts of benefits and effectively put you on a launching pad. And as if that wasn't enough, Saturn will be there to cover your arrears, stabilise gains, and import a concrete and durable form to what destiny offers you. This will be especially the case from mid-March on, when Jupiter and Saturn will embellish your heavens together, and most subjects will reap the benefit of this period in the autumn. It's highly probable that the value of your talents, personality and achievements will be recognised, and that people will at last 'render unto Caesar, that which is Caesar's'. It's a sure bet too that a lot of Aquarians will decide, despite their worship of independence, to throw themselves not only into a shared life, but a legally sanctioned one. This applies to the *first decan* before March, and to the *second* either in May, at the end of August/beginning of September, or at the end of October – which are all times I recommend for marriage. So a rare year is in store if you were *born before 13 February*.

If you were *born at the very beginning of the Sign*, you won't be neglected either. Quite the contrary, you'll be in total harmony with the events and planetary consensus of this year. The essential planetary configurations will have a positive influence and you'll find yourself in tune with things, and that a place in the sun awaits you – that's made to measure! Given the presence of Uranus (your planet) in your sector of the zodiac, this could correspond to a radical change in your life, if you were *born between 22 and 29 January*, while if you're at the *very beginning of the decan* it's highly likely that this change has been in the wings since last year, will become concrete either at the beginning of the year or in autumn. And if this Uranian influence could be a little disturbing in the sense that it's somewhat drastic, a reassuring sextile of Pluto will help increase your psychic strength and make things go your way.

Your most promising and exciting phase will be the first three months of the year, and most particularly before mid-February, when your impact on people and things will be virtually limitless and nothing will be impossible for you. You'll pack a knockout punch which will enable you to surmount all obstacles – not that there will be any! And simultaneously, Jupiter will provide opportunities almost miraculously. All you have to do is help yourself; while from March on, Pluto and Uranus will continue to safeguard your destiny and give rise to extraordinary circumstances that encourage you to evolve in the most positive way. In other words, if there's anything whatsoever you'd like to change in your life, this is the time to do it.

So pluck up your courage – and go for it!

### Pisces (19 February to 21 March)

Pisces, my friend, prepare yourself for a year of transition, without much in the way of relief, unless you were *born at the beginning or the end of your Sign.*

If you were *born before 27 February* you'll be subject to the dissonance of Pluto, which is going to tip you into another existence. You may have had a foretaste of this last year in the start of a slow but irreversible change, a real metamorphosis. While if you were *born after 15 March*, you'll benefit from a sextile of Neptune right through the year. And Neptune – which is your planet – will open you to hitherto ignored realities of an intellectual, philosophical, spiritual or artistic nature. This influence will quench inner thirst and bring you great interior calm and serenity.

This *last sector of the Sign* is most affected at the beginning of the year. In January in fact the extremely important conjunction of Jupiter and Neptune takes place in your heavens, and will put you on cloud nine! Many of you will experience an exceptional time in your life then: perhaps of illumination, of true joy; a moment when you'll suddenly perceive a new reality in a climate of plenitude, thanks to a vision in which everything suddenly finds its place. If you're religious, this could be a time of true mystical ecstasy, of revelation unique in a lifetime. Or if you're involved in politics this could correspond to real prominence, an exceptional moment of popularity. Whatever your area, in fact, this will be a peak in your life, though fortunately not the only one.

You'll again be very receptive to this kind of influence when Mars adds its rays to those of Neptune, in September and at the beginning of December. These are phases when your dynamism will be heightened in a spectacular way, when you'll undertake no matter what, *whatever your sector* of the Sign. But, from mid-March to the beginning of October, when Mars is in opposition to the *beginning of the Sign*, it will form a pretty explosive combination with Pluto and, if you are a *February Pisces*, it will open you to a certain violence, a diffuse aggression. So don't come on too strong then. On the road, for instance, don't counter-attack when someone cuts in front of you, or you could have an accident. And in everyday relationships try not to resort to force, which leads nowhere – except to break-ups.

And if you are one of those whom the stars seem to have forgotten or neglected this year, don't worry – 1998 will see you in a starring role!

# 1998

**The course of the planets**

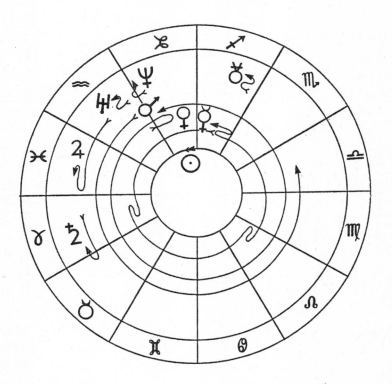

## World Events

1998 will be a year of transition in which new problems will come to light. There will still be an atmosphere of reform induced by the sextile of Uranus and Pluto, which has been in the air since 1994. But this will slowly dissolve, most probably affirming as it does the hegemony of Japanese power. As this sextile departs, the year contains only dissonance.

In March, an ill-aspected Jupiter and Pluto will bring the conjunction born in 1994 to a critical stage. But exactly what the effect of this will be is difficult to determine across the intervening years. What is far more certain, though, is that the square of Neptune and Saturn, which occurs twice – in June and in October – denotes a destabilising of existing political structures.

It could also entail a difficult time for the USSR – or what still exists of it – when this country will be in the news, perhaps because of military intervention. (The invasion of Afghanistan took place under dissonant aspects of these same two planets, as did that of Czechoslovakia in August 1968). It's also a virtual certainty that the problems thrown up by this influence will have repercussions in the spring of 1999.

## Your Personal Forecast

### Aries (21 March to 20 April)

Clearly, after the wonderful year the heavens have just sent you, Aries my friend, the one ahead is bound to seem less interesting and exciting, or a little less easy to live. Last year you experienced the rare appearance of Saturn in your Sign (which carries on this year), and had the good luck for it to be accompanied by a superb Jupiterian influence which diametrically transformed what might have been weighty or restricted. In other words, you probably only felt the constructive and serious side of Saturn which promotes durability.

In 1998, though Saturn continues to transit your Sign (starting the year by affecting those Aries subjects *born after 3 April*), it now unfortunately will not be sustained by the astral context, which means that, according to whether the influence of your natal Sun is harmonious or discordant, you will either: experience this transit as consolidating or gratifying, bringing you a long-awaited reward; or else, on the contrary, as a burden, involving additional responsibilities or a time of trial separation. This will be particularly the case for Aries *born between 3 and 10 April*, who were subject to Saturn last year between May and November. If you belong to this sector of the zodiac, there's a strong possibility you could see the recurrence of a problem that arose then, if you dealt with Saturn's influence in a negative way. But, in any event, don't worry about it, as after March, when this planet enters the *last decan*, you'll have been through the worst.

*Last decans* will have Saturn in their zodiac between April and the beginning of July and, as a result, experience repercussions between late October and the year's end (but only if they're *born between 15 and 20 April*). So, if your birthday is at the end of the Sign, avoid taking on too many responsibilities in the spring and watch out for mistakes which could have a boomerang effect and painful consequences at the end of the year. Though for many of you, once again, Saturn could prove entirely rewarding, bringing the recognition of your merits and worth, the esteem of your superiors.

One thing is, you'll quickly appreciate whether Saturn is negative or positive in your particular case; if you're *second decan* you'll know it in fact from the end of January on; and if you're *last decan* you can probably reckon on repercussions after April in your everyday life. Your general form – fatigue or increased physical stamina – and your moral form, which if you experience Saturn in a negative mode could mean you feel somewhat morose, will also serve as guidelines.

If you're an Aries of the *second half of the Sign,* however you experience Saturn's influence, you probably already know that it's of considerable importance in the course of our lives, since it leads us to eliminate the superfluous in order to attain what is essential. By distancing us from the environment, people and things, it causes us to suddenly look at life in a different way, more coolly and objectively. And one is often led to perceive that people and things fail to live up to their promises or our expectations. Hence the necessity, if we are criticised or, as we see it, undervalued, to put ourselves under the microscope and analyse ourselves in all objectivity and honesty. And so Saturn brings us the opportunity to discover ourselves and the world as we really are – and this chance is precious.

If you're at the *very end of the Sign, born after 17 April,* you could still suffer repercussions from a square of Neptune which little by little slips away from your heavens, much to your relief; you won't notice it much in January (thanks to the Jupiterian euphoria which will accompany this transit), but more in September, when in some way this Neptunian dissonance will form a prologue to the Saturnian repercussions due in October. A generally cloudy and confused atmosphere could thus characterise these last three months of the year: a climate of doubt, intrigue or trickery, which ought to awaken your critical faculties and vigilance. Mid-October will be totally typical from this point of view.

Now for the good news, which applies to the *first half of the Sign.* This will be uplifted and galvanised by a fine sextile of Uranus and a budding one of Neptune. Your pioneering spirit will be fulfilled. So you should throw yourself cheerfully into all the adventures which beckon you, all the pursuits which could extend your field of activity and open up new horizons. What's more, if you were *born before 2 April* and particularly *between 26 March and 2 April,* Uranus will widen your circle of friends, and perhaps incite you to enter into partnerships, participate in group activities or join a club. You may even take up a responsible post in a movement of solidarity. All told, you can count on widened perspectives, particularly as Neptune will reveal a superior spiritual, intellectual or artistic dimension, and greatly increase your intuition, which will guide you unerringly. And taking the reassuring trine of Pluto into account – which bears on the *second half of the first decan* (those *born between 25 and 31 March*) – it's likely that nothing will resist the impact of the psychic energy Pluto grants, combined with the increased intuition and galvanised willpower that stems from Uranus. In other words, if you were *born before 3 April*, you are invited to change, to improve everything in your life that doesn't satisfy you. The heavens will make it possible, and it's up to you to seize your opportunities.

Your willpower will be unwavering – you'll be a real steam-roller – in January, March to April (but watch out for excessive or misdirected energy), June and from the end of August to the beginning of October, when you'll be at the peak of your physical form. Love will be well aspected at the beginning of January, in March, May, July, the end of August, beginning of September, and at the end of November/beginning of December.

### Taurus (20 April to 21 May)

After the tidal wave you may have experienced last year, especially if you're an *April Taurus*, 1998 is going to seem a lot more mild, despite a square of Uranus which continues to crack down on your status quo. Uranus has moved a little in the heavens since last year and now will destabilise the lives of Taurus subjects *born between 26 April and 3 May*. Those who were *born around 26–28 April* will experience the repercussions or fulfilment of this change as they settle into a new life in October 1998, as the result of events which occurred at the beginning of the year. Depending on your personal chart, these upheavals could take various forms: a change of residence or profession or, sadly, an accident to do with health; but whatever their precise manifestation, they will all be unforeseen and of a sudden, brutal nature.

The advent of Saturn in your Sign between July and October

brings a phase of interiorising, perhaps of obstacles or setbacks to your progress. The result, for the *first decan*, of this double influence of Uranus and Saturn is quite problematic and difficult to assess, for the turbulence and agitation of Uranus are added to the static strength and gravity of Saturn. And you – who favour passive energy and the force of inertia – will without doubt be thrown off course by the destabilisation of Uranus. So it's worth knowing that the problem in your life which comes this summer will have repercussions in the spring of 1999. Psychologically speaking, this double influence has a strong chance of evoking an intolerant, rigid, even tyrannical and sullen climate. And you must combat this by reminding yourself that Taurus is a Venusian sign – therefore amiable and a charmer by definition!

Of all the Sign, the *first decan* certainly gets the worst of the cosmic aspects this year, as not only will you have to contend with Saturn and Uranus, but also with a budding square of Neptune which appears in February. This will disturb and blur your life, which you have a horror of, as you like everything straightforward, well-organised, clear and uncomplicated. But what Neptune does is precisely to introduce the irrational: sudden doubt about your objectives; irrational distress you can't find any good reason for; and a confused outlook on the world due to too much subjectivity. Neptune also inclines one to deceive oneself, and be deceived, and to make wrong decisions due to errors of judgement. Therefore this is not the time, if you can help it, to make important decisions to do with your future in whatever area. And if you must make decisive commitments in 1998, at least try to do so in February, when Neptune won't yet be fully active and you'll also have the support of Jupiter, the bringer of good luck.

On the subject of Jupiter, here's some good news: a fine sextile will favour your Sign from February until the end of the year. Those Taureans stressed by Uranus and *born before 3 May* will be protected by Jupiter until the beginning of April. While if your birthday falls in the *first ten days of May*, everything you sow between mid-March and the beginning of May will produce rich pickings between October and December.

This is the time, therefore, to take things on, to throw yourself into daring projects which, financially, promise to be highly profitable. If you are *third decan*, Jupiter will be protective and clement between May and July, inviting you to launch out in every direction and all sorts of undertakings, which you'll gather the benefits from – in terms of hard cash – at the beginning of 1999.

So here's to next year!

## Gemini (21 May to 21 June)

This is an ambiguous year, two-sided like you are, Gemini my friend, with positive and negative, rosy pink and grey.

The year begins well enough for *all the Sign* and particularly the *first decan*, who have all the trump cards it takes to change the direction of their lives in a positive way. In fact, on one hand the opposition of Pluto disrupts your life, and on the other, a trine of Uranus propels you towards the realisation of your aspirations and salutary change. This will be the ideal time, then, to clinch a business partnership or marriage which will bring radical change into your life. But you should equally take care not to exceed your limits or competence; and don't dive head foremost into some adventure you won't be able to find your way out of, especially as from March onwards Jupiter introduces an element of disorder, anarchy or complication, which fortunately has every appearance of being short lived.

In any event, if you're a *first decan Gemini*, you will have begun a process of change last year which will be unique in your lifetime. You'll alter your scale of values completely: for this is a time when you'll have to choose between past and future. A real turnaround will result, in either your everyday, amorous or professional life. But don't let yourself be seized by agoraphobia, a fear of open spaces, in the face of the unknown which opens to you, for Uranus will be there to serve as a guard-rail right through this process of transformation. In October particularly, if you're an *end of May Gemini*, you'll take giant strides towards a new horizon.

It's worth noting that the improvements and positive
surprises brought by Uranus are reserved in 1998 for those
Geminis *born before 5 June*, while for those whose birthdays fall
*at the beginning of June* the opening horizons and extension of
their activities will form a climate which they'll benefit from
until the end of next year, which is good news indeed! They'll
hardly have a single tricky period in 1998, except perhaps
between April and the beginning of June, when Jupiter could
well put a spoke in their wheels by dispersing them or bringing
them administrative worries or some financial problems. But
these will soon pass. And these same subjects will benefit at the
beginning of the year from a very rewarding period in which
they'll get their just deserts – and even more – thanks to Saturn
which will bring positive repercussions from last summer.

As for the second half of the Sign (Geminis *born on or after 7
June*) their life in 1998 follows quite a complicated pattern.
They'll enjoy a euphoric and highly gratifying start to the year,
thanks to Jupiter in January and Saturn in the spring; but from
mid-May they'll begin to experience Jupiter's dissonance, which
will introduce disorder into their lives (in an area that depends
on their natal charts). Whether it has to do with your love, day-
to-day life, career or finances, this turbulence will be manifest
from May till the start of October, when you'll then hold all the
cards and must play them as best you can to avoid suffering too
much at the beginning of next year (as a result of whatever your
problem was). But simultaneously, Saturn will be in the background as a sort of screen or shield and – particularly if you're
at the *end of your Sign* (*born after 16 June*) – it will come back
to reward you at the end of the year with the stabilisation and
consolidation of your situation, which makes it an influence
worth having, in view of the somewhat anarchic context of your
heavens. For example, you could get a distinction or a promotion at the end of the year (or next year) thanks to Saturn; yet
on the other side of the coin, Jupiter could cause ill-considered
or excessive expenses, whose worrying or frustrating consequences you'll be subject to at the end of this year and
beginning of 1999. Many other scenarios are equally imaginable
– like completing a long-term project which you'll benefit from at

the end of the year – and yet at the same time fundamentally call into question your professional life...

Subjects of the *first decan* will have every chance to get on the right footing in terms of their partnership; to breathe new life into a union or to have a significant new encounter. On the other hand, if you're a *June Gemini*, the heavens will let you stabilise and consolidate your emotional life and ensure it's long-lasting during the first four months, and at the end of the year. They will even encourage you to get married, if you decide to, at the very beginning of the year. Venus will favour these various emotional climates, and bring them maximum harmony, at the beginning of January, in March, May, the beginning of June, end of August and in October, which are the times you'll feel best with regard to yourself and others.

### Cancer (21 June to 22 July)

If you belong to the middle of the Sign – *born between 6 and 12 July* – you'll begin the year feeling somewhat down. But don't let your gloom turn into defeatism, as from spring onwards you'll be over the worst. It's true that during this first period you'll probably get it in the neck from Saturnian repercussions from last year – repercussions which, in your opinion, you could easily do without! In fact, this first period of the year could come to a head in an emotional separation which could take place at the end of January/beginning of February; or you could find you have a professional or physical problem in January. Or you might have to fight at the end of March against some impasse that demands a final assault... All these scenarios are probable and will depend on your personal chart. But whatever happens, when March is over, you'll be through with Saturn – for seven years!

On the other hand, as if to balance the books, the heavens will pour out Jupiter's manna in April. You'll benefit from it until the beginning of May, and reap its rewards in November (that's if you were *born before 12 July*). In the same way, if you belong to the *last decan*, you'll enjoy this fine influence of

Jupiter, the bringer of luck and expansion, between the beginning of May and the beginning of October – and get the final benefits from this at the beginning of 1999. But, whatever the timing of your Jupiterian influences, if you plant your seeds in the periods mentioned, you'll gather rich pickings from your initiatives. Found a company, launch a new project, decide to get married or form a partnership, organise a great voyage ... it's all within Jupiter's bounds.

If you're *last decan*, however, things become complicated, as virtually simultaneously you'll be obstructed by the opposition of Saturn, particularly in April to May, then in November to December. This will expose you to various obstacles, delays and limitations to your undertakings. As a Cancer, forewarned is forearmed: during the first phase try not to overload yourself with responsibilities whose consequences you won't be able to cope with at the end of this year or the beginning of next.

Without wanting to encourage your natural hypochondria, you also need to know that a square of Saturn is likely to lessen your vitality, exposing you more to overwork, major fatigue, vitamin deficiencies and skin or dental problems. Fortunately, you'll have a superb period – the best of your year – when your horizon will clear (Saturn being eclipsed for some months) between the beginning of June and October. You'll have a free rein to get on with your life then and gather the manna poured from Jupiter's horn of plenty.

The very beginning of the Sign – that's Cancer subjects *born before the 25th* – merits special mention. Between June and October it will benefit from a fine sextile of Saturn. This will help these subjects establish their status quo and consolidate their gains, and promises recognition from family or colleagues for past efforts, whether professional or private. This is, in fact, an excellent aspect and very promising, and it will incite these Cancerians to undertake a long-term work which they'll be rewarded for next spring. What's more, the whole *first decan* has a superb trine of Jupiter in February to March. It will put them in a good mood and great form, and serve them up all sorts of opportunities on a silver platter.

*All the Sign* will be in scintillating form in February, April to

May, and June to July, when you'll astonish those around you by your spirit of enterprise and dynamism (which is normally somewhat stifled by your phlegmatic temperament). October and November will also see you on the best of physical form.

So you see, Cancer my friend, apart from the *last decan* (which in October and the end of November will find itself in a difficult climate of irresolution and widespread obstruction) this year will have plenty to be said for it, and certainly won't be the worst of your life!

### *Leo (22 July to 23 August)*

*July Leos* will start the year in a spin. The opposition of Uranus will change their lives, and they'll feel they're taking off for new horizons. January, especially if you were *born on or after 26 July,* is absolutely magnificent and full of promise. You're going to be able to alter – and I encourage you to – everything in your life you don't like and make a clean sweep of it. And a magnificent planetary combination will help you make this alteration positive no matter to what area you apply your desire for change.

Subjects at the *very beginning of the Sign,* on the other hand, will catch it in the neck from the opposition of Neptune, which will make things difficult by complicating their lives to a greater or lesser degree. It will slow down positive influences and multiply obstacles, particularly between June and October when Saturn helps Neptune cause trouble. This opposition of Neptune, moreover, could well bear on a partner, or your relationship with one, which becomes blurred, troubled and less than frank, till you're all at sea with your 'other half'.

In some cases there could be a hard-to-diagnose illness which affects your partner. And this is all the more reason for both of you to have a preventative check-up, for Neptune encourages exposure to viral contagion. So if you were *born before the 26th,* be circumspect this summer – in every way – whether on holiday or at home; and in any event tell yourself that, if you're not on form either physically or mentally, this is only the reflection of a morose and disturbing planetary configuration. It's worth knowing, too, that this summer's astral climate will have an effect on next spring. So don't make point-blank decisions, but try to let them mature intelligently. And, given the debilitating nature of both the planets which affect you, don't make excessive demands on your body (as you often tend to believe yourself invulnerable). Take care of your heart and circulation, which are the weak points of your Sign, along with the eyes, and if you go in for surfing, gliding or golf this summer, watch out for falls or fractures, especially to the legs which are another vulnerable area. This warning applies particularly to the end of August.

The rest of the Sign, especially the second half, *born after 7 August* and those born at the *end of July* are this year's true winners. Until the beginning of July they'll be subject to a rewarding and extremely stabilising influence of Saturn which will bring them all sorts of rewards, particularly to do with their self-affirmation and the recognition of their true value. And if this doesn't occur for the *last decan* in the spring, it will in the last three months of 1998, or in January 1999. So this is the time, if you want to, to undertake a long-term project, which you can plan on completing in October to November, so that it bears fruit in December or January.

The *last decan* begins the year turbulently enough but this climate won't last beyond February. Curiously, it's in January that you'll most want to lash out with your cash and be prodigal (as your Sign tends to be) ... but then perhaps you missed out on Christmas! The *second decan*, for its part, begins the year in feverish activity and great output. *All the Sign* will be in exemplary form in March to April, June, from the end of August to the beginning of October (when the *first decan* should nonetheless be particularly careful), and from the end of November to the end of the year.

So ... have a go, Joe!

## *Virgo (23 August to 23 September)*

While most of your Sign had a fairly calm time of it last year
(apart from August Virgos who were subject to the destabilising
aspects of Pluto), only the *end of the Sign* looks as if it is still
sheltered from cosmic storms this year. And apart from those
*born after 19 September, all the Sign* will experience an astral
climate of turbulence and turmoil.

In fact, you'll be subject to the opposition of Jupiter, which
will make something of a shambles of your life (in an area which
depends on your personal chart, age and particular circumstances). In any event, it's worth knowing that, under this sort of
influence, there's little point in asking for tax relief or a rise in
salary, because dealings with hierarchic superiors or the authorities are not well aspected.

Special mention should be made of *first decan,* or in any
event, *August Virgos.* Until mid-March, they'll be under attack
from both Pluto and Jupiter at once, which could make them
feel the ground is slipping away beneath their feet and the
principles they've leaned on until now are collapsing. And
during this phase, these subjects could well be induced to
change completely their scale of values and objectives in life.
They might have to confront a problem outside their control,
such as redundancy. But, in any event, if you're an *August
Virgo* your life will be called on to change at the beginning of
1998. And you'll still experience the effects of this in the
summer of next year, especially if you were born at the *end of
August.*

It's also worth noting that the end of January/beginning of
February is a period to underline in red in your diary. You'll
feel pulled every which way, and it wouldn't be wise to make
long-term decisions. You'll be in an aggressive and passionate
mood, and won't be able to accept any form of compromise
whatsoever; and you may even momentarily abandon the over-
riding rationalism which in general rings out loud and clear in you.
The same applies to the end of February, when professionally
things seem to capsize. Fortunately, if you were *born before 26
August,* your best period in 1998 will be between the end of

July and the end of October, when Saturn will bring some calm, discipline and stability into a life that could feel as if it has been shaken by a cosmic tornado. Keep an eye on what's outlined on the horizon during this summer period, for it will have interesting spin-offs next spring.

If you were *born on or after 7 September,* you'll suffer the opposition of Jupiter from April till the end of the year; and this will plunge you into a climate of all-round instability. So be careful what commitments you make between April and July; and be equally sceptical about any promises made to you in this same period, as things could go wrong in the latter part of the year. Remember the adage 'Grasp all, lose all', for you'll have a tendency to go over the top and overestimate. And this could engulf you in June (if you're *last decan*) and have disagreeable repercussions in September. The same applies to November. Don't disperse yourself. And avoid – and this applies to *all the Sign* – taking on debts that are too much for you before July, or you could find they bleed you dry at the end of the year.

The luckiest Virgos in 1998 will be those *born after 19 September.* They'll benefit from a restorative and sublimating trine of Neptune, which will help them see life through rose-tinted spectacles. Even if these subjects are briefly bothered in mid-July by Jupiter, nothing will trouble their serenity; and they'll find the means to deal with their problems, be they legal, administrative or financial. A word of advice, nonetheless, if you belong to this sector: try not to go wrong through negligence or disinterest – to play the 'foolish virgin' – as Neptune's protection will no longer be there next year, when Jupiter will return to taunt you with repercussions from this July. So be on guard for possible errors of judgement this summer. And whatever happens, tell yourself loud and clear that next year – which will give you a foretaste of the third millenium – will be a lot more favourable for your sector of the zodiac.

Good luck!

## Libra (23 September to 23 October)

*All the Sign* begins this year in an atmosphere of some euphoria (despite the influence of Saturn which will somewhat spoil the lives of those *born after 8 October*). This is because, in January, Mars will infuse Librans with increased dynamism and new enthusiasm. What's more, Jupiter will touch the *last decan* with its magic – particularly those *born around the 12th/13th* – and bring tasty repercussions from last June, and spoil these subjects throughout the month.

The *first decan* appears to be blessed by the gods right through the year. Particularly if you're an *end of September Libran*, you'll have Pluto and Uranus together as allies, which will encourage you to take giant strides towards your deepest aspirations and to disrupt your life in a positive way. If you want to change job, partner, country ... this is the time to. Of course you won't have to decide on the spot in January, but it's likely that in this first month of the year things will take a sudden and exciting turn whose effects will spread out through the year and have concrete results, particularly in October.

Equally positive and almost as radical changes are in store if you were *born before 5 October*. However, they'll only really start around May and won't be finalised until next year. While if you were born in the *first week of October*, you'll have an irrepressible desire to break new ground in your life, feel plugged into whatever is topical or 'in' and find your place in the sun. There will be lightning promotions, spectacular improvements. And your field of consciousness will be extended inter-personally, geographically or intellectually.

Meanwhile, the opposition of Saturn will make life difficult for Librans in the *second half of the Sign* who will not be protected by Uranus, or any other planet, in 1998. You will have difficult or frustrating periods between mid-March and the beginning of June and from mid-October to the end of the year (if you're *born after the 17th*). While if you're *third decan*, and in particular *born between 12 and 17 October*, you're only affected by Saturn's transit between mid-May and the beginning of June. And though you won't be particularly aware of it, it could affect you emotionally by making you feel isolated, or threaten a break-up in May.

On the other hand, if you were *born after the 17th* Saturn's influence will bear on the end of this year and beginning of next. And if it affects you emotionally, it is quite likely you will have to go through something disagreeable in December or next January. Of course, if your relationship is solid, Saturn can do nothing to harm it, and the manifestation of its testing transit could then be limited to a general feeling of sadness, remoteness, or gloom. In other words, you'll feel on rotten form, that you've lost all appeal, and that your sense of insecurity is obvious to one and all.

As Neptune blends its dissonant rays with Saturn throughout the year, if you're at the *end of the Sign* you'll often find yourself in a tight corner, and be a ready-made target, if you've a tendency to depressing or morose speculation. So react vigorously against these mental and spiritual pitfalls. Impress on yourself that this is simply the effect of planetary dissonance, over which you can exercise your free will ... or at least try your best to. Repeat to yourself that this climate is both passing and purposeful: passing, because after next March you'll be free of it; purposeful, because all planetary dissonance is sent to test us; to make us aware of what we are and what we lack, of our weakness and limitations. We are here to learn and develop, and unfortunately man only learns when he's forced to, is pushed into it by Fate. So, if you're at the *end of the Sign* remember this, particularly in November, when you're discouraged and feel like giving up.

Collectively speaking, it isn't easy to assess the double dissonance of Neptune and Saturn, as they can take innumerable concrete forms according to particular cases. What's more, they can also fail to have any material manifestation and simply be confined to a depressing psychological climate, a total lack of spirit and spirit of enterprise (allied to possible anaemia). While for other Librans at the *end of the Sign* this period – especially round the end of the year – could produce a nebulous, deceptive atmosphere in which there's a risk – if they haven't shown basic prudence in their dealing with others at the start of the year – that they could find themselves victims or dupes.

For many of you this planetary tension will take the form of a professional or partnership problem, in which you'll be floundering about in a troubled and gloomy fog. So you'll need to be stout-hearted, to find a sense of harmony and peace that will link you to the bosom of your family. And, above all, knowing that Neptune is the planet of the irrational and nebulous, of confusion, where reason and logic no longer hold sway ... try to keep smiling! And keep your sights fixed on the horizon of 1999, when Neptune will trouble you no longer.

### Scorpio (23 October to 22 November)

Good news Scorpio, my friend: a harmoniously aspected Jupiter will lavishly favour *almost all your Sign* from the beginning of February until the end of the year. As a result, you'll be entitled to all the benefits Jupiter regularly brings: a souped-up vitality, the best physical and mental form, rejuvenated enthusiasm, a perked-up spirit of enterprise and, above all, the likelihood of material wellbeing – and, in all probability, financial expansion. That's the good news then, so even you – hard to please as you are at times – should still find something to write home about!

So, what's the catch? Jupiter's transit through the *first decan*, in February and part of March will, unfortunately, be rapid. So, if you were born in this sector, you must seize your opportunities while you can. On the other hand, though, this lucky Jupiterian influence at the start of the year *will* serve as a shield against worse to come: a virtual tidal wave of cosmic dissonance throughout the year in the form of squares of Neptune and Uranus respectively. Further dissonance will be added to this between June and the end of October, but only in the case of Scorpios *born before 26 October.*

For most of you *born before 4 November*, this planetary coalition will almost certainly bring the destabilisation of your family atmosphere. And particularly if you were *born at the very beginning of your Sign, before 26 October*, this will be marked by confusion, uncertainty or pretence. And this general haziness, this emotional fog (which could also have an effect on property) could evolve into a climate of deception which, in summer under the added dissonance of Saturn, could well give rise to a serious problem in terms of your relationship with your partner or family.

However – and this is good news – Jupiter will act as a guardian or shield for you during the first three months at least. So take advantage of this period to clarify relationships as best you can; to make them as good as possible and create a climate of harmony with your family and 'other half', which perhaps will minimise subsequent damage. Many of you could have a significant meeting during these three months (and particularly February to March) which could prove the basis for later contention with your partner. For Jupiter will favour love and your personal creativity until the end of March. So, if you were *born before 26 October*, don't overlook this potential partnership problem. Or, having made your bed, you may have to lie on it next year in the spring.

Uranus will shake up the status quo of Scorpios *born before 5 November*, and particularly those whose birthday falls in the first week of the month. For many, it's highly likely that this dissonance will have a concrete effect and entail a move or change of residence. For others, this ill-aspected Uranus will bring an unexpected family event, perhaps the temporary departure of a child or the more final departure of another family member. In any event, you won't have completely emerged from this climate of instability until next year, and possibly not till the end of it. This also means that a good many Scorpios of the *first week in November* will decide to emigrate – to settle down in another continent, country, culture – which will require a period of adaptation.

Scorpios *born after 4 November*, however, will have most reason to celebrate in 1998. For all they have in prospect is a positive and exciting trine of Jupiter, which opens all sorts of horizons to them and shields them from destabilising and otherwise worrying influences. If you belong to this sector favoured by the stars, you will see a climate of expansion blossom after the end of March: suggestions and ideas and plans will be in the air and captivate your interest before mid-July. And you can be sure that these projects or propositions will yield extremely positive results before the end of the year, particularly if you were *born before 13 November*. (Those born after this date must wait until 1999 to see Jupiter's promises realised.)

The most favoured Scorpios of all though, without doubt, are those at the *very end of the Sign* who were *born after 20 November*. They'll reach a sort of peak (in an area that depends on their personal chart) in mid-July, when Jupiter will add its beneficial and generous rays to those of Neptune. These subjects will certainly experience a time of rare serenity, happiness and enthusiasm then ... or simply downright pure good luck. Also in summer, from the end of July to mid-August, Mars will combine with Venus to generate 'an event'. And it's highly likely that this will be a Meeting with a capital M, that's destined to ripen into Love, with a capital L.

Mars, which brings increased pace, a spirit of enterprise and enhanced vitality, will in fact be favourable to *all the Sign* from the end of January to the beginning of March, in summer, and in October to November. Gifted with the joint backing of Jupiter and Neptune, many Scorpios will feel effectively invincible then.

And the facts will bear them out.

### Sagittarius (22 November to 22 December)

Just occasionally, the gifts of the gods are spread out in an equitable way. And this will be the case in the first five months of this year, when *all the Sign* will be favoured with lucky planetary aspects. But while Sagittarians *born before 5 December* are rewarded with threefold powerful planetary backing, while they continue to be the 'lucky victims' of this influence until the end of the year, it's quite different for the *second half of the Sign*. For clouds will gather in its heavens at the beginning of April that will spread and expand until mid-July, which could give rise to disagreeable news from then on till the end of the year. So, if you're a *December Sagittarian*, try not to rest on your laurels or doze off in all the rewards Saturn brought in previous months – rewards which were restorative, flattering and possibly soothing – for the wolf could lurk among the fold and cause you a good many worries to do with paperwork, finances or all sorts of bother before the end of the year, especially during the second half, if you don't take care. So don't get into a legal or administrative impasse. And watch out for the taxman!

From the beginning of the year till mid-March, Saturn will benefit Sagittarians *born after 5 December*. Many of you will reap rewards from last year then, or with great satisfaction come to the end of a long-term project, while many will also receive a distinction, award or honour, which they'll be more than happy to get!

If you belong to the *last decan*, between March and June of this year you will plant seeds which you will harvest great benefit from in or after October and until the beginning of 1999. And Saturn will save you from the worst and guard your back against Jupiter's dissonance. If you're *last decan*, between May and the beginning of October, you'll need to keep a watchful eye on everything that relates to over-optimistic commitments, fair-seeming but deceitful promises, overestimation of yourself and others, and a hang-up with authority, or else you'll regret it next January. The same applies if you're planning an important expenditure such as the construction of a house, or in fact any debt; for, while Saturn protects property or real estate – which is favoured for you this year – Jupiter could well bleed you dry financially!

Returning to Sagittarians *born before the 5th*, their heavens are at one and the same time serene and exciting. Lovers of change that they are by nature, they can totally trust their intuition and deep aspirations this year. The heavens dictate that they should fling themselves forward, dare ... should 'boldly go where no man has gone before'! For this is the time to be revolutionary in the right sense of the word. The planet of evolution and revolution, of emancipation and liberation, Uranus, will be positively aspected for you, encouraging progress and an enlarged field of consciousness. Pluto will also take a hand, inciting you to radical change, particularly if you were *born between 26 November and 3 December*; you'll want to turn everything topsy-turvy in your life, to bow out of your current scene and see what's going or somewhere else. In other words, adventurer that you are, nothing will hold you back any longer and you'll cast off your moorings.

So why not listen to these inner voices, especially when you have such exciting planetary aspects as protectors and guarantors?

### *Capricorn (22 December to 20 January)*

Capricorn, my friend, there's rose and there's grey in this year on the threshold of the third millenium. In other words, good and less good. Pessimistic realist that you are, I'm sure you'd rather I gave you the bad news first. If you're *second decan* – and especially if you were *born after 4 January* – you already had a foretaste of Saturn's dissonance last year, between spring and autumn; and this year, from January onwards, Saturn could well give rise to repercussions from last year's problem. The only consolation is that you'll be over this phase after mid-March ... and theoretically tranquil for seven years thereafter.

From the middle of March until the beginning of July, Saturn will hinder the *last decan*'s progress. It will then call a truce for some months. But after October repercussions will come – which you won't appreciate – of its first phase. As a result, some of you could well experience emotional disappointment or deception in May, which could enter a bitter phase at the end of October. A separation could ensue, though of course this depends on the quality of your existing ties. For a perfectly harmonious and solid relationship between two human beings is in no way as vulnerable to cosmic assault as ties which are already strained.

Special mention should be made of Capricorns at the *very end of the Sign, born after 17 January,* who from the end of August until the end of November will again be marked by the end of a transit of Neptune. For some this transit will mean a climate of increased intuition, greater serenity and an opening to an invisible dimension; for others, who experience it negatively, it will throw them off their aim, induce deceit, confusion, even a profound identity crisis. And after November a discordant Saturn will return to join this Neptunian influence in a strained configuration that, particularly at the end of December, could put a full stop to a number of relationships, which will unfortunately be a pretty gloomy way to end the year. But you must tell yourself that everything that happens is for the best, and one has to say 'yes' to life!

There's also some good news. Starting at the beginning of February, a harmonious sextile of Jupiter will bring all sorts of satisfaction to *almost all the Sign*. The only Capricorns exempt from this influence will be those *born after 17 January*, who'll have to wait for this fine aspect till the beginning of February next year. If you belong to this sector of the zodiac, keep an eye on the atmosphere in mid-July, which could well have a lucky effect on early 1999, through a phenomenon of planetary osmosis known as the 'Orb'. Briefly this means that, like radiation, an influence begins to be active *before* an exact aspect, and remains so, in terms of residual effect, *after* the precise aspect.

Jupiter will lavishly favour *first decans* between the beginning of February and almost the end of March. So, in this brief period, it's up to them to seize their opportunities and perhaps get on with a project they hold dear, while such good influences last. (The end of February will be particularly promising.) As if to compensate for this rigid transit of Jupiter, though, Capricorns *born before Christmas* will have a stabilising and rewarding trine of Saturn in their heavens from the beginning of June till the end of October, which will bring – or in any event promise – them a fine reward (most probably next year in the spring).

If you're *second decan*, Jupiter pours out his horn of plenty for you between the end of March and beginning of May. This promises you all sorts of material or psychological benefits and particularly a *jovial* (Jupiter is also known as Jove) good humour, and increased vital optimism, which is already a promise of luck. You'll also experience this climate between the beginning of October and the beginning of December, particularly if you were *born after 6 January.*

*Last decan* Capricorns will probably be the best off, as they'll enjoy a productive sextile of Jupiter from the beginning of May till the beginning of October. But then, this is only fair as they will also be the most tested by Saturn in the spring and at the beginning of the year. Their best period will thereafter be between the beginning of May and the beginning of October when not only will Saturn's effect be dimmed, but the excellent influence of Jupiter will intervene. If you belong to this sector of your Sign therefore, opt for this period which should prove the most fertile. And bank on September, which for *all the Sign* should prove an optimum time.

### *Aquarius (20 January to 19 February)*

If you belong to the *first half of the Sign* and especially if you were *born before 3 February,* you should step into the unknown and go for adventure, as boldness will certainly pay. Sustained by Pluto and Uranus, in an alliance which will favour you principally in January, you've every opportunity to change everything that needs changing in your life, and everything you dream of transforming. In fact, with the entry of Uranus in Aquarius in 1996, followed in 1998 by that of Neptune (something that only occurs every 164 years) you have every trump card up your sleeve to make sure of your positive evolution, or to bring about a real revolution in your life.

If you were *born between 26 January and 3 February,* Uranus will influence you particularly this year, and in its passage upset everything that isn't worthy of existence. Neptune, on the other hand, will affect those *born before 23 January.* As a result this year could have been difficult, confused, illusory, even catastrophic in some instances, but the solid protection of Pluto will make these dangers disappear. You can bank especially on January, which will be fantastically promising for you and effectively put you on a launching pad. Alternatively, if you were born at the *very beginning of the Sign*, you should be wary of July, as after June Saturn is ill aspected and could bring all sorts of worries, delays and disappointments. So be sensible, even at the beginning of the year, and don't overvalue either people or things.

Almost as if the heavens wanted to be fair in what they hand out this year, it's not only the first half of the Sign that is sustained, galvanised, stimulated and inspired by the planets already mentioned. The *second half of the Sign* will also get its share of manna from heaven. After the beginning of the year Aquarians *born after 2 February* will be rewarded with what last spring and autumn promised. They can count on a general consolidation of their life and improvement in their means of subsistence and emotional ties at the beginning of January, in mid-March and in May. And if you're *last decan* Saturn will promise you a special bonus, or encourage you to undertake a long-term work, between March and the beginning of June, which you should gather the fruits of at the end of the year. October, November and December will also be excellent months in several ways.

All told, then, this is a good year for *almost all your Sign.* Especially when we take into account the stimulating, even galvanising, influence of Mars, which in January, March to April, June and December will take you a long way – a very long way – forward on the road to your aspirations.

### Pisces (19 February to 21 March)

Pisces, my friend, if you were *born in February,* you can expect a year of disruption.

In fact, Pluto will upset your progress from top to bottom. And many of you will take advantage of this by changing jobs, country or partner – or even all three. The most unsettled period – and the most exciting too – will be in February to March when Jupiter, which is passing through your Sign as it does every 12 years, will provide you with opportunities you can put to good use as regards the great change in your destiny. If you have an ill-aspected natal Sun, however, this period could well be the most turbulent and, all told, extremely unsettling. The other critical times, or in any event disturbing, owing to decisions you will have to take, are: June, September and November to December.

More precisely, Pisces subjects *born on or after 24 Feburary* will be subject to a square of Pluto, and thus influenced by a climate of profound transformation. If you were born before this date, you will have already experienced a radical turn-around in previous years; and now, in contrast, thanks to a sextile of Saturn, you will enjoy a stabilising climate and general consolidation of your situation. You can expect to harvest the fruits of your past efforts – especially between June and October – and could also pave the way then for further gains from which you benefit next year.

The *first decan* isn't the only one affected this year by the astral conjunction. In fact, all your Sign will be transited by Jupiter which, as you already know, is the bringer of manna from heaven and all sorts of desirable benefits, both psychologically and materially. Only Pisceans at the very end of the Sign, *born on or after 17 March* won't be visited by Jupiter in 1998, and will have to wait until March 1999.

So *almost all the Sign* can look forward to a magnified spirit of enterprise, an unfailing vital optimism in fact, a starring role that's assured by a host of opportunities and a sort of natural complicity of events to tend to privilege you. In sum, you'll be starting anew on a 12-year cycle of opportunity and general expansion.

If you are *second decan,* good luck will most probably come knocking at your door between mid-March and the beginning of May: you'll have news about what happens then after October, and rake in your rewards before the beginning of December. The same applies, though on a slightly different time-scale, if you're *last decan.* Your lucky phase will begin at the start of May and spread out till mid-July, by which time all your cards will have been dealt. How you play them will be determined between July and the beginning of October. And the results of all this potential, of how you negotiated or exploited your chances, will come to light in December 1998 or January 1999.

There's a definite tendency to get married under a direct transit of Jupiter – which has been statistically confirmed – and you might also found a society or expand your business interests in a major way. Shifting focus, this is also a time the stars seem especially inclined to provide you with offspring. And whatever your plans or hopes, in professional or in private life, Jupiter will give you the chance to give concrete form to your dreams.

The most effective times to progress towards your objectives will be: between the end of January and the beginning of March; from mid-April to mid-May; and in July to August, which are all periods when Mars, the period of action, will help you find fulfilment in reality.

If your dearest wish is to get married, you should preferably choose one of the periods when Venus is well aspected: January to February, April, June, the end of July/beginning of August, the end of October/beginning of November or the second half of December.

Good luck!

# 1999

## The course of the planets

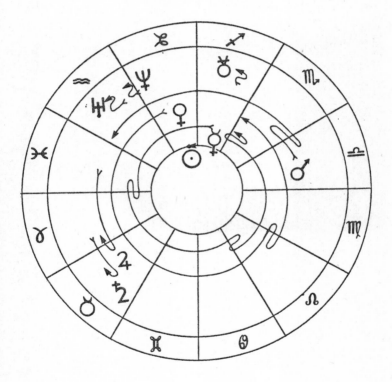

# World Events

After the total change in the USSR which took place in 1989–90, and was reflected by the great conjunction of Saturn and Neptune, 1999 sees a fundamental planetary configuration which will induce a new phase of this cycle. In other words, whether communism has totally changed, if it's had to rebuild itself under pressure from the ethnic demands of the various socialist republics, or whether it has disappeared altogether in its initial form (swept away by the immense astral current of Uranus and Neptune in 1993), in the spring of 1999 the USSR will come to a date of maturation, a decisive point in its historical itinerary. Perhaps the election of a new President of the Supreme Soviet? That is, if this post has not become obsolete...

Besides this planetary cycle, there is another extremely important one in 1999: that of Saturn and Uranus, which is generally attributed to the right wing in politics. And perhaps especially in the USA, this indicates a phase of hardening or even imperialism.

But what most compels attention is the prediction of the great visionary astrologer, Nostradamus, concerning the new moon of 11 August 1999:

> In the year 1999 and seven months
> From the sky will come a great King of terror
> To resurrect the great King of Angolmois
> Before and after Mars will reign happily.

(Quatrain 72, Century X)

As elsewhere, Nostradamus is referring here to an eclipse which will plunge the world into darkness for three days and which, on

11 August 1999 at 10.53 GMT, will in fact effectively result in a total eclipse of the sun. (As for the phrase 'seven months' one needs to take into account the difference between the Julian and the Gregorian calendars – a change which only came into force in 1582, after the death of Nostradamus. So August is a plausible hypothesis).

Looking at the heavens on 11 August 1999, one is immediately struck by how much dissonance there is, by the vast amount of cosmic tension between the beginning and middle of the fixed Signs (especially Taurus and Leo). This will especially bear on the France of the Fifth Republic (though this could perhaps be replaced by a Sixth Republic in 1997, during a conjunction of Jupiter and Neptune) and Germany. The chart for the original USSR will also be threatened by this conjunction, with the Sun and Saturn especially in 14 degrees of Scorpio and Leo. Finally, 1999 won't be a good time to stay on the east coast of the United States, as the mid-heavens of New York will be under multiple dissonance (between the Sun and Moon, Mars, Uranus, Saturn and the lunar nodes) which gives this astral climate a collective dimension ... and a solemn one.

What should we therefore expect or fear from this fateful moment, predicted four and a half centuries ago by Nostradamus? If we examine the heavens that day, at the moment of the eclipse, taking our bearings from the geographical coordinates of Paris, we see: a possible catastrophe of pollution (tied to the threefold dissonance of Mercury, Neptune and Jupiter) brought about by winds that come from abroad; and a cosmic outline that suggests the reflection of a battle, of a lightning war, either of a biological nature, or tied ... to an inter-planetary invasion of beings from elsewhere! (The Ninth House reflects foreignness or 'elsewhereness' in a chart.) And this dissonance therefore represents the inevitable shock of such a confrontation. This is a climate of trials of strength, of the clash of shields.

Two elements make me opt for a scenario which, all told, will without doubt be less catastrophic than a reversal of the magnetic poles or the melting of the polar ice-caps, resulting in a new Biblical Flood. The first is a trine between Mercury and

Pluto which indicates a 'message' that comes from somewhere else a long way away (Mercury in the Ninth House) and gives rise to a mutation in thought (Pluto in Sagittarius). The second factor is twofold: on one side a square of Jupiter and Neptune which tends to reflect the ideological, philosophical or religious disarray that would obviously result from so troubling a cosmic invasion; and on the other side, a trine of Venus and Jupiter which is a pledge of survival, even of bounty and love, perhaps of a safeguard assured by woman. Nature, with Jupiter in Taurus, seems in any event preserved: the world *can* and *must* continue. And didn't Nostradamus also date the end of the world in 3797? So we should still have a little breathing space...

*Note*: This extraordinary celestial conjunction will attack certain sectors of the zodiac in particular, while it will privilege others. Among the former are the *second decan* of the Fixed Signs: Taurus, Leo, Scorpio and Aquarius. Among the latter, the *first decan* of the Earth and Water Signs (apart from Taurus and Scorpio) which will be protected by Saturn and Venus. While the *first decans* of the Fire Signs – Aries, Leo and Sagittarius, along with Aquarius, Libra and Gemini – will be most receptive to the 'message of the cosmos'.

## *Your Personal Forecast*

### *Aries (21 March to 20 April)*

Aries, my friend, you can celebrate: there isn't a cloud in your heavens in 1999, despite the fact that, globally, this year is far from safe. So one must believe you'll be sheltered from the cosmic storm, which promises to be a memorable hurricane in the history of mankind. If there is a Flood, could you perhaps be another Noah? Your inventive spirit and taste for adventure will certainly be precious assets in any such scenario...

But seriously – apart from the *last decan* (and then only those *born after 15 April*) which in January will be disturbed, slowed down or depressed by the conjunction of Saturn – *all your Sign* will enjoy an absolutely outstanding year.

Those subjects *born before 25 March* will profit from a fine sextile of Neptune. This will guarantee them a greater opening to invisible things; an extension of their field of consciousness; a better receptivity or sensitivity to artistic matters, and to philosophy, religion, the invisible and the unexplained. It's an ideal transit for a poet or playwright, whose imagination will be increased tenfold. If you belong to this sector, you'll suddenly find yourself less pragmatic and realistic and more of a dreamer; you'll ask yourself questions which you'll feel no need to answer reasonably or rationally; you'll instinctively know the answers through pure intuition. Some of you will feel a new need to devote yourselves to others, to give a concrete form to your natural generosity. In any event, whether you're a business person, doctor or poet, your intuition will guide you and be a great help this year.

If you were *born between the 25th and the end of March,* a trine of Pluto will really favour you in 1999. This influence will help you make noteworthy social progress and find your true place in society. As an influence of profound and positive transformation, it will intensify your vital resources, increase your psychic strength and reinforce that potential vital energy which is frequently put to the service of society; and this will pay well, too, by seeing you're appreciated at your true value. And when Mars joins in, mixing its rays with Pluto's, your tenacity will make you frankly invincible; you'll be impossible to keep up with, have a tiger in your tank! In January, May, September and the end of November, you'll thus take giant strides towards your objectives.

*First week in April* Aries subjects will be protected by Uranus this year. And it will bring them the chance to extend their field of consciousness, relationships, circle of friends and intellectual knowledge, while sudden and unforeseen events will allow you to leap ahead in terms of progress. For example, you'll meet someone highly placed who will help you realise a plan or idea (perhaps by sponsoring you), which without him or her would have stayed on the drawing board. Or perhaps 'by chance' and in a totally sudden way, you'll stumble upon the house or flat of your dreams.

Between mid-February and the end of June, *all Aries subjects* will have Jupiter in their zodiac. This rapid transit which in four months or so will encompass your entire Sign, won't have a particularly drastic or radical impact on most of your lives, precisely because it is so speedy. Unless, that is, you were *born after 14 April*; for at the end of the year (after October) Jupiter will return to, in some way or other, bring you the fruits of opportunities or suggestions which occurred in May to June. If you are *last decan*, therefore, you should be attentive and receptive to this late spring climate; you'll certainly have news of it – and in the majority of cases very good news – at the end of the year. And if you were *born after the 14th*, you can look forward to Jupiter's savoury fruits at the beginning of the year 2000. In sum, if you're *last decan*, Jupiter will help you see things on a grand scale and lay solid foundations in the spring, to reap your rewards in the autumn or winter. Many of you, in fact, will decide to found a society or get married, but won't actually do it until the end of the year, or January 2000.

All told, then, at the dawn of the third millenium, you've a year that looks as if it will spoil you rotten!

### Taurus (20 April to 21 May)

Without beating about the bush, Taurus my friend, you're not in a splendid phase – far from it, particularly if you were *born before 8 May*. Only the *last decan* this year benefits from a very fine sextile of Jupiter, and then only from the beginning of the year until mid-February. (This influence will give it the chance to gather the fruit it planted last year.) If you belong to this sector of the zodiac, you will thus have had your good times by mid-February – and your norm throughout the rest of the year will be a benevolent astral neutrality. In other words, from February on, you'll enter a phase which theoretically will be without clashes or hitches, but not marked by any extraordinary luck either. This transitional period will last throughout the year, and have its highs and lows of course, but they'll all be rather feeble.

Not so, unfortunately, for those *born before 8 May*. For they'll have to confront a sort of planetary coalition consisting of Jupiter, Uranus and Neptune together. And their dissonance will have different effects on the sectors of this first half of the Sign. If you were *born before 25 April*, Neptune will seed your life with confusion this year. And even the appearance of Jupiter between July and October won't be of any great help; in fact will only serve to in some way throw oil on the fire. In all honesty, there's a risk this summer and autumn that you could find yourself totally swamped in confusion. From July to the end of October is particularly powerful, even relatively dangerous, when Jupiter could increase your confidence in yourself and others and make you overestimate people and situations – while Neptune could well cost you a painful awakening and bitter disappointment after a phase of exaltation. And be wary of castles in the air, and other illusions, from the beginning of March to the end of May, when Saturn pays you a visit, as it does every 29 years. In this difficult phase of interiorisation, doubt and uncertainty, you could well call into question the very principles on which you have built your life.

In any event, it's worth knowing that during this delicate phase you'll be exposed to all sorts of misfortunes, setbacks and disappointments. Realistic Taurus that you are, you'll realise that you have to fight on and that the world is less rosy than you imagined. But, instead of losing faith ... react. For under these doubly dissonant influences you'll tend to see things as all black (which isn't your nature) and the glass of life as half empty rather than half full. So put your sights right and don't give in to depression, which would serve no purpose.

The *second decan* is also highly affected by the astral conjunction, especially Taurus subjects of the *first week in May*. If you're one of these, you can expect to call a lot into question as the result of Uranian tension, which will sweep away a good many established situations. Uranus, as you know, is the planet of sudden and unforeseen change, which we have to take on by somehow foreseeing the unforeseeable. And this is hardly in your make-up, Taurus, my friend, as you like things organised and detest improvisation. All the same you will have to improvise now; and particularly after the end of May, when the dissonance of Saturn will be added to that of Uranus until the end of the year. As a result, you'll feel yourself somewhat tossed about and put down by contradictory forces. On one side, due to Saturn, you'll be tempted to interiorise; to retreat into self-analysis and assess your life, and suddenly have an irresistible desire to eliminate all its dross, its superfluous and useless elements. But alongside this major influence, you'll also have to contend with the destabilisation and stress of Uranus, which has a propensity to impose severe tension on our nervous systems. (One tends to sleep poorly, for example, under Uranian dissonance.) Possessed by these very different energies, you'll often feel disturbed, physically off-balance, or ill at ease with yourself. So don't dramatise or come to definitive and terrible conclusions. Bear in mind that this is a relatively fleeting configuration, which ought to help you tidy up your life. It's not impossible, for example, that you could split with your partner in June or November. But keep your eyes fixed on the blue horizon of the year 2000, whose spring will bring you recognition, the all-round stabilisation of the new situation you've settled into and, in sum, a warrior's rest.

One last piece of advice; if you were *born in the first half of the Sign*, be extremely careful between the end of January and the beginning of May. This is one of the most volatile periods of the year, as Mars will make you particularly impulsive or rash, with potentially explosive consequences. Particularly if you're at the very beginning of the Sign, this period could also entail grater vulnerability to viral illness. But *all your Sign* will be crossed by a dissonant Mars in July to August, and then during December – two phases of the year in which the same advice to moderate and control your aggression holds good. For you'll tend to be lacking in consideration for others and attack those around you needlessly ... perhaps because you'll feel so ill at ease with yourself and put upon by others: in sum, a vicious circle, which you'll have to defuse. Be confident that your cheerful Taurean calm can do it...

Which said ... have a good year – on this eve of millenial change!

### Gemini (21 May to 21 June)

If you're *last decan*, you'll have to suffer the consequences of errors of judgement you made last year. For example, you'll be faced with an uncomfortable financial settlement, or a trial will end in a way that bothers you. But whatever these Jupiterian concerns may be, a happy outcome seems guaranteed by Saturn, which in January to February will shield you and guard your back. Furthermore, after mid-May, Jupiter – which was ill aspected at the beginning of the year – becomes your ally, and hands you on a silver plate all sorts of opportunities and enticing suggestions whose effects you'll harvest – often in the form of hard cash – after October, and beyond 1999 into the beginning of the year 2000. So you see, if you're *last decan* you have very little cause for complaint. With your legendary adaptability, one can be sure that you'll know how to make the most of the opportunities which come your way in the spring: whether these have to do with an expansion (perhaps going international) of your existing business, or the decision to set up in business on your own, or even get married ... whatever your objectives, they should be protected by the heavens.

The *second decan*, too, can be well pleased with its cosmic influences this year. In fact, Uranus, the planet of abrupt change, aspects your natal Sun in a magnificent trine that's bursting with promises. If you belong to this sector, profit from this Uranian influence to speed up your business and throw yourself boldly into the unknown. Uranus will assist you, though you'll need to be on the lookout for all the possibilities for expansion and progress which occur in the first five months of the year. In fact, the pieces will be laid out on your chessboard before May; and after October you'll enter a phase of realising your aspirations. Many of you will go for communal activities, will join a club or pursue something which will benefit their fellow man. Others will be more inventive than they've ever been before; while others still will have a sudden and unexpected promotion, courtesy of Lady Luck. And in April there will be a beneficial and effective aura that will change their lives in a radical and hyper-positive way.

Among *first decans*, we need to distinguish between those *born before 26 May* and those *born between 26 May and 1 June*. The first group will be favoured by a trine of Neptune. This will open new mental and psychological horizons, widen their perspectives artistically or mystically, and bring them a new serenity. And given the appearance of a fine sextile of Jupiter which will add its note of pure luck to their lives in mid-February, one can bet that this month (especially towards the end) will be a marker point in 1999, or even a longer period of time. If you belong to this first group, then, you'll most probably go through a period more positive than any you've known for a very long time. This need not necessarily be materially – though that's highly likely in terms of sudden stardom and an un-expected luck – but could be manifest on the mental or psychic planes, and as such produce great inner happiness, rare fulfil-ment, even a moment of illumination. Perhaps in February you'll have the fleeting – but nonetheless vivid – impression that everything is suddenly explicable, that the world is coherent and comprehensible, and that you've found your place in it.

Geminis *born between 26 May and 1 June*, on the other hand, are the only ones this year who are somewhat ill treated by the astral conjunction. For they will have Pluto in opposition and this will disrupt their lives. Not that this disruption need necessarily entail drama or catastrophe – far from it, especially when, like you, one has a passion for change for its own sake and a horror of all monotony. Pluto will give you the chance to indulge this fundamental tendency – and then some! – through the psychic transformation which its influence provokes. You'll question your standards and frame of reference; and after this Plutonian phase (which you won't emerge from until the end of the year 2000) you'll no longer be the same Gemini. You'll be transformed. (And as Pluto is in your solar house of Sagittarius, it's even possible for many of you that your partner is also affected by this metamorphosis.) According to your natal chart, this change will, of course, be more or less difficult to live through: ranging from a hard-to-diagnose illness to a professional about-turn and including a divorce or some other painful separation. But whatever happens, your perspectives and manner of seeing things will be totally altered.

If I may give you some advice, expose this change – and steam ahead with it. And good luck as you round the headland of the twenty-first century!

### Cancer (21 June to 22 July)

You'll enjoy the heavens' favour in 1999, Cancer my friend, especially if you were *born before 10 July*, in which case you'll gather the fruits of past efforts and consolidate your gains in an appreciable way. Particularly if you're at the very beginning of your Sign, *born around 25 June*, you'll profit after March from the extremely satisfying results of a climate that held sway between last June and October. For example, some of you could receive a distinction resulting from this period, or others do brilliantly in an examination they were working for last year.

All the *first decan*, in fact, will find all sorts of causes for satisfaction between March and May. Being more precise, we have to eliminate March itself, when a briefly ill-aspected Jupiter could induce a certain amount of disorder and lack of organisation. But April and May (and also July to October) are among your best periods of the year, with Jupiter replacing a lucky influence of Saturn, and bringing suggestions and plans which you only have to develop to reap rewards from in February 2000.

In conclusion: if you're *first decan*, you'll hardly have a tricky period apart from mid-February to mid-March, when Jupiter brings problems of choice, which for some could be emotional and for others professional. (It's also possible that this climate induces some short-lived confusion in another area.)

*Second decans*, for their part, will see signs of consolidation and an affirmation of their worth after the end of May; these signs will become clearer from the end of August till the end of the year. And in the first months of 2000, you should glean the results of past efforts in a reward which has been germinating for you since this spring. For many of you this will correspond with a long-term project you'll undertake then, to see it finalised to your great satisfaction next year. So you have the fine prospect of entering the third millenium with long-awaited laurels!

Whether you're *second decan*, or *born at the very beginning of the Sign*, your most fruitful and constructive period will be July to August. In fact, *all the Sign* will be overflowing with enthusiasm then, with a spirit of enterprise and exceptional vitality, due to a stimulating trine of Mars which will galvanise you during these summer months.

If you're *last decan*, you'll begin the year in a contradictory climate, probably of stress and overwork brought on by a square of Saturn – but equally of success and positive fulfilment, thanks to a trine of Jupiter which will bring the rewards of what you achieved between last May and September. However, don't neglect the fatigue (which might be quite exceptional) which could grip you in January and February. The result of last May's or the end of last year's astral climate, it could take concrete form as an illness that has been brewing since then, and now shows itself at the beginning of the year. For other Cancerians this influence could involve a separation that has been germinating since the spring or end of last year and which will take place at the beginning of 1999. In any event you'll have to count on starting the year in a spin which will not ensure your serenity. So be extremely careful in January: it could conceal all sorts of unpleasantness, and even accidents due to overwork and fatigue, or lack of luck, though this won't be totally absent as Jupiter's trine will serve as a guard-rail and protective influence. Finally, many *last decan* Cancerians will experience these contradictory aspects in terms of a separation, alongside a new relationship which will simultaneously root itself in their lives.

Nonetheless, if you belong to this *last sector* of your Sign, from May to the end of June Jupiter will cause trouble in your administrative affairs, problems to do with paperwork or financial worries, which you must not neglect, given their likely repercussions on the end of the year. I don't advise you during this period to be too active administratively or to start proceedings in court: the omens in this respect are in no way good. And if you go wrong through overestimating situations, people or yourself, you'll be sorry for it between the end of this year and beginning of next. Still ... forewarned is forearmed and you know what to do: keep your eyes wide open in the spring, so you won't end up gnashing your teeth at the end of the year!

### Leo (22 July to 23 August)

Leos *born between 29 July and 5 August* are the darlings of this year. For (along with the *last decan*) they'll get the best of the influences in 1999. If you belong to this first sector, you'll profit from an exceptionally rewarding and regenerative trine of Pluto, which will change your existence in the right way. In March, in particular, you'll have the chance to start again from scratch: to rebuild your life as seems best to you, with the maximum likelihood of success. For many of you, furthermore, this will be a period of pure good luck, such as a lottery win, the meeting of a soulmate, or a once-in-a-lifetime business deal. So keep your eyes open, so that you don't waste your opportunities or take a wrong turning – and miss out on an amorous encounter!

If you were *born before the end of July*, you'll also get your chances, but in February, which is your best month and also a lucky one. More specifically, at the end of February you'll be exposed to a short-lived trine of Jupiter, Venus and Pluto, which will transform the influence of otherwise dissonant Neptune into general harmony. For example, this will be a dream of a time to form a partnership or get married; to set up an advertising or publishing firm; to do business abroad; or launch a company in the travel or tourism area. You should exploit this unique period to the full. For the rest of the year the opposition of Neptune (which will disturb Leos *born before the*

*28th*) could well obscure your vision; rob you of your objectivity and critical sense; and expose you to all sorts of errors of judgement or breaches of trust.

If you were born in this sector, it's also possible that your partner could pose problems for you: that your relationship could suddenly take on a sort of confused distance, a foggy quality which makes all authentic contact difficult, if not impossible. In brief, there will be dishonesty in the air (either imposed or suffered) and deception. March and April, in particular, will be marked by an especially sullen and confused climate which could depress you and take away your self-confidence. So react against this depressing atmosphere vigorously, and don't allow any person, situation or event to take away your leonine serenity, your lofty view. Cultivate positive thinking, as Saturn will place its lead cowl over your everyday life between March and the end of May. And if a door or two closes on you, hope that a third will open, which is wider and more grand.

Another time to watch is between July and October, when Jupiter's tension replaces Saturn's, creating a climate of agitation, turbulence and all sorts of excess and disorder. In fact July and October will be months that demand the utmost self-control on your part. And you should also know that (provided you were *born before the 28th*) Jupiter will probably give rise to worrying situations between July and October, which expose you to difficult choices and have repercussions next year. So don't get involved in hazardous undertakings this summer and don't get into debt, or you could have trouble paying it off next year.

Almost all the *second decan* is likely to be disrupted by Uranian tension. So, if you belong to this sector, you can expect dramatic turns of events in your life, 'electric' relationships with those close to you at certain times of the year, and probable changes in a joint venture, association or partnership. These changes could be outlined in the first six months of the year and become concrete any time from autumn onwards. And from the end of May until the end of the year, when Saturn will mix its tension with that of Uranus, you'll be least at ease with yourself

and others. A problem at work, a period of frustration, delays
and setbacks in your career, even perhaps a crisis of orientation,
will do nothing to sort out your possible relationship problem
either. So, rein yourself in hard when Mars makes you want to
kick off the traces in July to August. And take care then not to
exceed the limits of your own interests and aspirations. Caught
up in a sort of whirlwind, you could make decisions which later
you will regret.

All told, the *last decan* gets the best of this year. And from
January or February on, these subjects will gather the fruits of
previous efforts, in the form of a (probably professional) reward
or recognition of their worth; or through a strengthening of
their emotional ties. What's more, from the beginning of May
till the end of June, a lucky Jupiterian influence will present
them with all sorts of desirable windfalls, including the prospect
of a promotion at work, or the expansion of their business.
These Jupiterian benefits will also have repercussions after
October on the end of the year. If you're *last decan*, it's also
worth knowing that July and the beginning of October will
witness considerable progress towards your objectives; in fact,
you'll advance with giant strides. As you also will in January,
when nothing will limit your self-assurance or put you down!

### Virgo (23 August to 23 September)

Last year, Jupiter caused you all sorts of troubles in terms of
administrative worries or financial problems, particularly if you
are a *September Virgo*. And it's quite likely if you're *last decan*,
that at the start of 1999 you will suffer from the repercussions
of this tense Jupiterian period. Some of you will perhaps have
trouble repaying a debt; others will have problems with the
authorities; while others still will be victims of misunderstandings with their superiors at work. There's something for
everyone, and in February you could also have an emotional
problem, Virgo my friend (perhaps involving a difficult choice).
Happily, though, you'll be out of the woods from mid-February
on, and the stars will leave you in peace. So – if you're *last*

*decan* – you'll enter a calm period after mid-February, without any clashes or drastic changes (provided there's nothing to counter this on your personal chart).

Not so the *other decans*, however, who'll be strongly influenced by the end of this century's astral conjunctions. To be as precise as possible here, we need to divide the zodiacal cake into different slices – and remember, these forecasts are still collective...

If you were *born before 28 August*, you can celebrate. Firstly, Saturn (in March), then Jupiter (between July and October) will be there to protect your back and bring you (as a result of what has been brewing since last summer) a long-awaited and well-deserved award. Conscientious and efficient Virgo that you are, your worth will at last be recognised! From July on, Jupiter will lend its outgoing qualities and pure luck to your everyday life. And this will take the form of interesting opportunities and a renewed vital optimism, a positive attitude to life and people that will encourage and induce good luck.

If you were *born before 5 September* you can expect your life to be turned round from top to bottom in 1999. This fundamental change could well be to do with your family, perhaps involving the departure of a family member, or a separation, or it could simply entail moving home, which will deeply disturb your old habits and mark a new stage in your life. But whether or not this Plutonian tension brings you anything concrete or material, you can be sure it will generate a profound transformation in you, a sort of metamorphosis, which will totally modify your vision of the world. And you'll be a different person afterwards.

You, who so love your security, must try to avoid clinging onto the past. For this only encourages the sentiments of distress, remorse or guilt which often accompany a dissonant Pluto. Instead, swim with the tide towards the future; wed yourself to change, even if in a sense you have to die to be born again. Retain your faith in life and try to go beyond everyday trivia, to abandon the microscope in favour of the telescope, as it were, even though this is especially difficult for Virgos as they love detail. And bear in mind this paraphrase of the Bible: you have to be lost to find yourself again.

If you were *born between 3 and 11 September*, you'll benefit from a fine constructive trine of Saturn, which will give you a sense of stability from the end of May until the end of the year. More precisely, between the end of May and the end of August life will bring you – perhaps without your knowing it – the germ of some reward which you may only get at the end of the year or, more probably, next year. So be patient, and don't lose hope if you don't see results before the end of 1999. Your reward is just around the corner!

Saturn's stabilising influence on your life could also very well be manifest in an emotional tie, to which you suddenly attribute a fundamental and definitive importance, as could be the case at the end of May, in October or in December. Equally, a business matter from earlier in the year could begin at last to pay dividends in September or November. All told, then, a fine year – rewarding and constructive – is in sight, and an ideal one from which to enter the third millenium.

## Libra (23 September to 23 October)

1999 will be a golden year for the *first two decans*. And for the *last* it could hardly be more difficult, which is at least worth knowing if you have to show courage in the face of adversity and do battle against ill fortune!

The *last decan*, then, is the only one to have trouble with the heavens in this final year of the century. At the beginning of the year – particularly if you were *born after 17 October* – it's likely that you'll have problems in terms of your relationship with your loved one, or family in general; and that this will stem from last year. Given that Saturn is in your opposite sign of Aries, this problem will without doubt bear on your partner (private or professional) him/herself. For example, he or she could have contracted some illness last summer which will only be diagnosed at the end of 1998 and come to a head this January. Equally, in another scenario, troubles in your relationship with a business associate, which will date back to last summer, could reach their full magnitude at the beginning of 1999. Either way, though, things settle down after February and you should then have a trouble-free period until mid-May to the end of June; after which, more aggro! But this time to do with administrative, financial or legal difficulties, or a problem with the authorities or your superiors at work, which are all things you must not neglect if you don't want to suffer unpleasant consequences round the end of the year. As forewarned is forearmed, try not to make official approaches or take legal action during the spring – which will most likely have a negative effect on your winter.

If you were *born before 27 September*, on the other hand, you can celebrate. For February could bring the fulfilment of a dream and more luck than you ever hoped for. For some of you this could well be the lucky break of a lifetime, involving a totally unexpected gain, like winning the pools or a lottery. For others it will entail a leap into the limelight, artistically or politically, or in any event socially; in sum, a gift from the gods that's as unforeseen as it's significant.

*Beginning of October Librans* are protected by a sextile of Pluto. This will incite them to modify the framework of their environment and undertake wide-ranging negotiations. March will be the most propitious month, when they'll exceed their expectations and perhaps clinch a once-in-a-lifetime business deal. If your situation calls for it, you have every chance to start again from scratch and reconstruct your life on firm foundations. If you're ill, this is an ideal time for recovery and a spectacular cure, in other words to undergo medical treatment with the optimum chance of success. In brief, this is an assurance of much greater wellbeing, of quite extraordinarily moral and material luck. (By 'moral' I mean a disposition to see things in a positive light, which is already halfway to victory.)

Finally, if you were *born before 10 October*, Uranus will aid you in 1999, will give rise to sudden positive situations which could entirely change your life. If you belong to this sector you'll open yourself to new disciplines, perhaps astrology or computer science, which are both governed by Uranus. Or you could make the discovery of a lifetime. But in any event it's a certainty that something extraordinarily desirable will take place in your life in April, so much so that later on you'll look back and say, 'It happened in April 1999'!

### Scorpio (23 October to 22 November)

Glancing over your chart for 1999, a lot of red (dissonance) springs to my eyes, and not much blue. But as William of Orange said, 'One need not hope, to try; nor succeed, to persevere.' And being a Scorpio you know that well. You like adversity, in that it gives free rein to your well-known fighting spirit.

From the start of the year until mid-February, the *last decan* will harvest what it sowed since last spring, perhaps in the form of a business it founded then; or a marriage which it planned then and now goes through with; or some beneficial undertaking which· turns out entirely satisfactorily. From mid-February on, though, the year becomes more neutral, lacking any great tension, but equally without any great strokes of luck.

If you belong to the *first or second decan* (and particularly the latter), however, your heavens are more turbulent. So if you were *born before 10 November*, you'll be directly affected by this year's astral conjunction.

If you were born at the very beginning of the Sign, that's *before 29 October*, you'll have to face up to an ill-aspected Neptune right through the year. As a result, this planet will bring you confusion and perplexity, errors of judgement and castles in the air. And that's not all. Saturn will mingle its discordant rays with those of Neptune between March and the end of May; and from July to the end of October will be replaced by Jupiter, which is as good as saying you probably won't have much in the way of peace of mind or spirit in 1999, especially in March, April, July and October. So fortify yourself against the cosmic winds and tides with patience, optimism, faith in life and in yourself (which, in particular, you're not lacking anyhow). Try to think of the glass of life as half full, rather than half empty, and don't let yourself get beaten down by gloomy ideas which are entirely due to the negative rays of Neptune and Saturn. Above all, remind yourself that we attract what we radiate or emit; and if you emit negative and sombre thoughts, if you doubt yourself and the world, good luck will pass you by.

In more concrete terms, it's highly likely that March and April will bring the outcome of a problem which dates back to last year (probably last summer) and which up to now you weren't aware of. This could have to do with your partner, could entail trouble in your relationship, a progressive distancing or, in some instances, an illness he or she will have contracted.

Between July and October, Jupiter will join his contrary ways to those of Neptune, increasing your spiritual confusion; you'll feel pulled hither and thither by circumstances, be perplexed and not know where to turn for a solution. So try to understand what your problems are, to reflect on them calmly and if possible rationally, even if Neptune's dissonance tends to deprive you of all objectivity. Get the advice of a lucid and honest friend, who seeks neither to flatter nor deceive you. Finally, be extremely careful financially around July, and don't take on obligations or debts that you won't be able to honour in the future. For you'll still have to contend with Jupiter in the year 2000, and any mistakes in the summer of 1999 could very well have ill-fated results. By getting to grips with your problems now, though, you'll diminish their repercussions early next year.

All told, you'll have one of your most difficult periods of the year in July, and particularly mid-July. You'll find yourself in an extremely stressful situation then, which you must counter with the greatest calm you can muster. For Mars will add to the cosmic turbulence and tend to make you careless or brutal in your decisions, which you must avoid at all costs.

Scorpios *born between 27 October and 2 November* can expect a relatively calm year lacking in major turbulence. But those *born between 2 and 10 November* will be simultaneously disturbed by a square of Uranus and the opposition of Saturn. The former could bring all sorts of changes and dramatic events to your life during the first six months of the year, which will have repercussions until next year (when you'll be settled into a new situation); while from May on, Saturn will contribute its planetary tension until the end of the year. So it's a sure bet that, for the great majority of you, the resultant conflict will involve their family or an emotional partnership.

August, in particular, should be watched in this respect, as it will encourage untimely reactions on your part which could pass the point of no return. Watch out for accidents in this period, too. For a dissonant Mars and Uranus – especially when supported by Saturn – give rise to all sorts of disappointments, incidents or accidents ... including those of mechanical origin. And under this influence one is also exposed to falls and fractures, which in your case are most likely to be to the legs, which are one of your Sign's weak areas. So take care if you're water-skiing or windsurfing.

In general, then, my advice is to hold fast against the cosmic winds and tides. And if nothing else, by measuring yourself against adversity, you'll come to appreciate your true limits and capabilities.

And as Clint Eastwood once said, 'A man's gotta know his limitations.'

### Sagittarius (22 November to 22 December)

Sagittarius, my friend, you have something to write home about! Your Sign is one of the luckiest and most protected of all in 1999. Only the beginning of the year could be disturbing, and this only for the *last decan*, which will be somewhat bothered by Jupiter. If you belong to this sector, in fact, your planetary ruler could well bring you the bill for your errors which you committed between May and October last year. For example, if you took legal action, or someone tried to take you to court ... or if you took on a heavy debt, now comes the disagreeable time for settlement. But you can console yourself in that, after the middle of February, these worries will have gone like a puff of smoke.

Actually, you'll clearly feel the supportive influence of Saturn from as early as mid-January; and this will serve as a shield against your troubles and help you find surprise solutions. In a totally different area, you'll also be the lucky beneficiary of a reward or recognition of your merits, which will satisfy your prestige, quite apart from your Jupiterian worries. Staying with the *last decan*, from the beginning of May till the end of June a trine of Jupiter – your ruler – will bring you all sorts of possibilities for expansion and extrovert activity which I'm sure you'll know how to get the best from. This should yield results in the last two or three months of the year, with the prospect of a delightful prolongation into the beginning of 2000. So, if you belong to the 'tail' of your Sign, the Centaur, you have little to complain about this year, which will probably reach its peak of effectiveness and good luck in May to June: a period you should not neglect.

If you were born in the *first two decans*, on the other hand, the omens are even more positive. In fact, if you were *born before 10 December* (the remaining days of the *second decan* are neutral, I'm afraid), you can congratulate yourself on this year's influences. They'll take you far and wide, place you on a launching pad, and promise you luck and success, positive changes and all sorts of windfalls, right through this year.

*First decans* will have their hour of glory and good luck in February to March, while *second decans* must wait until April to enjoy absolutely spectacular opportunities, which are as unexpected as they are exciting. What's more, round mid-April, they can expect a real stroke of luck which will allow them to change their status quo completely and improve their current position in a noteworthy way. Some can count on a promotion at work, others on being put into orbit by a business enterprise in which their personality, originality and daring really blossom. If you belong to this sector, you'll often have both the desire, and the opportunity with it, to set yourself up in business on your own, to become your own master – and in the best possible conditions, with the maximum chance of success. In fact, if you belong to the *first two decans*, on the whole the first three months of the year could be so profitable they will have you saying 'Nothing's impossible for a Sagittarian'!

Subjects born in the *first week of December* deserve special mention. For they will be marked by the direct transit of Pluto, which will radically transform their lives – much to their delight, I'm sure. For isn't Sagittarius (along with Aquarius) one of the Signs that most loves change? It's worth knowing, in any case, that Pluto will influence your situation in such a way as to alter it entirely, and transform you inside as well. And in March, especially, you can expect to make a new departure – and one which I hope will be mighty and crowned with success!

### Capricorn (22 December to 20 January)

The celestial favours in 1999 are clearly divided, Capricorn my friend. And the *first two decans*, and particularly Capricorns *born before 8 January*, are clearly favoured, while the *last decan* has problems with this year's conjunction.

Let's start with the *first two decans*, though we have to distinguish between the first and second. If you were born in December and more specifically *before Christmas*, you'll have the leisure and pleasure to gather the fruits of your labours last year. This will happen from March onwards, but especially in the summer. Some subjects could be rewarded with success in a competition or an examination; others could see the long-awaited fulfilment of a major project; others still can expect important recognition in their career, possibly a distinction or promotion. And even if, in March itself, Jupiterian dissonance comes to trouble the atmosphere and inject disorder into your daily life, you'll feel the stabilising effects of Saturn. (In any case, the possibly difficult choices and problems of paperwork Jupiter brings will be short lived and inconsequential.)

What's more, from the beginning of July, Jupiter will be well-aspected for you and admirably favour your aspirations and undertakings, especially if you were *born before 26 December*. Keep your eyes and ears open during this phase which ends in October. For the opportunities which could occur now are likely to have extremely fortunate repercussions next year, the first of an entirely new century. Many of you, for example, will decide this summer to get married next year, in February to March. Others will conceive a child in July, which will be born in March. Others still will think about founding a business which will have every chance of success early in the year 2000.

If you're *second decan*, some very fine aspects await you in 1999. But they'll nonetheless put your patience to the test, as you won't enjoy their rewards until next year, though what satisfaction you have in prospect then! And, as a result of Saturn's positive influences from May until December, you can hope to end the century duly recognised by your peers. You will reassert your position; consolidate your gains; find your true place in the sun – all as the result of repercussions from the second half of this year. So this period, which promises to be so explosive in global terms, will be especially propitious for you; you'll be swept on towards your objectives at a gallop and, whatever happens, be protected by the cosmos – which is essential, given the worrying situation in the world at large. For many *second decans* this will also be the time to consolidate an emotional tie, particularly at the end of October or end of November.

As we mentioned earlier, the *last decan* is less favoured. Its year begins with a mixed climate: problematic, on one side, as a result of last year (perhaps the last phase of an illness or emotional worry which could lead to separation); while on the other side the coin is positive, even if only in terms of a reinforced vital optimism, the sort of serenity that goes with a nudge from Lady Luck, and serves as a shield against adversity.

At the end of February, Saturn will cease to manhandle you, but you won't be out of the woods. For Jupiter enters the cosmic dance at the beginning of May, to complicate your business life, bring disorder to your everyday life and upset your dealings with the authorities or those senior to you at work. Pay particular attention during this spring phase to potential worries and try to nip them in the bud, or you could have disagreeable news after October. In other words, this is not the time to take legal action or incur major debt, which you could find unacceptable at the end of 1999 or beginning of 2000.

Still ... as a Capricorn, forewarned is forearmed, you're now equipped to cheat adversity! And, you'll be pleased to hear, next year will be better by far.

## Aquarius (20 January to 19 February)

Aquarius, my friend, you are one of the Signs most affected by the astral conjunction of 1999. As you already know, Neptune has been in your zodiac since last year, which only happens once in a 164-year cycle. What's more, Uranus, your ruler, has been there two years as well (in itself a rare occurrence, as this planet only visits your Sign every 84 years). So it's easy to see, under the influence of two such rare and powerful transits, that both one's psyche and where one is going in life can be radically marked and distorted. Though, of course, these transits do not affect all your Sign...

In fact, Neptune traverses the first four degrees of Aquarius, having a disturbing effect on your life if you were *born before 25 January*. According to whether your natal Sun is harmonious or dissonant, this planet's influence will be very different, going from one extreme to another. At its best, in a positive mode, Neptune introduces a climate of extraordinary expansion, of sudden brilliant stardom. And on another plane, one develops an almost mediumistic intuition and exceptional sensitivity and receptiveness. At its worst, however, in a negative mode, Neptune can signify ruin, loss of prestige, scandal or breach of trust, and a climate of intrigue which results in false manoeuvres and catastrophic muddles. Neptune can make you a poet, musician, prophet or cosmopolitan businessman. And it can see you a tramp, or a drug addict, as it also favours flight from reality, the artificial paradise. If you're in any doubt, then, distrust this climate. For, whatever happens, it will rob you of much of your objectivity and critical faculties. And when our judgement is less certain, reality diminishes.

If you belong to this *first sector of the Sign*, you'll feel this influence very clearly, if ambiguously, in March. In fact, the dissonant Saturnian energy which suffuses this spring month could blur your family situation and might possibly cause a problem there. Yet after mid-February, Jupiter – the planet of fullness, wellbeing and pure luck – will effectively guard your back, and could even push you to the forefront in a significant way. This influence could also be manifest on a mental or psychic plane, causing you to blossom, and bringing you an irreplaceable inner peace. However, on the purely material level, I think if I was a very early Aquarius I'd buy a lottery ticket or do the pools in the last two weeks of February!

Nevertheless, Saturn's negative energy continues to expand throughout the spring, leading – in its critical phase – to a possible family problem. And this is certainly not the time to move or buy a house, as the omens regarding this are far from propitious.

Between May and the end of June, you'll enjoy a sort of truce. Then from July to mid-October, Jupiter will appear with a vengeance, throwing oil onto the fire: perhaps making you spend huge sums on setting up house; or simply scattering confusion, disorder, and lack of organisation into your present home. So be careful, if you're this sector, not to take on excessive debts which will fall due in the spring of 2000. They could bleed you dry.

If you were *born between 28 January and 7 February*, you can sleep easy. You'll have Pluto to act as a guardian and source of psychic energy for you. In March, Jupiter and Pluto together are simultaneously favourable. So this is a period of pure luck, which you mustn't miss out on. Business people could sign the contract of a lifetime; while other Aquarians will throw themselves into the unknown – in terms of a new enterprise – with a guarantee of absolute success (that's if there's nothing in their personal charts to contradict these auguries).

This extremely positive phase will extend into April, when Uranus will be well aspected. So if you were *born in the first week of February*, profit from this, by changing everything in your life that bothers or displeases you. But do it while you can. For after May, Saturn will enter your Sign and stay there till the end of the year. It will put spokes in your wheels, cause all sorts of inconvenience, and slow down and hinder your progress. What's more, the Uranian energy, which during the first five months of the year proved positive, will suddenly change under Saturn's dissonance and make you more nervous than ever. You'll be almost 'electric', and seem to people around you to be verging at times on the hysterical. This is because the vibratory rate of Uranus is very high and powerfully bears on the nervous system, so insomnia is common under this influence. And when one also has to take on a negative energy like Saturn's at the same time, the resultant burden can be heavy. You could even find yourself going through cyclical phases ranging from feverish exaltation to despondency – the first caused by Uranus, the second by Saturn. Certain phases will cause you to make decisions at a moment's notice, and perhaps not always fortunately (particularly between July and mid-September), while at other times, under the influence of Saturn, you'll come to a dead halt in a rigid and intolerant attitude. And angelic Aquarian that you are, you'll be unrecognisable!

React by trying to master these spiritual states, which is best achieved through meditation, yoga and relaxation – all powerful antidotes to mental over-excitement. You should also avoid taking risks in terms of health as here too – particularly in July to August – you'll be exposed to all sorts of feelings of discomfort, probably of a psychosomatic origin. Watch out for overwork and stress, for throat infections, circulatory problems and eye troubles, which can also have a nervous or psychic origin. And if you're the sporty type, avoid violent games in mid-February, July to August, and in December.

Finally, if you feel worn out, it's worth remembering that your trace elements are manganese-cobalt, and your Schussler salt is sodium chloride.

### Pisces (19 February to 21 March)

Pisces my friend, there's a fine optimistic curve on your chart this year, and something for all tastes and every sector of your Sign!

The heavens will start by spoiling the *last decan* between the beginning of the year and mid-February: Jupiter will bring you the realisations of your dreams then, in an absolutely superb and virtually cloudless astral climate. This will be an ideal time, for instance, to get married, if you haven't already done so last year, or to launch a new business. A time, then, that for *last decans* could prove a real milestone in their lives.

But last decans aren't the only ones rewarded with celestial favours. Between the beginning of March and the end of May, Saturn will bring *February Pisceans* a long-awaited bonus. This will most likely be in the form of spin-offs from last summer or autumn, especially if you were *born before 25 February.* You'll be rewarded and stabilised in your situation and gains, socially anchored in a greater wellbeing. And simultaneously Saturn will make you want to organise your time better, to cut out superficial or useless pursuits, which will suddenly seem just a waste of effort. And when an excellent Jupiterian influence dawns between July and the end of October, you'll have no desire to stay cloistered at home. On the contrary, you'll be burning to express yourself and follow up some, or all, of the offers which pour from Jupiter's horn of plenty. Be sure not to neglect these. They could have delicious results in the spring of next year.

If you're *second decan,* you're really in luck. From the end of May till the end of the year, Saturn will give a more solid basis to your mental, social and working life – and perhaps your love life, too – while between the beginning of June and the end of August many Pisces subjects will see the dawn of possible promotion or some major professional satisfaction; though they'll have to be patient, as the real results won't come until early next year. What's certain is that Saturn will bring you the need to be more selective in your social relationships, and more serious in your intellectual pursuits. So it's possible you could become interested in a science or austere discipline; or that you'll take on a long-term project which won't see daylight till the first three months of 2000.

All the same, some Pisceans will be unsettled in 1999. By and large, these are born in the *first week of March.* And they've some disruption in prospect! Many of you will totally change your career, your aims, your destiny; others will find spectacular stardom socially, but be uncomfortable in their private lives. Others still will change partner. But whatever the semi-obligatory change which takes place in your life – and especially in your system of reference or vision of the world – try to adapt yourself to it. It's in your Piscean nature anyway. And this way you won't succumb to the distress, destructive emotions or negative thoughts which Pluto's adverse energy can give rise to. Watch out, too, for psychosomatic illnesses. It has been statistically established that there is a correlation between the appearance of certain tumours and Plutonian dissonance, though I believe these negative physical manifestations can only come about if one lets oneself be so open to depressing situations and thoughts that they set off a self-destructive force in us.

So concede. Let go. 'Let it Be', as the Beatles said. For this is the only way to wed yourself to change, to swim with the current, to say *yes* to Life. And that's what I wish you, Pisces my friend, on this eve of the third millenium.

# *2000*

## The course of the planets

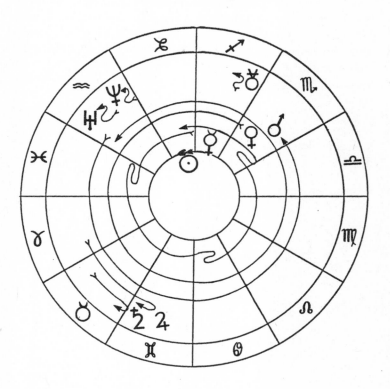

# World Events

In March, under a square of Jupiter and Neptune, there will still be confusion in the air, flowing on from the summer of 1999. Beware of false prophets, gurus and other 'wise men' who seek power over impressionable minds...

In May, Saturn and then Jupiter will be in opposition to Uranus. This will result in a hardening of authority combined with a spirit of revolt and insurrection, that will make this first spring of the century a 'hot' one. These dissonances introduce a solemn conjunction of Jupiter and Saturn, ending a cycle that began in 1980-1 (when the 10-member Europe was born) and beginning a new cycle which will open a new and constructive phase for the European entity ... until 2010. The king is dead, long live the king! The twentieth century is dead and gone, long live the third millenium!

And at least this begins with a good-looking trine of Jupiter and Neptune, which symbolises a world at peace, inspired with a rediscovered faith: perhaps a faith in man and in humanity.


# Your Personal Forecast

### Aries (21 March to 20 April)

Aries, my friend, magnificent prospects lie before you in this first year of the new millenium. There's not a false note or cloud in your heavens. Quite the contrary, your skies radiate planetary harmonies, which will lighten your journey and protect your progress. And the first *two decans* are the most spoiled of all.

Nonetheless, it's the *last decan* that opens the year with a fanfare, thanks to the presence of Jupiter in its sector of the zodiac. These subjects will reap the rewards of opportunities that have been germinating since last May; and their prospects will be superb, though unfortunately somewhat short lived, as after mid-February Jupiter passes into Pisces. Not that this is anything to worry about for, even without 'the Great Bene-factor', your year is no more difficult or burdensome as it's entirely without dissonance.

And though the *last decan* will have its best times in an hour of glory at the beginning of the year – when you'll attain virtually all your objectives and can realise a dream, which for many of you will mean marriage or an emotionally significant meeting – you won't be without planetary support later on in the year. In fact, Mars, your ruler, will fill you with new energy that will further the success of your undertakings, particularly in the first two weeks in June and first two weeks of September.

If you belong to the *first two decans*, sustained by the planetary trio of Pluto, Neptune and Uranus, you have nothing to fear from your entry into the third millenium. If you were *born before 27 March*, you'll benefit from a sextile of Neptune which will open you to new realities, often of an invisible, subtle, mystical or artistic nature. You'll have a less pragmatic and realistic (though real enough!) vision of life and your intuition will flourish, which even in practical life can be a great help. You'll instinctively know what's right for you and choose the correct solutions. In love, you'll be idealistic and tend to sublimate your emotions, while for some subjects this year offers growing notoriety or even sudden stardom.

In the first ten days of April we need to distinguish between those *born in the first four days of the month* and those born afterwards. The former will enjoy a superb trine of Pluto, which will give them the opportunity to start again from scratch, to fly off in a new direction in life. There will be fundamental changes in situations which dissatisfy you, health readjustments, and spectacular improvements accompanied by cosmic protection. This is because Pluto enhances our physical tone, increases our strength of character and, in addition, develops an instinctive awareness in us of what's good for us. What's more, it tends to favour a positive consensus around us, which helps give concrete form to our aspirations. As Pluto this year is in Sagittarius, a Sign allotted to travel and also philosophy, you could be seized by a desire to move abroad, or take a sabbatical year touring the world; equally, you could devote yourself to detailed intellectual, philosophical or metaphysical research.

And if you were *born after the 4th*, you can be equally pleased, as in your case Uranus will focus on your fate and give rise to exciting situations. You'll have the chance to widen your field of consciousness in every sense of the term, to open your horizons and undertake all sorts of new and exciting activities. As Uranus will be in its own Sign of Aquarius, which also stands for friendship and projects, these two areas will no doubt be highlighted in your life as well. In brief, you'll be in on, 'turned on' to, everything that's happening, and you'll have the desire to innovate more than ever and steam ahead. And, more than usually, you'll also want to share, to show solidarity and play an effective and fraternal role in society and your own immediate circle. On the personal level you'll also have every chance to climb the social ladder and, overnight, see spectacular improvements in your material conditions thanks to a promotion or similar surprise.

I tell you, this is a wonderful year. Make sure you get the very best out of it!

## Taurus (20 April to 21 May)

'There's always sunshine after rain' ... and the reverse. After the exceptional years you had at the end of the 1980s and beginning of the 1990s (thanks to planets in Capricorn which sent your Sign positive energy), you are at present, unfortunately, down in the dumps. For the zodiacal wheel turns, and after the ebb comes the flow. Not that this sort of explanation really satisfies the realistic and pragmatic Taurean you undoubtedly are. And even if I promise you that, after 2003, everything will go really smoothly, this may not do much to console you...

If you belong to the very first days of your Sign – were *born before 24 April* – you will probably have experienced Neptune's vaguely depressing climate last year: will have felt you were 'cycling in sauerkraut' and not known which way to turn. And, unfortunately, this climate will continue this year and perhaps with a fresh outburst of confusion and woolliness.

As by nature you are a vital and positive Sign, call on your innate sense of life to thumb your nose at Neptune and its phantoms of distress. Even if things become complicated, if the atmosphere of your business and daily life deteriorates, if you feel that the more you try to inject some order into your existence, the more muddled it becomes ... don't use this as an excuse to throw yourself into an eating binge, or seek escape in drugs or alcohol, which are useless remedies. As Neptune also makes you more vulnerable to drugs or intoxicants, that makes this a double warning.

As it's helpful to know what's coming, the better to confront it, it's worth knowing that Neptune's confusion will probably reach its peak in March. So don't take any important decisions then, as you'll lack objectivity; and be careful when Jupiter enters your sector of the zodiac, as it will increase your confidence in yourself and others, and tend to mask Neptune's deceptive influence. Watch out, too, for viral contagion and for food or medicinal poisoning at the end of March/beginning of April and the beginning of August. And don't build castles in the air, emotionally, at the end of February, in March, at the end of June, or end of September.

If you were *born in the first ten days of May* the presence of Saturn in your Sign, coupled with the energy of Uranus, will destabilise your life and fill it with turmoil. From April on, the entry of Jupiter into Taurus – which normally should be excellent news – will only throw oil on the fire and amplify your existing problems. You won't know which way to turn, and run the risk of acting impulsively as the result of false inspiration. In brief, from the beginning of the year, you'll be plunged into a contradictory climate of dramas, unpleasant surprises, abrupt changes, and you'll want to retreat into yourself, to review and sort out your life. The tidal wave of Uranus could well do it for you, when April and May bring this stressful, and somehow electric, climate to its peak. You can expect radical changes in your situation then, particularly if you were *born between 5 and 12 May.*

Some advice: take time to relax, to lose your tension and calm a nervous system which has too many demands made on it. Don't be hasty or too nervous, which could result in wrong moves and accidents, particularly in April and August. As a self-respecting Taurus, you naturally detest improvisation; but this year you'll be obliged to deal with the unforeseeable. As a last resort, then, tell yourself that everything that happens is for the best; and that positive thinking is one of the most valuable antidotes to adversity.

All told, only the *last decan* seems favoured with good influences this year as – particularly between June and July – it will experience the double, and extremely constructive, presence of Jupiter and Saturn in its natal Sun, which sould be a guarantee of considerable concrete fulfilment. If you're *last decan*, these two months will definitely be the best of the year. And if you take on long-term work then, or someone puts a proposition to you, you'll most probably have news of it after October, with interesting echoes or results in 2001.

Saturn's transit will bring many *last decans* consolidation of their gains, a recognition of their merits and sometimes even a sort of consecration; while for others it could induce a relatively painful period, which could entail separation and a harsh reassessment, in which you're forced to see things and people unembellished, as they really are. This climate could well affect you between mid-October and the end of the year, when you'll no longer have Jupiter to sprinkle its vital optimism into your heart and life. Having said that, bank on June and July, which promise to be a major turning-point in your life, and in most cases a fantastically constructive one. This should generally be an ideal time to launch a business, form a partnership, conceive a child: in other words, a major landmark in the course of your life, which I hope it will be.

Good luck!

## *Gemini (21 May to 21 June)*

Gemini, my friend, if you were *born at the end of May or very beginning of June*, you probably felt the beginnings of a Plutonian change last year. Most probably in terms of your partner or associate, Pluto has already begun to unsettle your status quo. And it will continue its undermining work until radically new conditions prevail in your life.

This year Pluto will bring Geminis *born around 2 June* the completion of this fundamental change. It will most probably come to fruition in August, September or October (the most critical months of the year for you) when you'll most need to call on your inner resources. This influence will also extend to subjects *born on 6 June*, for whom it will open up an era of profound transformation which will only be realised next year. So, as it's better to be safe than sorry, have a thorough medical check-up to assess and remedy any possible deficiencies. For Pluto favours the appearance of all sorts of illnesses which are difficult to diagnose, and especially benign – or even malign – tumours. And as you are an easily influenced Sign (because you're always prepared to see two sides of a question) it will be necessary for you, under this compulsion, to change, to choose between the past and the future. So accept change, swim with the current, and you'll be all right in the long run.

Geminis of *around 21–23 May* (as well as *very early June* subjects) could well have a rough ride from the rare appearance of Saturn this year. For, though Saturn can bring the realisation of hopes and reward for past efforts, it frequently symbolises a period of turning in on oneself, of limitations and setbacks, and least luck: in essence, then, a period in which one has more trouble making progress or imposing one's point of view. As a result, one tends to tidy up one's life, eliminate frivolity, and only keep what's essential. For you Geminis who often flit from one thing to another and have relatively short-lived and frivolous relationships, it's an influence which will hardly delight you. But it's nonetheless necessary, if you want to make progress on the path to wisdom. Between August and October, very early Geminis will feel the effects of this influence strongly, and have repercussions from it next year.

I've only good news for the rest of the Sign, though. And particularly those *born between 23 May and 13 June* (excluding, of course, those born in the first week of June). If you're *first decan*, you'll benefit from a trine of Neptune. This will widen your mental and psychic horizons, accentuate your subtle intuition, and open you to superior realities, which have nothing to do with everyday pragmatism. In July to August, and then from October till the end of the year (thanks to Jupiter joining Neptune in your zodiac), you'll enjoy an absolutely superb, extremely fertile period, when all your hopes will be viable. This will encourage many of you to get married, or to start up a business in which you'll find the independence that's so dear to you. And for many a Gemini this phase will even bring fame, as Neptune will magnify Jupiter's luck,

*Second decan subjects born after 6 June* are also very well aspected, thanks to Uranus this time, which will lift them to higher spheres and fill them with an irresistible desire to change their lives and fly off to new horizons. This is because Uranus not only widens our intellectual perspectives, but also gives rise to all sorts of fortunate and unexpected events that help us on towards our aspirations. Overnight, as it were, you could meet the person who will change your destiny, either in business or in love.

The most favourable times on the heart side for *all the Sign* will be: from mid-February to mid-March, in April, at the time of your birthday, the end of July, September and the end of December. You are already sociable and communicative and, under Uranus' exciting trine, you'll widen your circle of relationships. And many Geminis will want to devote them-selves to the community, to undertake an activity involving humanism and solidarity.

The *last decan*, for its part, will be somewhat left out this year, except during the first two months. But they'll really be lucky and take off then! They'll make an enviable impact on people and things and move forward with giant strides, fulfilling many of their secret aspirations. What's more, for many *last decans* this period will see the fulfilment and realisation of

promises that have been in the air since last spring or autumn.
All the best!

### Cancer (21 June to 22 July)

Apart from a slightly cloudy start for the *last decan* in January,
your sky is blue in the year 2000, all blue. In fact, overall, your
chart for this year, that opens a new millenium, presents a
delightful picture!

If you're a *second decan* Cancer, what you did between June
and the end of last year will at last bear fruit, which you'll
harvest in the first four months of this year. For some, this will
mean success in a competition or examination; for others, the
successful completion of a project which cost them a lot of effort,
patience and time. For others still, there will be a reward: some
recognition or other of their worth, most probably professional;
while others again will stabilise an emotional tie, which will then
be long-lasting.

So there's only good news, in sum, which ought to have the
maximum chance of happening between April and mid-May,
when Jupiter will mingle its beneficial rays with Saturn's positive
influence. So if you're born in this sector of the Sign, this will be
your most constructive period. This is also a good time to put your
plans into practice, for they'll have everything going for them.
Your friendships will be set fair too, and, to your delight old
acquaintances will resurface. So profit from all this to give concrete
form to your aspirations and to delight in the joys of friendship.

If you're *first decan*, from mid-February to the end of March
will be the most beneficial time for you, thanks to Jupiter.
That's not to say that this is the only positive and fertile period
of the year, but it's certainly the most constructive and lucky. If
you belong to the *last decan*, on the other hand, the period
May/June/July will bring you the most satisfaction, possibly in
the form of promises that are only fulfilled after October. In
prospect, though, is a secure consolidation of your situation, a
reward for past efforts and a gratifying recognition of your
merits. It's also possible that, if you were *born after the 17th*,

you'll only enjoy these rewards in 2001. All the same, you'll still have an exquisite and very lucky time in May to June. Jupiter will see to it! And as these influences will still be present, though waning, at the time of your birthday, it's a safe bet you'll experience their constructive benefits all year long and until your next birthday.

*All the Sign* will enjoy a greatly increased vitality and revived spirit of enterprise in April, from mid-June to the end of July, and from mid-September to the end of October. And love will shine on your horizon from mid-March to the beginning of April, in May, from mid-June to mid-July, in August and in October. So, you see, you have a good many sunny periods in this solemn year of 2000.

## Leo (22 July to 23 August)

If you were born at the very beginning of your Sign, *around 23–24 July*, I've excellent news for you. In August, September or October, you'll take on something that will have long-term effects on the year 2001, effects which will be entirely satisfying. You'll establish your position, and your true leonine value will be recognised.

There's also good news for the first half of your Sign, more precisely those *born before 6 August.* Your best period will be in the last six months of the year, between July and December, when Jupiter will enter your zodiac and cover you with his heavenly manna. This will take the form of offers or propositions which further your objectives. And the period September to October will be especially beneficial, giving you the opportunity to change what you want to in your life, with every chance of success. It's also likely that you profit then from a context that favours you but could bother others, and thus are the beneficiary of a strained or litigious situation.

Pluto will act as a catalyst of change for you: change which will come about gently and which you'll be able to control, and very profitable and beneficial it will be. That's if you were *born between 2 and 6 August.* If you were *born around the 2nd or 3rd* you will have already seen this start last year. And now Pluto will help you to fit more effectively and happily into your social situation, to move up a notch, and in fact find yourself in some way or other in the driving seat.

For some Leos, Pluto will definitely bring a highly lucrative deal ... even fortune. (The word 'plutocrat' comes from Pluto and, as you know, means somebody very rich!) But it's chiefly on the psychic and philosophical plane that you'll go through an important and positive change which will open you to other, hitherto ignored, realities.

However, we need to make a slight exception in this first half of the Sign. While the *first decan* will be positively influenced by Jupiter in the last six months of the year, if you were *born between the 24th and the end of July*, Neptune will bring negative energies into your life. Its dissonance could well encourage you to believe that the moon is made of green cheese and to build castles in the air, either in business or in love. In business, the danger of this will be acute at the end of January, and end of April/beginning of May; while on the heart side, you run the risk of throwing yourself blindfold into a nebulous and possibly disappointing affair at the end of February or beginning of May. On the health side, too, Neptune will make you more vulnerable to viral infection, particularly at the end of March/beginning of April.

As for the *second half of the Sign* – with the exception of January, when Jupiter's generosity will bring the *last decan* all sorts of satisfaction and happiness, – things won't be that great this year. Particularly in April, May and June (which probably are your most difficult times) things could well become remarkably complicated and really unsettle your life. You will be pulled hither and thither by astral influences and for many of you this will result in a professional or partnership problem. Watch out particularly in April, when there will be flying crockery if you don't succeed in controlling yourself. April and August are the two periods when Mars adds its discordant notes to the already strained cosmic concert. So take care then to avoid being too forceful with your family; and watch out for a mechanical accident, too.

For some of you a trial or other legal matter could be in the air, and become defined, in all probability, between April and May, when Jupiter will also be involved. In any event, I advise you in this coming astral storm to try to keep calm at any price and to slow down, as Uranus incites our nervous systems to excess; predisposes us to thoughtless and regrettable acts, and inclines us to an abruptness that does not lend itself to harmony. As a square of Saturn could also establish a distance between you and others, try to compensate for these difficult cosmic influences through conciliation and regard for others.

If you belong to the *middle of the Sign* (*born around 7–8 July*), changes introduced by Uranus at the beginning of the year will only be fulfilled at year's end when, without doubt, you'll be settled into a new situation.

The *last decan*, for its part, will be afflicted by a square of Saturn between the beginning of May and the beginning of August; and you mustn't underestimate the troubles which could loom on the horizon as a result; they could multiply at the end of the year and even be prolonged into 2001.

Happily, Mars will give *all your Sign* a renewed vigour and spirit of enterprise, which will help you take the bull by the horns, from mid-February to the end of March, from the beginning of May to mid-June, and all through August – when this Martian energy could even be excessive or untimely, and should therefore be watched. Mars will also be beneficial, and galvanise you, in November to December.

Make the most of it!

## Virgo (23 August to 23 September)

If you're *second decan*, you'll be delighted to learn that your merits will be recognised and rewarded during the first four months of this famous year 2000. More precisely, you'll reap the benefits of something put forward in, or germinating since, the end of May 1999 (when you may yourself have started a long-term project, which will now be happily realised).

What's more, Jupiter in Taurus will sustain Saturn's already positive influence from mid-February till the end of June. And this applies to *all the Sign.* So the first six or seven months of the year will be the best in the world for you, Virgo my friend. Travel, foreign lands, publishing, advertising, even politics are all areas particularly protected by this conjunction. In the same way (via Saturn) going abroad or buying a house are highly favoured.

If you belong to the *last decan*, it's possible you could start looking for this house between May and the end of July, find it between October and December, and only actually buy it in 2001. This is more or less the timing that will govern what you achieve, whatever particular field it may be in. But, in any event, it will prove rewarding, constructive and secure.

For *second decans*, April and May will be an absolutely unique time this year – and perhaps for some years to come – as many Virgos will attain the goal they set their sights on a long time ago, and build a solid and lasting future as a result. This will be a period of extraordinary expansion, fulfilment and success, no matter what your activity. On the heart side, in business, in terms of health ... everything will go well – and as you want it to.

Nevertheless, the dissonance of Pluto, which is in the background, throughout the year, will alter the lives of Virgos *born in the first week in September.* A family problem could be more or less directly linked to a deep transformation that will take place in your mind and, no doubt, in your life. What's certain is that, if you belong to this sector of the Sign, you won't emerge from this influence the same. Your personality, your conception of life, will be changed. There's a 'before' and 'after' with Pluto. And when it destabilises us, we're obliged to choose between the past and the future.

You'll most strongly feel this astral shock and its repercussions on your spiritual state in September to October, when Jupiter will team up with Pluto to help destabilise you. You'll have the impression – rightly – that family and professional problems are tangled up and interdependent, the one bringing on the other. In fact, the lives of many *beginning of September Virgos* could well capsize at this time, their destinies change radically. So a warning is necessary here. As Mars will also transit your Sign at this time it will throw oil on the fire and turn a wise Virgo into a foolish one, ready for every excess and liable to every pitfall. So stay circumspect and keep yourself on a tight rein during this period, in order to avoid mistakes which will be irreversible. Your family will help you out, and a dialogue with friends or loved ones will guide you.

### Libra (23 September to 23 October)

It's extremely pleasant for an astrologer to see such a brilliant chart! In fact, looking at the auguries which concern you, one's struck by the planetary harmony that affects all sectors, apart from the *last decan* which, unfortunately, is not on this year's prize list. It will even suffer at the beginning of the year and until mid-February from the opposition of Jupiter, which will bring the bill for last year's mistakes or overestimation. For some this will be tax audit, or settlement of a legal matter; for others money worries or problems in their relationships with their partners or superiors at work. Fortunately the worst will be over by mid-February and the rest of the year will flow by peacefully without a hitch, even it is equally devoid of any great promise.

Librans *born around 26–27 September* will probably get the best of this year. They'll have an absolutely exceptional July, which looks set to show that all their dreams and expectations are right! There's no doubt that luck will come knocking at their door. Many will have a gambling win, while others will think about getting married, even if they don't do it till the beginning of 2001. All the *first decan*, protected from the beginning of July until the end of the year, will feel buoyed up by new inspiration, and by a faith in itself, other people and life that will encourage Lady Luck.

Whether you're a business person or a poet, Neptune and Jupiter will team up to guide you towards success. And if you're a *first week in October Libran*, Pluto will help you transform yourself, to go forward and evolve in a positive way that will bring you in range of your ideals. Thanks to Uranus, if you were *born between 6 and 12 October*, you'll progress with giant strides to surprise windfalls, which will change your life overnight. Generous and fair-minded Libran that you are deep down, you will suddenly have every chance to devote yourself to society and contribute your share of innovation and imagination in a spirit of solidarity. And some of you will take up a humanitarian cause or become absorbed in a totally unexpected pastime which will transport you to unknown realms.

For *all the Sign*, the months of May and June, August and September will be among the most fruitful. Your impact on things and other people, your inner harmony, will be almost perfect.

In fact, you've a veritable cascade of fine aspects ahead!


### Scorpio (23 October to 22 November)

As you know, Scorpio my friend, some years 'have it'. Others don't. And I'm afraid this is going to be a rather grey year. There will be tension, quandary and change for some of you; doubts and queries for others; and for others still, a distancing and isolation.

*October Scorpios born after the 25th* will be affected by the dissonance of Neptune, which will tend to blur and confuse their lives. Not normally lacking in self-confidence (which can irritate those around you) you will suddenly find yourself in the grip of basic metaphysical questions, will be obsessed and distressed without apparent reason. So chase away these disturbing phantoms through meditation and objective analysis of what you're trying to do. Try to see people and situations as they are, so you're not deceived, and don't build castles in the air. The peak of this Neptunian climate will be March, a month of total confusion when you won't know which way to turn. But ride out the storm, and you'll see more clearly later.

The origin of your worries and possible depression could well lie with your family. And a destabilisation of your family environment, a sudden event that takes place in your home, could bring about an important change in your life this year. If you're *second decan*, this problem will peak in April to May. And, if you were *born around 7 November*, this change will begin at the start of the year and won't take concrete form till after October. In fact it could be the consequence, or aggravation, of a latent problem which existed in essence since last spring. And I have to say that, for some of you, this situation could come to a head in divorce. So take care not to be stubborn. And avoid power plays – which will be difficult – particularly in April, when Mars joins this discordant astral concert and complicates things still further. April and May could well result in a sort of explosion in terms of relationships. And another explosive period, which will be physically dangerous too, will be August to September, when Mars is equally ill aspected.

My advice is to practise meditation; and perhaps even martial arts, to defuse the excessive energy which often characterises you and risks turning into aggression. For this year, especially, that aggression could turn against you like a boomerang.

If you're *last decan*, you'll have to monitor your relationship with your 'other half' from the beginning of May on, when it will be heavily compromised. This difficult phase will last until the beginning of August and start again after mid-October. So do nothing your partner could reproach you for in the first phase, and you won't have to pay for it in the second at the end of the year, or even at the beginning of 2001.

So ... chin up – and the best of luck!

### Sagittarius (22 November to 22 December)

In the first six months of this year the stars will bring you an exciting, immensely optimistic, time. In fact everything should go extremely well in this period. However, afterwards things are less good for the *first decan*.

From January to July, Jupiter will pour heavenly manna on you; and particularly favour the *last decan* in the first six

weeks of the year. Those *born after 16 December* will have the
good fortune to gather the fruits of opportunities that have been
germinating since last May or June (and which you will have
already had news of, late in 1999). As Venus and Mars will
both be equally favourable to you in January, it's highly likely
that many Sagittarians will swing into action, implement a
decision they took last May or June, and get married then. Or if
you started a business in those months last year, it will really
begin to prosper now. In brief, this is a time of good luck,
success and concrete fulfilment.

The *first and second decan* can also look forward to a superb
period. If you were *born in the first week of December,* the
transit of Pluto in your Sign will alter the lives of some subjects,
who will each experience this in different ways. But as, in
general, you love change, you should heartily applaud this
promise of transformation, of true Plutonian metamorphosis.

It seems to me that the period from May to June – when the
other planets will be in opposition to you – is the only one
which could be a bit uncomfortable, as your family won't be
keen on your vague ideas of change then. The tension which
could result may lead to clashes in your relationships. So you
must try to lessen these through self-control and tolerance,
especially as Mars will make you particularly aggressive and
impatient in May to June, and heedless of others. The same
applies to the periods January to February, and September to
October, which are equally danger points on your route. Be
prepared then for resistance from family members and a general
climate of conflict and rivalry, which won't always be that easy
to live through.

In happy contrast, Mars will be well aspected for *all the Sign*
from mid-February to mid-March, in August, at the beginning
of September and in November to December. These periods
will favour your progress in a spectacular way. And they'll be
times of greatly increased vitality.

If you were born in November, Neptune in particular will
affect you this year, will make your destiny more mellow, will
give you a loftier and more serene view of life, and increase
your intuition, subtlety and curiosity towards the world unseen.

It's the sort of period in which we idolise our partner and those around us, in which we have more of a tendency – which your Sign already has – to see the glass of life as half full, rather than half empty. And this will apply in January, April, July, September, and the end of October/beginning of November when, for *all the Sign*, the flame of love will burn bright.

Thanks to Uranus, Sagittarians *born between 7 and 12 December* will have the opportunity to take giant strides on the path to victory. They'll widen their field of consciousness as well as their circle of relationships, and improve their living conditions in a subtle and unforeseen way. For some of you this will result from a proposition made in January, which becomes concrete in October. While if you were *born around the 10th to the 12th*, promises made in May will be fulfilled in December. But, either way, the year should be full of good surprises.

During the last six months, on the other hand, *first decans* will have some loose ends to tidy up. Particularly in September and October – when the opposition of Jupiter and Pluto will hit them head on – they'll have to confront a pretty delicate problem to do with a partnership or association. And if these are not solid, they'll shatter when Mars joins the fray in October. Still ... a Sagittarian forewarned is forearmed, so take care what you do or say in these times – or it'll come back to haunt you in 2001!

## Capricorn (22 December to 20 January)

In all probability, tenacious and self-willed Capricorn that you are, you had to fight your way through a pretty stormy path last year. But if you're *second decan*, Saturn will bring you its reward during the first four months of 2000. To their great satisfaction, many of you will accomplish a long-term project; others will stabilise an emotional tie (probably at the end of January/beginning of February); while others still will buy themselves the house they've always dreamed of and settle in there at last. For all of you this will be a time of abundance, of reward; a time when the world at last recognises your worth and 'renders unto Caesar that which is Caesar's'! And, when Jupiter joins Saturn in your zodiac in April to May, this influence is certain to be at its height and takes on a wider scope, coloured by the good luck which Jupiter brings. So, if you were *born in the first ten days of January*, this spring could well be memorable for you.

The *first decan* will, unfortunately, profit quite briefly from Jupiter's generosity, between mid-February and the beginning of April. The *last decan* will be protected and assisted by Saturn, their ruler, from May on, and particularly in May to June, when Jupiter accompanies Saturn. In fact, they'll probably have the pleasure of starting something between May and the beginning of August that will yield extremely rewarding results after October, though the final fulfilment or realisation of this gift from the gods may not come until the beginning of 2001. Not that this matters to a patient Capricorn. For your worth *will* be recognised and your prestige enhanced – and that should be enough for you.

*All your Sign* can be delighted you've got the backing of Mars. This will put your ego to the fore and endow you with a surplus of effective energy in January to February, at the beginning of May, and from mid-September to mid-November, which are your most dynamic periods. And there is a strong chance you could make an emotional tie solid and long-lasting – and legal, too – at the end of March/beginning April, or in May.

The question, though, is do you want to?

### Aquarius (20 January to 19 February)

You had a foretaste last year and now, once again, will be strongly influenced – and not always comfortably – by the stars' conjunction, though there's an exception in the case of *first-week-in-February Aquarians* and particularly those *born between 1 and 4 February*. If you belong to this small segment of your Sign, you'll be protected by Pluto. This will orientate you towards a greater wellbeing and be an appreciable plus in your life, on both the psychic and material planes. In other words, you'll have the ability to turn your life in the right direction, and people and events will seem to tie in with your wishes. This will be particularly so (and this also applies to the *first decan*) in the second half of the year. In fact, you'll benefit from a trine of Jupiter then which, allied to a sextile of Pluto, will give you every possibility of expansion you could hope for or imagine. September and October will be extremely promising: privately, in terms of love or friendship, in September; and professionally, at the beginning of October. It's a fair bet that you'll profit from surrounding tension then, from contentious legal situations, if need be, in which somehow or other you'll be the lucky winner.

The rest of the Sign, on the other hand, has no such delightful prospects, particularly the *early first decan.* If you were *born around 24 January,* March could be nebulous and confused, could generate breaches of trust, loss of prestige, overestimation and regrettably bad choices. So during this period, don't make any drastic decisions which could affect your future, particularly at the end of the month, when Mars will make you foolhardy and reckless.

If you were *born before 27 January,* you'll experience the very rare (every 164 years) transit of Neptune, which can bring the worst and the best. In the case of the 'worst' one can expect depression, viral illness, loss of prestige, bankruptcy, scandal, a sudden and powerful attraction to drugs or alcohol. While in the case of the 'best', the prospects are quite fantastic. A positive Neptune can mean notoriety or fame, good luck and fortune, inspiration and total illumination, even union with the universal spirit of the cosmos. Your personal chart will decree which category applies to you – and let's hope it's the second!

Aquarians *born between 3 and 11 February* will be aspected by Uranus, your ruler. This planet could change your vision of the world entirely, and also your situation *in* the world, by creating various dramas, surprises and abrupt changes, which are more or less positive according to the position of your natal Sun. Here, too, it's difficult to forecast precisely on a general level, as the effects of Uranus also range from one extreme to another. On the rosy side, we find a miraculous promotion, a lottery win, a professional turnaround which is the opportunity of a lifetime, the most significant meeting of your life, love at first sight. In the negative extreme, however, there's divorce, accidents, all sorts of bad luck. The only thing both sides have in common is the unforeseeable and sudden nature of what they bring.

One can be less ambiguous, unfortunately, in the case of the *second decan*. For, under the square of Saturn which affects it in the first four months of the year, it's hard to predict any positive outcome. This is because, added to the sudden changes of Uranus, the restrictive and limiting energy of Saturn will delay or destroy their potential. Or, put another way, Saturn will give the kiss of death to a cocktail of Uranian dramas which may be pretty sour in the first place!

To counter this hostile conjunction, try to remain as serene as you can through meditation, yoga or other disciplines which calm the nerves. It's well known that Uranus makes us live on a higher vibratory level that makes considerable demands on our nervous system, particularly when it is located in its own Sign of Aquarius. But we mustn't allow its influence to excite us mentally to the point where it produces an effect analagous to hysteria in us. And a mental discipline like meditation will really help you keep your footing and courage during these difficult first six months of the year 2000.

If you belong to the *last decan*, you'll have to gather your courage and maintain a god-like calm from May onwards. So watch out for troubles which could come between May and the beginning of August. They could result in disagreeable news after October which could last until 2001.

Knowing the worst, it's up to you now to go out and deal with it!

### Pisces (19 February to 21 March)

Whatever your sector of the Sign, the first six or seven months will be the best of the year for you. First of all, there's an echo of last year's promises for subjects of the *second decan*, and they'll collect the resultant rewards in the first four months of 2000. You'll establish your situation and enhance your prestige through a general recognition of your merits. Your physical resistance will be reinforced, and emotionally you'll consolidate your ties and anchor them in time, particularly at the end of January/beginning of February or at the end of March. However, in April to May you'll reach the summit of your year. You'll be building on really solid foundations then and, being far-sighted, will have the maximum chances of giving concrete form to your dreams.

If you belong to the *first decan*, Jupiter will reward you between mid-February and the beginning of April with extra opportunities and vital optimism, which will bring you luck. You'd do well to exploit this to the full as, between July and December, the wind turns. Particularly if you were *born at the end of February/beginning of March*, September to October could be difficult. A considerable degree of tension could affect both family and professional sectors, robbing you of your calm and inner peace.

Pluto will destabilise the status quo of Pisces subjects *born in the first four days of March*. And the change it will bring about in and around you will be irreversible. This could be linked with a professional choice which itself is generated by Juptier's dissonance. In brief, you'll be sailing on troubled waters, particularly towards year's end. But Pisceans are essentially adaptable and you'll know, if not how to run with the hare and hunt with the hounds, at least how to go with the flow. Above all, try not to lose your inner unity or let yourself be damaged by these adverse influences, which could disturb you emotionally in August, professionally in September, and in terms of health and everyday life in October. And if you don't get your nerves and emotions in hand, there's the danger of an accident then.

The *last decan*, for its part, will be utterly spoiled in this turning-point year. If you're *born after 10 March*, you'll benefit as the result of a fine constructive sextile of Saturn between May and August, when you'll be approached regarding an award, distinction or promotion. You'll get further wind of this after October. And it will finally happen early in 2001. But in any event, from May on you'll consolidate your situation in an extraordinary way. And you'll also reap the rewards of past efforts, which for many of you could include the satisfaction of completing a long-term project. You'll also have a much greater ability to concentrate (which is useful as Pisceans are often absentminded and have their heads in the clouds).

What's more, as Jupiter will mingle its beneficial rays with those of Saturn in May to June, nothing will seem impossible to you then. In fact, this period could well be the high point of your year in terms of success and fulfilment. Durable and advantageous contracts will be protected by the stars' conjunction; mental work will be favoured; and you'll have the taste and capacity to construct an attractive and coherent philosophy. This will be an ideal time for writers, philosophers, journalists; also for representatives, business and contact people, intermediaries and agents. You'll all enjoy an increased vitality and a renewed desire to get on with life from the end of March to the beginning of May, and from mid-June to the end of July, thanks to positive Martian energy. Your personality will be radiant and you'll have the maximum impact on those around you at these times, which is a good way to end the century and open the third millenium.

All the very best!

# A Glance At Your Next Five Years

### Aries

You are one of the favoured in almost every way in this period. Thanks to Pluto, a positive change awaits you and you'll be able to start again on the right foot. The years ahead are almost as good as they could be. **2001** is excellent (especially the first half). In the second half, despite an extraordinary planetary context, there's nonetheless a risk of judicial, administrative or financial problems, perhaps even of a tax audit, which could rebound on mid-**2002**; but you'll no doubt come out of it for the best and find some miraculous solution. The last six months of **2002** are cloudless, excellent in every way, and fantastically promising, as is **2003**, especially in its first half. And if **2004** is somewhat mixed, in **2005** your heavens will be all blue again, without a cloud in the sky, and the maximum chances of success.

### Taurus

With its ups and downs, you can expect the next five years to be a somewhat confused and chaotic period in which you're seeking to find yourself. If in **2001** and **2002** you catch a glimpse of changes which are often marked by confusion and doubt, in **2003** and **2004** they'll turn positive and a degree of good luck will save the day. On the other hand, **2005** looks quite difficult. A year of 'cycling in sauerkraut'!

## Gemini

Radical alterations will unsettle your life in the five years ahead. But how you love change! You'll be lucky. The passage of Saturn, which is often dreaded and dreadful, will act – thanks to your cosmic context – in a stabilising way in **2001** and **2002**, following drastic, but excellent changes. In the middle of **2003** and until the end of **2004** the wind turns ... fasten your seat belts! In **2005** Jupiter saves the day, and alterations take place in your life which are as fundamental as they're unexpected.

## Cancer

In **2001** and **2002** the passage of Jupiter through your Sign promises expansion and success. You'll begin a twelve-year cycle. (What happened to you around 1990? Did you start on something good?) In **2003** you'll see the positive stabilisation of your situation. In **2004** things change ... but for the better. In **2005**, on the other hand, watch out for financial or legal matters which could have a doubtful outcome. All the same, thanks to Uranus, you'll progress and change many things in your world, will extend your field of consciousness, and discover a new dimension to life.

## Leo

Despite some general confusion, you'll be favoured by the gods in **2001**, and lucky, despite possible problems with a partner. In **2002** and **2003** there's a hazy atmosphere involving hesitation and a climate of deception. So look out! However, Pluto should watch over and protect you. You'll change everything for a greater wellbeing. And in **2005** you'll establish yourself, eliminate the superfluous, perhaps even win life's major prize.

## Virgo

There's total change in prospect in these five years if you belong to the second half of the Sign. In **2001** and **2002**, despite radical upheavals, you'll enjoy the protection of Jupiter which will make things go your way. Till June **2003** will be a more uncomfortable year. Then from the last half of **2003** to the end of **2004** you'll settle into a new situation. In **2005**, though, you'll be sailing on stormy seas. So take care – and hang in there!

## Libra

Generally speaking, you can take what liberties you want to in this five-year period, as Pluto will protect you. And so will Neptune and – for the first two years – Uranus. So you've got *everything* going to help you succeed! In **2001** and until the end of **2003** you'll experience an extraordinary phase, perhaps the most fertile of your life. And, despite some setbacks or pitfalls from Saturn, in **2004** you'll triumph, while **2005** is once again great. You can count on a once-in-a-lifetime phase.

## Scorpio

**2001** and **2002** add up to stress, uncertainty and doubt. In **2003** it's a question of eating the hair of the dog that bit you, thanks to Uranus which brings positive changes in the second half of the year. In **2004**, you stabilise things, relatively speaking. Despite persistent doubts and general confusion, finances are very well aspected. While in **2005** you'll need to watch out for depression. Innovate. Dare. Throw yourself into the unknown – as Uranus invites you to.

## Sagittarius

You are going to make a clean sweep of your life during these years, especially if you were *born after 8 December.* In **2001** and **2002**, despite general instability, you'll keep the faith and even make progress. In **2003** you can count on stress and abrupt change, but luck will protect you. **2004** is a rout, so be careful; then, despite a square of Uranus which promises drastic change, by **2005** the horizon is clear again – a super and fertile year – and don't you love change anyhow?

## Capricorn

In **2001** you enjoy spectacular consolidation during the first six months. But in the second six, and until mid-**2002**, watch out. You'll have to cope with some legal problems and the taxman cometh! **2003** is a superb year. You're on a launch site. You'll progress and luck will help you from mid-**2003** right through **2004**. In **2005** there's a mixed climate: of difficult decisions, money problems, or conflict with the authorities. Thanks to Uranus, though, and perhaps to unexpected intervention, you'll find miracle solutions.

## Aquarius

A positive metamorphosis takes place in these five years. **2001** is mixed. You'll change a lot in your life (*last decans*) and positively, but there will be setbacks and problems in the first six months. The *first decan* keeps the faith despite more or less muddled situations. After mid-**2001**, everything turns to your advantage. You'll settle into a new reality and be happy. From mid-**2002** to mid-**2003** you'll be faced with difficult choices, but they'll end in something new and rewarding. In **2004** the *last decan* gains better social integration and makes spectacular progress. **2005** is even luckier. The caterpillar has every chance of turning into a magnificent butterfly. A golden year!

*Pisces*

Five years of radical destabilisation and change, in which you grow up! In **2001** you'll experience change, shielded by Saturn during the first half of the year and Jupiter in the second, as you will in the first half of **2002**, when Jupiter will guard your back and your optimism. From mid-**2002** to mid-**2003** is a critical, not very jolly period. Then from mid-**2003** to the end of **2004** Saturn will return as a guardian and more or less preserve your gains. **2005**, unfortunately, is a real shake-up, with Pluto and Jupiter toppling your status quo. Perhaps you need to swim with the current and let the unknown surprise you. But whatever you do, stay positive!

# How the Signs Divide into Decans

**Aries**
1st: 21–31 March
2nd: 1–10 April
3rd: 11–20 April

**Taurus**
1st: 20–30 April
2nd: 1–10 May
3rd: 11–21 May

**Gemini**
1st: 21–31 May
2nd: 1–11 June
3rd: 12–21 June

**Cancer**
1st: 21 June–1 July
2nd: 2–12 July
3rd: 13–22 July

**Leo**
1st: 22 July–2 August
2nd: 3–12 August
3rd: 13–23 August

**Virgo**
1st: 23 August–2 September
2nd: 3–12 September
3rd: 13–23 September

**Libra**
1st: 23 September–3 October
2nd: 4–13 October
3rd: 14–23 October

**Scorpio**
1st: 23 October–2 November
2nd: 3–12 November
3rd: 13–22 November

**Sagittarius**
1st: 22 November–2 December
2nd: 3–12 December
3rd: 13–22 December

**Capricorn**
1st: 22–31 December
2nd: 1–10 January
3rd: 11–20 January

**Aquarius**
1st: 20–30 January
2nd: 31 January–9 February
3rd: 10–19 February

**Pisces**
1st: 19–29 February
2nd: 1–10 March
3rd: 11–21 March